D0251550

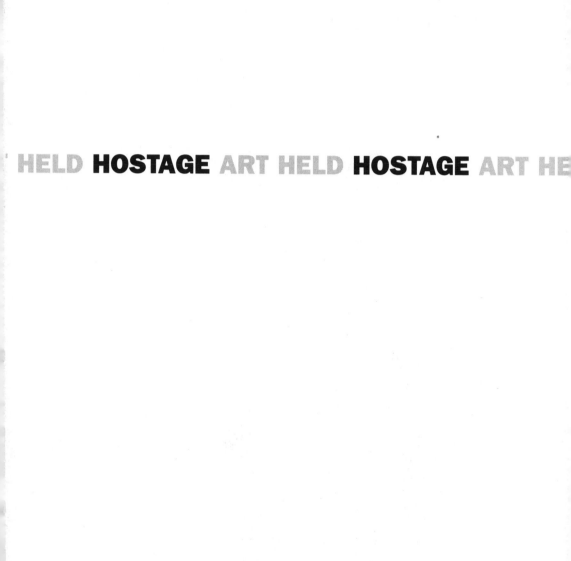

HELD **HOSTAGE** ART HELD **HOSTAGE** ART HE

ART
HELD
HOSTAGE

The Battle over
the Barnes Collection

JOHN ANDERSON

W. W. NORTON & COMPANY • NEW YORK • LONDON

Copyright © 2003 by John Anderson

For information about permission to reproduce selections from this book,
write to Permissions, W. W. Norton & Company, Inc., 500 Fifth Avenue,
New York, NY 10110

Manufacturing by Courier Westford
Book design by Dana Sloan
Production manager: Julia Druskin

Library of Congress Cataloging-in-Publication Data

Anderson, John.
Art held hostage : the story of the Barnes collection / John Anderson.—1st ed.
p. cm.
ISBN 0-393-04889-6 (hardcover)
1. Barnes Foundation—Management. 2. Art—Private collections—
Pennsylvania—Merion. 3. Barnes, Albert C. (Albert Coombs), 1872–1951.
4. Glanton, Richard. I. Title.

N5220.B28 A53 2003
708.148'12—dc21   2002154148

W. W. Norton & Company, Inc.
500 Fifth Avenue, New York, N.Y. 10110
www.wwnorton.com

W. W. Norton & Company Ltd.
Castle House, 75/76 Wells Street, London W1T 3QT

1 2 3 4 5 6 7 8 9 0

For Hilary

CONTENTS

ACKNOWLEDGMENTS

In the course of researching and writing this book, I have built up many debts. I would like to acknowledge my appreciation to all those who helped in the making of *Art Held Hostage*.

From the beginning, I was greatly aided by the fact that the principal actors in the more recent aspects of this drama gave generously of their time and opinions. I wish to thank the following, in particular, for their cooperation: Richard H. Glanton, Niara Sudarkasa, Eugene L. Cliett, Jr., Cuyler Walker, Carl Singley, Paul Diamond, and Kimberly Camp.

Numerous others in the story shared their insights—sometimes in brief, but often at length—with me, and I thank them as well: William R. Adams, Anne Barnard, Richard L. Bazelon, Julia Bond (Mrs. Horace Mann Bond), Julian Bond, Christopher Booth, Earle Bradford, David Bright, William H. Brown III, Larry Cesare, Larry Ceisler, David Cohen, Mark Cohen, Murray Dickman, Richard Feigen, Loren Feldman, Lucinda Fleeson, Kathleen Frederick, Richard Goldberg, Antonio Guizzetti, Roosevelt Hairston, Jr., Ron Javers, Gregory B. Jordan, Eliot Kaplan, Hilton Kramer, Matthew D. Lee, Laura Linton, James Lopresti, E. Roger Mandle, William Marimow, David Marston, Richard McElroy, Jonathan Neumann, Mary Ann Nolan, Michael

Pakenham, Lewis Piccini, Joseph Rishel, David W. Rawson, Paul Rosen, Stephan Salisbury, Robert Montgomery Scott, Michael Smerconish, Peter Smith, Richard Spiegelman, Michael Stiles, Sidney Steinberg, Robert J. Sugarman, Robert Ferris Thompson, Nicholas Tinari, Jr., Joe H. Tucker, Jr., Gary Tuma, John Unkovic, Frederick Voigt, Lois Wark, Bob Warner, Bernard Watson, Richard J. Wattenmaker, Shirley B. Williams (Mrs. Franklin Williams), and Ethel P. Wistar.

Some of my best sources wished to remain anonymous or virtually anonymous, and I have honored their desires. I think it is fair to say, however, that among them are Lincoln trustees; members of the Philadelphia legal, educational, and philanthropic communities; and high-ranking state and federal officials.

I am especially indebted for their help to Kimberly Camp, the current CEO and executive director of the Barnes Foundation, and her colleague Andrew Stewart.

For their advice and insights on various matters, I would like to thank the following: Catherine Aman, Michael Apstein, M.D., Eric Asimov, Camelia Cassin, Margaret Daisley, Thomas Daly, Joan Ferrell, Jon Gertner, Ronald C. Gordon, Jr., Karen Hall, Martha Hevenor, Ashby Jones, Andrew Longstreth, Judy Lopatin, Douglas McCollam, David Marcus, Fleming Meeks, John Morris, Mark Obbie, Elisabeth Preis, Todd J. Schwartz, Amy Singer, Morris Stubbs, Kevin Pierce Thornton, Nicholas Varchaver, Mark Voorhees, Rob Walker, and Phil Waller.

Professors David Musto and John Warner, at Yale University, and professor James Havey Young, of Emory University, kindly shared their vast knowledge of the history of science and medicine with me. Mary Ellen Bowden, of the Chemical Heritage Foundation in Philadelphia, and Edward Mormon, of the Library of the College of Physicians, also in Philadelphia, were also most helpful in this regard. Evan Towle, of the Urban Archives of the Temple University Libraries, and Diane Worrell, of the Special Collections, Morris Library,

Southern Illinois University at Carbondale, were both of great assistance in the photographic research for this book.

Readers will notice that there are no source notes. As I point out in the introduction, *Art Held Hostage* is neither a scholarly biography nor a work of art history. It is journalism. I do, however, wish to note my obligation to a number of earlier works about Dr. Barnes and the Barnes Foundation. These include: Henry Hart, *Dr. Barnes of Merion: An Appreciation*; William Schack, *Art and Argyrol: The Life and Career of Dr. Albert C. Barnes*; Gilbert M. Cantor, *The Barnes Foundation: Reality vs. Myth*; and Howard Greenfeld, *The Devil and Dr. Barnes: Portrait of an American Art Collector*. More interesting, by far, however, is the essay on Barnes in John Lukacs's stimulating book, *Philadelphia Patricians and Philistines, 1900–1950*. Also highly recommended is Richard J. Wattenmaker's splendid short essay, "Dr. Albert C. Barnes and the Barnes Foundation," which can be found in *Great French Paintings from the Barnes Foundation: Impressionist, Post-Impressionist, and Early Modern*.

Others who read and commented on portions of the book in manuscript include: my old teacher and mentor, Howard Roberts Lamar, retired Sterling Professor of History and former President of Yale University; David J. Garrow, Presidential Distinguished Professor of Law at the Emory University Law School; Professor Kevin Van Anglen of the Boston University Department of English; Lois and Tom Wark, retired editors at the Philadelphia *Inquirer* (Lois helped edit the Girard Trust series that plays such a prominent role in chapter twelve); and my old friend Lawrence Walsh, also of Philadelphia. Lawrence and Mary Williams Walsh not only hosted the author on a number of his visits, they also gave him good counsel and encouragement.

Colleagues in the magazine and newspaper world who read and commented on all or part of the manuscript—and gave invaluable advice—include R. W. Apple, Jr., Geoffrey Precourt, Craig Unger, Loren Feldman, Jon Rizzi, and Robert Friedman. I thank them all.

At *The American Lawyer*, editor-in-chief Aric Press encouraged me to pursue the Barnes story, then gave me the time I needed to report it. I am grateful for that. Senior writer Allison Frankel read and commented on the manuscript; and I particularly thank managing editor Dianne McDonald, whose infectious enthusiasm for this project was much appreciated by the author. (Dianne, there's not a writer alive who doesn't need a fan; and you were a great one to have.) Two other people at *The American Lawyer* deserve applause: executive assistant Eileen Vella, for her good care and keeping; and *Corporate Counsel* executive editor Anthony Paonita, who helped rescue me from all sorts of pitfalls.

I am profoundly indebted to two quite special readers of this manuscript. The first is my friend Denise Martin, the executive editor of *Money* magazine—and the best line editor I know. Her careful eye and fine ear made this a vastly better book than it would have otherwise been. The other is Richard J. Wattenmaker, the director of the Archives of American Art, whose acute reading of the text saved me from many an error—and taught me much about Dr. Barnes (for whom he is or will be the ideal scholarly biographer). I thank him—and absolve him of any errors that might persist in my book. *Santé*, Richard.

My agent at International Creative Management (ICM), the indefatigable Kristine Dahl, has been a friend and a comfort throughout; and I thank her and her assistant, Jud Laghi, for all their help and support.

At W. W. Norton & Company, I have been blessed with having as my editor "the prince of publishers," as Kris Dahl once called him: editor-in-chief Starling Lawrence. It was Star who rang me up one day and asked if I'd like to write a book about the Barnes. Well, yes, I did; but it was Star who made it happen. And when, midway through the process of writing a first draft, I found myself bogged down and dispirited, Star never wavered.

He just said, "You write it, and I'll publish it." Three and a half years later . . . I thank you, Star, for staying the course with me.

Star's assistant, Morgen Van Vorst, has been both patient and kind with me throughout the process; and the same goes for the book's photo researcher, Ruth Mandel, and the art director, Eleen Cheung. Janet Byrne was my copyeditor; and, God knows, she has done her share of work. I thank her for all the improvements she has wrought in my book. For her good judgment in all things legal, Norton's outside counsel, Renee Schwartz, also deserves my kind thanks.

This being in many ways a legal tale, many another lawyer has also played a significant role in shaping this book. Daniel Kornstein of New York's Kornstein, Veiz, and Wexler has long been my principal counsel and able advisor. Dan's legal instincts are unerring; and his literary instincts are just as keen. Kevin Goering, the head of litigation at Coudert Brothers, is, like Dan, one of the good guys of the First Amendment bar—and a very strong advocate as well. I thank them both profusely for their thoughtful and wise readings of my manuscript. I also thank my old friend Mark T. Millkey, senior litigator at Milberg Weiss Bershad Hynes & Lerach, for his support not only on this book but throughout the years; and my newer friends, First Amendment lawyer-cum-author Cameron Stracher; litigators Thomas Moore, of New York's Proskauer Rose, and Paul V. Kelly, of Boston's Kelly, Libby & Hoopes; and counselor and bon vivant George Sape, of Epstein, Becker & Green.

Finally, and most especially, I'd like to thank my family. My wife, Hilary Hevenor, is the painter in the family; she's also a rock in difficult times. Surely, this book could not have been written without her. She and our Valentine's Day boy, Charlie, were magnificent throughout the long process. My mother, Lois Croft Anderson Newton, step-father, Oakley, mother-in-law, Frances, father-in-law, Bob; and all the rest of the extended family deserve thanks, too, for their support. I only wish my beloved father, Charles Wyatt "Tap" Anderson, were still around to have seen this book go into print. I think he would have enjoyed it. This I do know: I miss him every day of my life.

It goes without saying that any errors of fact or judgment in this book are mine alone.

ART HELD HOSTAGE ART HELD HOSTAGE ART HELD HOSTAGE ART HI

THIS PARADISE OF ART

Buried inside the *New Yorker* issue of September 22, 1928, was a brief but tantalizing story by a long since forgotten writer named A. H. Shaw. His subject: a place virtually unknown in its day.

> *In the midst of a twelve-acre park in Merion, a suburb of Philadelphia remote from the beaten path of art museums and galleries, stands a French Renaissance palace of bluff limestone, which houses the finest collection of modern paintings in the world with the one possible exception of a museum in Moscow. . . .*
>
> *The name of this paradise of art is the Barnes Foundation and presiding over it is the gentleman who collected and owns the pictures—Dr. Albert C. Barnes.*

"De Medici in Merion," Shaw called him. And the point, as Shaw made clear, was that the Barnes Foundation was neither a museum nor a gallery. It was, instead, a nonprofit institution dedicated to advancing Barnes's own brand of art education and appreciation. Housing thousands of works of art, including some of the greatest works of impressionism and post-impressionism, the Barnes Foundation was unique. Admission was by invitation only. The gentleman who owned and collected all those works of art got to decide who saw them.

Shaw described the iron-willed master of this curious art foundation thusly: "Fifty-five years of intense living have turned his light hair almost entirely gray, but he still radiates strength and inexhaustible nervous energy." Barnes, Shaw noted, was broad shouldered, stood "an inch or two short of six feet," weighed 190 pounds, and had "piercing blue eyes," which frequently darted "quick, suspicious glances" at his interviewer.

Barnes was, by all accounts, a difficult sort. A self-made man, he'd made his fortune in pharmaceuticals, in particular in the production and marketing of something called Argyrol. As Shaw reported: "The laws of most states require that a few drops of Argyrol be put into the eyes of newborn babies to prevent ophthalmia neonatorum, which often leads to blindess." To "guard his rights" to the exclusive manufacture of Argyrol, Barnes bragged to the reporter of how he'd "had to wage lawsuits in almost every country under the sun."

The "ultimate destiny of the pictures" housed at the foundation, Shaw wrote, "will probably not have to be decided for a long time, however, for Dr. Barnes is in excellent health and takes every precaution to remain so."

That was still the case almost fourteen years later, when Carl W. McCardle of the *Saturday Evening Post* stopped by for a visit. His portrait of the almost seventy-year-old Barnes was hardly changed from the one Shaw had painted so many years earlier: "He is heavy-set and muscular. He always appears to be bursting at the seams with energy." Up every day at "exactly 6," Barnes "hikes 5 miles [a day] and goes to bed around 10."

His competitive energies were still keen, too. Barnes's father had worked in a slaughterhouse alongside another young butcher named Pete Widener. More than three-quarters of a century later, their children, Joseph E. Widener and Albert C. Barnes, were both multimillionaires—and rival art collectors. In 1937, Joseph Widener had gone to Europe and returned with Cézanne's *Bathers*, for which he'd reportedly paid $110,000 and which he promptly donated to the Philadelphia Museum of Art. The local newspapers reported that "another 'smaller' version was at the Barnes Foundation." Barnes, McCardle wrote, "boiled over" at the news. (Barnes's own *Nudes in the Landscape [Les grandes baigneuses]* of 1900–1905 is regarded as one of the jewels in the collection.)

The "sequel," as McCardle put it, was a voyage to Europe a few months later in which Joseph Widener and Albert Barnes found themselves on the same ship, seated in neighboring deck chairs: "Neither spoke during the voyage." Or, as Barnes put it: "We just sat there, side by side, a couple of millionaires on the luxury liner *Normandie* . . . just as his old man and my old man had once worked side by side in a slaughterhouse."

By now, the paintings in his collection were said to be worth over twenty million dollars. Barnes told McCardle that he'd paid less than a quarter of that amount for them. "I just robbed everybody. Particularly during the Depression, my specialty was robbing the suckers who had invested all their money in flimsy securities and then had to sell their priceless paintings to keep a roof over their heads."

A case in point was the tale of how he'd gotten hold of Cézanne's *Jeune homme à la tête de mort* (*Man and Skull*). According to Barnes, another rival, "a Chicago Art Institute benefactor," had offered $150,000 for the work, but its owner, a wealthy Swiss businessman, held out for $200,000. During the

Depression, though, the Swiss owner used the painting as security; and when the bank pressed him for cash, he sold it: to Albert Barnes, for a mere $50,000.

It was probably true, but who knows? Barnes spent a lot of time pulling reporters' legs. The reporters—and their editors—made up for that by tweaking the great man, often mercilessly. The caption for one photograph accompanying the opening article in the *Post* series read: "Inside the main Barnes gallery, from which snobs, swooners, celebrities, and YOU are rudely barred."

McCardle was more fair-minded than his editors. The Barnes Foundation, he wrote "is a $500,000 palace built out of cream-colored limestone imported from France. It is set in a twelve-acre tract containing some of the rarest trees and shrubs in the United States. A tall iron-spiked fence encircles the grounds protectively. It is a walled-in little universe."

■

The history of the Barnes Foundation, this "walled-in little universe," has from the beginning been one of mystery, controversy, contradictions—and court cases.

Following Barnes's death in 1951, his acolytes, led by long-time education director Violette de Mazia, insisted that foundation art could never be reproduced in color. To do so, they claimed, would violate Dr. Barnes's most strongly held beliefs. It comes as a surprise, then, to find that McCardle's *Saturday Evening Post* articles were illustrated not only with black and white reproductions of the paintings but also with "color photographs by the Pinto Brothers," including one of Barnes himself in the gallery standing next to Matisse's *The Red Madras Headdress*. *House & Garden* ran Barnes Foundation art in color just a few months later in December 1942.

Nor was it true, as de Mazia later claimed, that Barnes never lent out paintings from his collection: There were loans to the 1934 Maurice Prendergast memorial at the Whitney, and, later, of three Glackens to the Whitney in 1939 for a Glackens memorial. What is certainly true, however, is that Albert Barnes had a litigious soul. He made his fortune by going to court and ridding himself of the cofounder of his pharmaceutical company, Hermann Hille. Barnes, as a good monopolist, also didn't hesitate to threaten unlicensed Argyrol imitators with suits. And, as Shaw reported, he gave contractors and developers legal hell when they proposed putting up homes across the street from his beloved foundation.

The Barnes Foundation, it could be argued, was built on litigation. A half century after the death of its founder—and despite a series of court cases that threatened to open wide its doors—the Barnes has retained its unique identity. But thanks now to one of the strangest examples of litigation this century—a case over a parking lot brought in federal court under the Ku Klux Klan Act—the Barnes Foundation today is on the brink of insolvency.

■

This book is not a history of the Barnes Foundation, and I am not an art historian. Nor is this a biography of Dr. Barnes. These are tasks for other writers and scholars. My book is instead the story of how Dr. Barnes's legacy, the greatest private art collection in America—valued at more than $6 billion and including some 69 Cézannes (more than in all the museums in Paris), 60 Matisses, 44 Picassos, 18 Rousseaus, 14 Modiglianis, and no fewer than 180 Renoirs—became captive to the roiling crosscurrents of race and politics, ego and greed.

Above all, though, this is a tale shaped, for good and for ill, by the extraordinary character of the Barnes Foundation's former president, Richard H. Glanton, who, like Albert C. Barnes before him, was born into poverty and rose by dint of intelligence, energy, and pride to become a power in the American art world of his day.

Glanton's enemies write him off as insincere, arrogant,

manipulative, and mean. His friends counter, saying that he's charming, brilliant, and brave. I once asked Glanton how he would describe himself. "The best politician you'll ever meet," Glanton replied without hesitation. He is an enigma.

"So what's your book about?" friends keep asking me. The answer: Race, culture, politics—and Richard Glanton.

Where, some would say, is the art in this picture? It's still held hostage.

CHAPTER ONE

PORTRAIT OF
DR. BARNES

In his long lifetime (1872–1951), Albert Coombs Barnes made two fortunes: the first in marketing a preventive treatment for gonorrhea known as Argyrol, the second and greater one in amassing a remarkable art collection. The former made the latter possible, but it is for his spectacular art collection that Barnes is remembered today.

Barnes, who grew up impoverished in the teeming slums of late nineteenth-century Philadelphia, had to work for everything he got in life. And when he finally had money and his interests turned to art, he *worked* at collecting. Perhaps it's why he chose to buy so much contemporary, or at least near-contemporary, art. Anyone with sufficient money and desire could collect Old Masters, whose very names form the roll call of art history books. But to collect first-rate contemporary art required judgment, passion, and the keenest possible intelligence, all of which Barnes possessed in abundance. It also didn't hurt that life had taught him to be a hard bargainer. No dealer was ever going to gyp Albert Barnes—at least not if he could help it.

His origins showed. He was rough at the edges and caustic—prickly, quick to find fault in others, and quicker still to take offense. But he was also brilliant, energetic, and shrewd. Those who were not put off by his manner found an engaging partner, with intellect to spare. His circle of friends was surprisingly wide and included, among others, Leopold Stokowski, William Bullitt, Leo Stein, Horace Mann Bond, William Glackens, James Johnson Sweeney (head of the department of paintings and sculpture at the Museum of Modern Art and later the director of the Guggenheim), John Dewey, and the actor Charles Laughton. Pretty good company for a poor boy from Philly.

When Carl Van Vechten photographed him in late middle age, Barnes was still ruggedly handsome, "a big, raw-boned man, with a determined face," in the words of the historian John Lukacs. It was not for nothing, after all, that women liked him—or that he returned the liking. In Van Vechten's photographs from 1937, Barnes at age sixty-five looks tough and able, a man neither diminished by time nor dissipated by privilege: a powerful and virile character, to be sure.

The Giorgio de Chirico portrait of 1926, *Dr. Albert C. Barnes*, is more enigmatic. The subject, seen in semi-profile, seems lost in thought, brooding perhaps, his seated body angled to the right, his eyes gazing away from the viewer. One large hand dangles at his waist, while, balanced above it, the other rests against his cheek. It's a portrait at once cool and melancholic—a point emphasized by the palate of grays, pale blues, and browns.

An unkind critic, Aline Saarinen—she preferred writing about more gentlemanly collectors (her best-known work was entitled *The Proud Possessors*)—wrote that Barnes had "the face of a dentist," making him sound more like the loutish McTeague in Frank Norris's eponymous novel than an M.D. from the University of Pennsylvania School of Medicine. But then that's the sort of treatment Barnes always tended to receive in conventional art circles, "iconoclastic" being the kindest adjective used to describe him. As Lukacs says, Barnes's reputation "became that of a vulgarian, flaunting his collection acquired by a large and perhaps inexhaustible checkbook: a ham-handed boor, a rich Don Quixote who, unlike the tattered Spanish comic hero, lived in his own windmill laden with riches."

Though far from being an unsympathetic critic, Lukacs has offered his own, memorable description of Barnes. His face, Lukacs writes, was that "of a first-rate president (rara avis) of a second-rate university. Beneath his eternally wrinkled brows and behind his rimless glasses his eyes glared strong and clear. His preferences were singular; his hatreds were puissant."

■

Barnes's father, John, began his working life as a butcher in ante-bellum Philadelphia and ended it as a watchman in his son's pharmaceutical factory. In between, he drifted through a variety of other jobs, never wholly succeeding in any of them.

Working side by side with Barnes in the Philadelphia slaughterhouses was the young P.A.B. Widener (1834–1915). But where John Barnes plodded along, Peter Widener saw an opportunity and took it. The Union army, he correctly reckoned, would require a steady supply of mutton. Widener undertook to provide it—and made the first of several fortunes. Today, the main library at Harvard University owes its name to descendants of that same Peter Widener.

John Barnes, on the other hand, enlisted in the 82nd Pennsylvania Infantry on February 5, 1864. By then, the American Civil War had entered its fourth year. The first great battle of the war, at Bull Run, had started out as something of a picnic, with ladies in parasols and gentlemen in buggies accompanying the Union army's jaunty descent on Manassas Junction from Washington—only to finish as a rout. Since that time,

Shiloh and Antietam, Vicksburg and Gettysburg had come and gone. Thousands of soldiers, Rebel and Yankee alike, had returned home maimed or in caskets. Surely, the human cost of the war was there for all to see. The wealthy could buy their way out of fighting, while many among the poor seethed. By 1864, with a presidential election scheduled for the fall, race riots had erupted in the north, especially in the big urban centers. When so many were trying so hard to avoid fighting, why then did John Barnes choose to enlist?

The answer is, almost certainly, more prosaic than patriotism or blood lust or desire for glory. Four days before Barnes enlisted, President Abraham Lincoln had ordered America's first half-million-man draft. As a young man with no wife and no family, John Barnes was subject to the draft, indeed, was likely fodder for it. If you were drafted, you got nothing. Voluntary enlistment in the Union army, however, carried with it a $300 signing bonus. For a poor man, that was a lot of money.

It would cost him dearly. At the Battle of Cold Harbor, four months after his enlistment, Barnes's right arm was shattered. It had to go. He would spend the rest of the war in government hospitals in Washington, D.C., Baltimore, and Chester, Pennsylvania. Barnes was lucky to be alive. Most often it wasn't the bullet that killed, rather it was the mortification or gangrene that set in later. The fortunate ones, like John Barnes, came away without limbs, the gangrene having been lopped off together with the infected arm or leg. Barnes, in any case, left the Union army with a three-quarters disability and a pension of eight dollars a month for life.

His old career as a butcher was now over. His new career as a letter carrier had already begun when he married Lydia A. Schafer, on April 4, 1867. She and John would have four children, all boys: the first, Charles, and the third, Albert, survived into adulthood. The other boys died in early childhood, ages one and two.

Albert was born on January 2, 1872, the place of his birth the family's small two-story home at 1466 Cook Street, in the Kensington section of Philadelphia. Kensington was a tough neighborhood then, and it's a tough neighborhood today. In the words of a recent student of Philadelphia, the journalist Buzz Bissinger, "No area embodied the tradition of industry and the white working class better than Kensington, with row house and church steeple and narrow street and the El and the spew of factory smokestacks all within its boundaries."

At the turn of the century some one hundred thousand people "filled its row-house corridors, an assemblage of Irish, English, Scottish, and German immigrants pocketed in a neighborhood two miles northeast of the grand spire of City Hall, and the estimated worth of its manufactured products was said to be $100 million annually. 'A City Within a City,' touted one local booster, 'filled to the brim with enterprise, dotted with factories so numerous that the rising smoke obscures the sky. . . . A happy and contented people, enjoying a land of plenty.'"

It was a land of plenty where a one-armed vet who'd once been a butcher found it hard to stay afloat between jobs with only a small government pension to support his family. When John Barnes couldn't pay the rent for the house on Cook Street, the family was forced to move into squatter slums in South Philadelphia. The Neck—or the Dumps, as it was also called—was overgrown, unpaved, and filthy. There were rats everywhere, and few houses had running water. The litany of everyday life—especially as regards a small boy living amid destitution—ran its predictable course. Bullies and fighting came with the turf.

Lydia Barnes did what seemed possible for her sons—and a great deal more besides. Albert was taught to paint, and he was given musical instruments to play. He was also made to go to church—Lydia, who came of Pennsylvania German stock, was a devout Methodist—and taken to camp meetings. At the age of eight, Barnes made a discovery that would have a profound influence. It came at an African American camp meeting held at Merchantville, just beyond Camden, New Jersey, across the Delaware River from Philadelphia.

Years later, Barnes recalled the impression made on him that day as having been "so vivid and so deep that it has influenced my whole life, not only in learning much about the Negro, but in extending the aesthetic phase of that experience to an extensive study of art in all its phases, and particularly the art of painting." Thenceforth, Barnes would be, in his own words, "an addict to Negro camp-meetings, baptizings, revivals, and to seeking the company of individual Negroes."

The idiosyncratic Dr. Barnes, it seems clear, was shaped by a highly unusual childhood, one that pitted poverty against extreme maternal strength of will, but also quotidian urban lower-class existence against events and experiences quite removed from the norm for the day and for his class. If the character of the later Dr. Barnes seems contradictory, surely the tectonics took form early in his life—often at the instigation of Lydia Barnes.

The image one has of Barnes's mother is of a serious, respectable, grave woman proud of her bright son and ambitious for him. All things considered, she did remarkably well by the boy, above all in seeing to it that he got a first-rate education. In June 1885, when he was thirteen, Albert Barnes entered Philadelphia's Central High, considered at the time to be one of the top public secondary schools in the United States. The academic program was rigorous: not merely English grammar and literature but four years of Latin, three of French, chemistry, physics, and a strong dose of mathematics.

While at Central, Barnes, who seems to have been a popular student—he was elected vice-president of his senior class—made at least one significant friendship, with William Glackens (1870–1938). Barnes and "Butts" Glackens were only once in the same class, from February to June 1888. Nevertheless, according to Barnes, "We became close friends, partly through my interest in his drawing . . . and because we had the same interest in sports. We were members of the . . . baseball team for several years."

During Barnes's third year at Central, the family finally escaped the Neck, moving into their own, small house at 1331 Tasker Street, just off Broad. By now, John had a full-time job in the *Public Ledger*'s circulation department; but the deed was in Lydia's name.

Central was empowered to grant baccalaureate degrees, and, after eight consecutive terms, Barnes was graduated in June 1889, with a bachelor of science degree. His class ranking, twenty-fourth of twenty-six, is surely misleading. How many Central students, after all, got up every day at four A.M. and delivered newspapers?

Henry Hart, a journalist who knew Barnes well in his successful late middle age, says that it was Al's mother's dream that he should be a doctor. She must have prayed that someone would prove successful in the family; older brother Charles wound up a lead worker.

In the fall of 1889, Albert Barnes matriculated at the University of Pennsylvania Medical School. Despite his ranking at Central, he was given a small scholarship. It wasn't enough. For the next three years, Barnes supported himself by tutoring and by boxing—he later claimed to have developed his skills in the ring by necessity, while growing up in the Neck and by playing semi-pro baseball, at ten dollars a game. Fortunately, too, Penn in those days was a commuter school. If you lived at home and were willing to do odd jobs when not in class, you might be able to get by.

Barnes thrived in medical school. His three-year cumulative average was 84.5. Many, indeed most, of his marks were outstanding: 94 in physical diagnosis, 95 in chemistry, 91 in morbid anatomy, 92 in therapeutics, 93 in clinical medicine, and 95 in practice.

At age twenty, Albert Barnes found himself a doctor of medicine.

■

Eighteen ninety-three was the year of the Great Panic—and the beginning of a nationwide depression, the likes of which would not be seen again until the 1930s. For Albert Barnes, it was the year when he discovered a startling fact: He wasn't cut out to practice medicine. A series of internships—one of them at the State Hospital for the Insane in Warren, Pennsylvania—convinced him that his real interest lay in chemistry. Boldly, he set out to study the subject in earnest.

Most of the great chemists of the late nineteenth century were German; and it was to the University of Berlin that Barnes went for advanced study in chemistry and physiology. When he returned to America in 1896, he found work as a consulting chemist for the H. K. Mulford Company, a well-known Philadelphia pharmaceutical concern. Mulford had two years earlier, in 1894, produced the first diphtheria antitoxin in America. It had also been the first American firm to produce smallpox vaccine commercially.

Barnes took a second job writing ads for Gray's Glycerine Tonic. From the beginning, his business career would successfully mix science and marketing. According to the journalist Henry Hart, the two jobs paid Barnes close to $10,000 a year—the equivalent of $150,000 or more today. By the late 1890s, Barnes was employed full-time by Mulford as its advertising and sales manager. It was in this role that he convinced the company to send him back to Heidelberg's Ruprecht-Karls Universität in 1900 to do course work in pharmacology and to recruit a well-trained German chemist for the firm and bring him back to America. Late that spring or early summer, Barnes found his man: Hermann Hille, a young Ph.D. from Heidelberg who had studied pharmacology at the University of Würzburg. A promising student, Hille had worked with the great physicist

Wilhelm Röntgen, whose research led to the discovery of the X ray.

Barnes returned to America in late summer. Shortly afterward, while visiting a cousin in the Poconos, he was introduced to a small, thin, reserved young woman with blue eyes and blonde hair. She was pretty and single. Her name was Laura Leggett. In the course of less than six months, Albert Barnes had met both his future business partner—the man who would help make him a millionaire—and his wife.

■

If Barnes hadn't been smart and tough—and his mother determined—he would never have escaped the Neck. The city was not kind to those of his lot. Welfare didn't exist, and, if it had, the Republican town fathers of Philadelphia wouldn't have been for it. Philadelphia's wealth was mostly derived from manufacturing, finance, and especially transportation: railroad money, in particular—The Pennsylvania Railroad and the Baldwin Locomotive Works—and the Main Line was the artery that bound them together.

The Main Line was exactly what its name said it was: a suburban railroad line thrusting out of Philadelphia and into the surrounding lush countryside. All along it wealthy suburban towns sprang up, many of them with Welsh names, such as Bryn Mawr and Bala Cynwyd, to provide retreats for the mighty railroad executives and their fellow members of the downtown institutions, the Union League and the Philadelphia Club. It happened that way, not by accident but by plan, for the Pennsy not only laid the lines, it sold the land, and often the houses as well. It was a good way to make money—and a good way to isolate and protect the well-to-do from the Irish, Italian, and Jewish immigrants who were pushing their way into the heart of the city.

Immigrants or no immigrants, Philadelphia politically was still Protestant and Republican, if anything as Republican then as it is Democratic today. A smooth-running machine handed out patronage, put down streets, and built buildings. The well-connected prospered mightily. Not for nothing did the turn-of-the-century muckraker Lincoln Steffens describe Philadelphia as "corrupt but contented."

Home for the machine was Philadelphia City Hall, begun in 1879, dedicated in 1901—but not completed until 1909, after thirty years of construction, at an astronomical cost overrun of $17 million, and for a final price tag of $24.5 million ($500 million today). Filthy though it has long been, City Hall is by turns magnificent, decadent, inspired, and depressing. In the freshness of youth, though, with its 650-plus rooms, Second Empire mansard roof, high-ceilinged courtrooms, and tower (designed to be the tallest in town) topped by a twenty-seven-ton cast-iron statue of William Penn (the largest and heaviest such statue in the world), it was the very symbol not only of Philadelphia's wealth but also of the machine's power.

In his 1927 novel *The Llanfair Pattern*, Francis Biddle (1886–1968) wrote of the building:

> *City Hall, symbol of dishonesty and ugliness, squatting over the city's heart, its immense meaningless bulk blocking traffic where it was thickest, wasting space, shutting out sun and air from the gloomy rooms within: great corridors that every day were littered with the refuse of the crowd; ill-ventilated courtrooms, where the fetid air lay heavy over judge and jury, witnesses and accused; imitation marble, velvet plush grown dingy with the grim, meaningless decorations, carving of slaves and Cupids where they could not be seen; fly-specked portraits of forgotten nonentities; gilded Venetian ceilings with checkerboard patterns; a Philadelphia architect's dream, perhaps, of the vanished Tuilleries.*

Biddle, then a young lawyer, was both an aristocrat and a reform-minded Democrat in a city that was 2-1 Republican, and his words read today like a mock elegy. John Lukacs has given us a rather more balanced portrait of turn-of-the-century Philadelphia:

> *There was in Philadelphia none of the coruscating glitter of the late afternoon of Western civilization in 1900, when London, Paris, Vienna glowed like the night-blooming cereus and when the steel and stone fingers of New York were reaching up to the top of the world. Unlike Boston, with its intellectual tradition, and with the drawing card of Cambridge across the river, Philadelphia was almost indifferent to intellectual achievement. . . . There was something almost English in this indifference to aesthetic and cultural professionalism, this preference for amateurism. . . . The preservation and the collection of art were still largely a private matter. . . . The art museums were in a deplorable state.*

Philadelphia was a big city, with about 1.3 million inhabitants in 1900, making it the third largest U.S. metropolis after New York and Chicago. Oddly, given the city's size, wealth, and long history, Philadelphia was not known for its support of the arts. If you wanted to see great art, you had to have entrée to one or the other of the city's two most important private collections. One belonged to the Wideners—the ex-butcher Peter Widener's scions—the other to John G. Johnson.

Like Albert Barnes, Johnson (1841–1917) grew up poor, was educated at Central High, and worked his way through the University of Pennsylvania—in his case, its law school. A brilliant student, he also proved a brilliant lawyer and was widely considered the preeminent corporate attorney of the day. Twice Johnson was offered a seat on the United States Supreme Court and twice declined the offer. It was said that he preferred to remain "a Philadelphia lawyer."

Johnson loved art. He collected widely. And by happy circumstance, this great art lover was also the lawyer for Henry and Louisine Havemeyer, the sugar trust barons who were themselves important collectors. Over time, Johnson's large, unpretentious home on South Broad Street came to resemble an art gallery, with its paintings hung in "every nook and corner."

In philistine Philadelphia circa 1900, there was no one like John Johnson, and no collection quite like his. The day would come, though, and in the not very distant future, when the Johnson collection finally met its match. Johnson, I suspect, would have welcomed the competition.

■

The Leggetts were the polar opposites of the Barneses. Laura's father, Richard, had been a captain in New York's fabled 7th Infantry Regiment during the Civil War and had gone on to establish a highly successful Brooklyn wholesale grocery business known as Francis H. Leggett & Co. The Leggetts lived in a comfortable four-story brownstone set in a genteel Brooklyn neighborhood. Even the church in which Laura and Albert were married, on June 4, 1901, bespoke a safe, middle-class existence: St. James Episcopal. It could have been a million miles from the Neck.

Following their wedding, Albert and Laura honeymooned in Europe, taking the ocean liner *Waesland* to Bremerhaven and going from there to Heidelberg—where Barnes showed his bride the university and introduced her to his old teachers. After that came a journey through the Black Forest, thence to Switzerland, to Rome, and finally to Genoa. It was exactly the kind of honeymoon expected of an upper-middle-class late-Victorian couple.

When the Barneses returned from Europe, Albert got down to business. While he had ostensibly hired Hermann Hille on behalf of Mulford, Barnes had other, more profitable uses in mind for his talented new colleague—and he had no intention of sharing those plans with his superiors at the Mulford company. Like his father's old friend Peter Widener, Albert Barnes was about to prove himself a first-rate opportunist.

For almost two decades—since 1884, when K.S.F. Credé had first proposed its use—silver nitrate had been put into the eyes of newborns as a preventive measure against gonorrheal infection. The use of silver nitrate, however, was not without serious side effects, the most worrisome being argyria (which could result in discoloration of the eye, the skin, and membranes).* A basic solution to the problem, put forward in 1896, had called for a protective colloid—colloidal silver—to be combined with dextrin, a nonirritant. The resulting product, unfortunately, lacked the therapeutic power of silver nitrate. It was too weak to do the job properly.

For some time, Barnes had been experimenting with silver compounds. What he was hoping to find, as John Lukacs has written, was one whose "antiseptic qualities would be strong while [its] caustic qualities would be weak (the very opposite of his personal characteristics)." Clever as he was, Barnes wasn't chemist enough to solve the problem.

Now, though, Barnes had Hille to help him. The German chemist proposed using the protein vitellin, which occurs naturally in egg yolk and in certain plants, in a colloidal solution. Subsequent experiments confirmed that he was correct.†

---

*According to the sixth edition of *A Manual of Pharmacology*, "The antiseptic action of silver nitrate is complicated by irritation, pain, astringency, and corrosion. These may be desirable for the destruction of tissue or the stimulation of indolent wounds, but when they are not necessary for such purposes, they are distinctly undesirable."

†The class of silver protein to which Hille's discovery belonged "contains 19 to 30 per cent of silver, of which only a small fraction is ionized; together with alkali proteins which confer well-marked demulcent properties. They are therefore not irritant, but rather soothing" (*A Manual of Pharmacology*, 6th ed.).

Convinced that they had in hand the discovery that would make their fortunes, the two men resigned their jobs at Mulford. Overnight, Albert Barnes and Hermann Hille went from being well-paid employees to being the bosses of a company that was little more than a name, Barnes & Hille. But they also had what every entrepreneur dreams of: something the world wants to buy.

Clinical trials for the new drug were held at Barnes's alma mater, the University of Pennsylvania Medical School; the results were successful. Hille's breakthrough was announced by Barnes at the third annual meeting of the American Therapeutic Society in New York, on May 14, 1902. Ten days later the findings were published in *The Medical Record*. The news immediately caused a stir. With capital of $1,600, much or all of it borrowed from Laura's mother, the two partners set up offices at 24 North Fortieth Street in a poor black neighborhood. Their rent was $25 a month. In the beginning, Lydia Barnes worked as part-time bookkeeper, and John Barnes as caretaker. Hermann Hille lived on the third floor. The company's two full-time employees were a pair of young women. Each was paid eight dollars a week. Later that year, they were joined by a tall, sturdy, blonde, and blue-eyed young woman from Pennsylvania Dutch Country. Nelle Mullen, 18, was the new bookkeeper. With her sister Mary, who joined the company a few years later, Nelle would spend the rest of her life associated with Albert Barnes and his work.

In the early days, Barnes & Hille was about as small a man-ufacturing business as you could have. It worked because of the partners' disparate abilities: Hille oversaw the laboratory and production side, while Barnes marketed and sold the products. Barnes spent much of 1903 on the road, making sure that Hille's invention—Argyrol, they called it—was put into the hands of some of the most renowned physicians of the day. That year alone, he made visits to London, Dublin, Berlin, and New York, handing out samples and explaining the drug's benefits.

As a physician whose M.D. had been granted by a first-rate

American medical school, Barnes was welcome in doctor's offices and on hospital wards in a way that few pharmaceutical salesmen were. The Argyrol road show proved a thundering success. When he returned home, Barnes carried with him a packet of glowing testimonials. He soon worked them into circulars aimed at fellow physicians. Of particular importance to this incipient ad campaign, four of the world's most distinguished specialists, two from Philadelphia, one in New York, and another in Berlin, had given Argyrol their imprimatur.

Within months, the firm of Barnes & Hille had to move its lab into larger quarters in order to keep up with the orders that were by now pouring in. By the spring of 1903, the company had cleared close to $40,000 (about three-quarters of a million dollars today). Meanwhile, however, the relationship between the two partners began to sour. Barnes had a domineering personality, but Hille had the formula. Argyrol was just a trademark. The drug itself was never patented because that would have meant revealing the formula. And Hille had no intention of letting anyone—especially Albert Barnes—in on his secret.

In April 1903, Barnes and Hille drew up a five-year partnership agreement. Hille was to continue in charge of the laboratory, while Barnes was to handle sales and marketing. Neither was to overstep his stated bounds. Meanwhile, the money-making machine that was Argyrol just kept on humming. The drug, after all, was both cheap to make and easy to distribute. By the end of 1904, sales had reached the $100,000 mark. Worldwide demand was rising.

The following year Barnes made his first tentative moves on Philadelphia society. The conventional steps were to build a big house, join a country club, and learn to ride to the hounds—in short, to join the horsey Main Line set. The later Albert Barnes was the least conventional of rich men. But the younger Albert Barnes was something else—a pretty familiar type, when you come right down to it.

From the early 1890s through the end of the first decade of the 1900s, the Philadelphia nouveaux riches—the George Wideners (Peter's son) and their ilk—had vied with each other by building ever grander estates along the Main Line. In 1905, Albert Barnes built his, a mansion in Merion that he called Lauraston, in his wife's honor.

As befitted a rich man with a mansion in the countryside, Barnes began taking riding lessons and joined the Rose Tree Fox Hunting Club. He soon found, however, that riding and the pleasures of the idle rich—the less hedonistic pleasures, in any case—did not suit his temperament. Whenever he could, Barnes preferred, instead, to take in afternoon baseball games featuring the Athletics of the American League. A connoisseur of the sport, Barnes particularly admired the hardnosed business sense of its crusty owner-manager, Connie Mack. But unlike Barnes, the straightlaced Mack was one hundred percent his own boss, his many hats including field manager, general manager, president, and team owner.

That's a degree of control Barnes may well have envied, given his own, ever more tenuous relationship with Hille. In 1906, sales of Argyrol had topped a quarter of a million dollars, with net profits of over $185,000. It didn't take a medical or scientific genius to see that control of the company was potentially worth millions. On May 31, 1907, Barnes entered a bill of equity against Hille in Philadelphia's court of common pleas. As would be the case throughout his life, he spared no expense when it came to hiring legal counsel. Perhaps it was the medical man's training: When you needed specialized help, you went to the specialist. Whatever the reason, Barnes went straight to the top, and, in the process, made a friend of the great corporate lawyer—and art collector—John G. Johnson.

The legal wrangling persisted for about a year. Finally, in 1908, a state court judge ordered the firm dissolved. As part of the severance agreement, the two former partners were to bid against each other for the totality of the business, winner take all. When the day came, Barnes prevailed. Hille might have invented Argyrol, but Barnes believed in it and was willing to bet that demand would not only hold firm but grow steadily. In the end, he staked just about everything he had on Argyrol—and came away with one of the bargains of the century.

When Barnes upped the ante to $350,000, Hille walked away from the table. He did not, however, walk away with the secret formula. As part of the settlement, Hille not only had to show Barnes how to make Argyrol, he had to watch as the new owner learned to make it himself. It must have been a galling task. Not until Barnes was sure that he could produce Argyrol successfully was Hille finally excused from coming to work at the newly opened A. C. Barnes Company.

What Connie Mack had been to the Athletics, Albert Barnes would be to the Argyrol pharmaceutical works: The undisputed one hundred percent boss.

■

Now that he controlled the company, Albert Barnes imposed his will on every aspect of it—often in ways that were deemed, at the time, highly eccentric. The working day he set at the A. C. Barnes Company factory, for example, was remarkably humane: eight hours, of which only six were devoted to manufacturing. For another, the workforce was mixed-sex and racially integrated. There were never more than twenty employees in the company at any one time, but among the most prominent were the Mullen sisters and "Argyrol Jack," an African American with a local reputation as a prize fighter. Everyone was expected to attend the daily two-hour discussion group presided over by Barnes.

It might seem strange to imagine Argyrol Jack and the Mullen sisters—fresh from Pennsylvania Dutch Country—sitting around a factory room reading Sigmund Freud, but we know they did. Above all, though, Barnes was an admirer of the work of the

Harvard philosopher William James (1842–1910), the novelist Henry James's influential brother. It was William James's concepts of intelligence as applied to the conduct of everyday life—Pragmatism, it was called—that Barnes found most appealing. And it was Pragmatism, as the noted Barnes scholar Richard Wattenmaker has said, that came to provide "the intellectual underpinnings of Barnes's eventual life work in education."

For the first two years, the A. C. Barnes Company "seminars" were, in fact, mostly devoted to the study of James. The curriculum was later expanded to include Bertrand Russell's "The Free Man's Worship," John Dewey's *How We Think* (1910), and George Santayana's "The Sense of Beauty" (1896) and *Reason in Art* (1906). The factory was, by all accounts, an unusual place. There was a lending library for the workers—and original paintings on the walls, at least one of which was by Barnes's high school chum William Glackens.

Sometime in 1911, Barnes reestablished contact with Glackens. By now, Glackens had become an established painter. A former student at the Pennsylvania Academy of the Fine Arts, he was a contemporary and friend of Robert Henri and had begun his career as a realist. Early in 1912, Barnes commissioned Glackens to go to Europe on a shopping spree. Glackens's marching orders were simple enough: He was given $20,000 to spend and told to buy what he liked.

Would that it had been as easy as that. From Europe, Glackens wrote his wife in frustration: "You can't touch a Cézanne for under $3,000, and that for a little landscape. His portraits and important pictures range from $7,000 to $30,000." Later, he wrote her, "Hunting up pictures is not child's play." And, on February 21, "I am mighty glad it is finished and I am sick of looking at pictures and asking prices."

Glackens returned triumphant, bearing with him twenty paintings that included Cézanne's *Mont Sainte-Victoire and Valley* (1878–1880), Picasso's *Woman with a Cigarette*, a van Gogh

(*The Postman*), and a Renoir (purchased for $1,400). By April of the same year, Barnes himself had begun to make purchases from the Parisian dealer Durand-Ruel—a Renoir and a Monet bought in New York.

One month later, in May, Lydia Barnes, ravaged by brain cancer, died at age sixty-six, the immediate cause of death lobar pneumonia. Lydia had lived to see her son not only an M.D. but also a very wealthy man indeed. She had done well by him—and he had done well by her. The man who hadn't done particularly well by either of them, John Barnes, would live on for many a year (until his death in 1930) in the house on Tasker Street—but it was his successful younger son Albert who took title to the home.

The 1912 fall musical season marked the start of yet another important friendship, this with the talented—and equally idiosyncratic—young Leopold Stokowski, the newly installed conductor of the Philadelphia Orchestra—a man with as extreme a personality as Albert Barnes's own.

Early that winter, Barnes found himself in Paris. It was then that he first met the fabled Stein siblings, Leo and Gertrude. At their initial encounter, in December, Gertrude offered him two Matisses. Barnes came away with the pair. While Barnes and Gertrude never took to one another, he and Leo were to become friends and correspondents. By March 1913, Barnes wrote Leo to say that he now owned a dozen Renoirs.

In February 1913, Barnes attended the first great exhibition of modern art in America at the 69th Regiment Armory in New York—the fabled "Armory Show." That summer there would be visits to all the important museums of London and Paris.

In October, William Glackens underwent surgery at Jefferson Hospital in Philadelphia. The event brought out a side of Barnes that would have surprised many. Though he hadn't practiced medicine in almost twenty years, Barnes had stayed abreast of current medical issues and had maintained close contact with some of his old classmates. Determined now that Glackens should get the best possible medical care, he donned a surgical gown and mask and stood by throughout the successful surgery.

Barnes continued to collect and to read widely. By early 1914, he told Leo Stein that his collection contained more than two dozen Renoirs and a dozen Cézannes. Meanwhile, Barnes had become active in supporting liberal causes and the arts, among them *The New Republic* (founded in 1914 and for which he also occasionally wrote), *The New Masses* (briefly), and the Provincetown Players.

With the entry of the United States in World War I in 1917, research at the A. C. Barnes Company seems to have focused on chemical warfare. In a short biographical entry in the 1922 edition of the *General Alumni Catalogue of the University of Pennsylvania*, Barnes was said to have done "experimental work on Gas Masks for U.S.A. War Dept." Curiously, the same entry incorrectly showed his date of birth as being January 2, 1892.

Barnes enrolled as a special student in John Dewey's Columbia University philosophy seminar in 1917. Dewey (1859–1952) was William James's intellectual heir, and his *Democracy and Education* (1916) stirred Barnes as perhaps no other book ever had. Surely, it can be said to have given focus and framework to his innately liberal sentiments.

■

Eventually, Barnes and John Dewey became far more than just student and teacher. A close and enduring friendship—"as between equals," in the words of Richard Wattenmaker—ensued between "Al" and "Jack," as the two men called each other in frequent correspondence. In one letter, dated May 21, 1921, Barnes told how Leo Stein had decided to sell some of the remnants of his collection, using Barnes as a middleman. The proceeds, Barnes wrote, came to more than $30,000. As for his own, ever-growing collection, Barnes estimated that he now owned more than a hundred Renoirs, at least a score of which he'd bought in just the past two years (1919–1921).

The years 1922–1923 would arguably be the most important of Barnes's whole career as a collector. During that period alone, he made more than one hundred purchases, working with the Parisian dealers Bernheim-Jeune, Vollard, Durand-Ruel—and, above all, the young Paul Guillaume.

According to one of Barnes's several biographers, Howard Greenfeld, Guillaume "first attracted attention in 1913 when at the age of twenty-one and apparently without money or family connections, he struck up a close friendship with Guillaume Apollinaire, the enormously influential poet and critic then at the height of his fame among the Paris avant-garde. Initially their bond was a mutual interest in African sculpture. . . . [But in] time Apollinaire introduced the well-mannered, soft-spoken young man to the world of modern art, and before long Guillaume set himself up as an art dealer." Among the artists whose works the dapper Guillaume handled were Cézanne, Renoir, Matisse, and Picasso, as well as two who became close friends, André Derain and Giorgio de Chirico.

In 1917, Guillaume had opened a large gallery on the fashionable Faubourg St.-Honoré. There, recounts Greenfeld, he "dazzled Parisians with the first comprehensive exhibition of African sculpture to be seen in the French capital." When Barnes first met Guillaume in the early 1920s, he was barely thirty years old, but charming, sensitive, dynamic, and intelligent. Under his influence Barnes—already from his childhood fascinated by African American culture—would develop a passionate and abiding interest in African art.

■

Barnes had to find a place to put all the art that he had collected in the past two years. The big house in Lower Merion (Lauraston—known today as "Dietrich House"—still stands on the Episcopal Academy campus, cheek to jowl with the Barnes

Foundation) wasn't, after all, *that* big. In 1922, Barnes had added acreage to his domain by purchasing the twelve-acre Wilson Arboretum from his friend and neighbor Captain Joseph Lapsley Wilson. But that didn't solve the problem of where to house the paintings.

Meanwhile, steps were being taken to ensure the ultimate destiny of the collection. That fall, the noted Philadelphia attorney Owen J. Roberts—John Johnson having died five years earlier—was retained by Barnes to draw up an indenture of trust. Barnes once again hired first-rate legal talent—Roberts would eventually serve as an associate justice of the U.S. Supreme Court. The indenture, dated December 6, 1922, followed by two days the grant of a corporate charter for a nonprofit entity to be known as the Barnes Foundation. Via the indenture, Barnes conveyed $6 million (about $70 million in 2002 dollars) in money and stock—900 shares of A.C. Barnes Company common stock—specifying that the foundation's endowment could be invested in his lifetime "in any good securities," but after his death only in federal, state, and municipal bonds. For several years thereafter Barnes contributed an annual $450,000 to the foundation endowment. Also conveyed to the foundation were twelve acres of land and a gallery to be built by the donor—plans for which already lay on the drawing board of Paul-Philippe Cret (1876–1945), a graduate of the Ecole des Beaux Arts in Paris and professor of architectural design at the University of Pennsylvania.

The bylaws of the foundation give plenty of insight into the character of the donor. If Barnes had involved himself in the minutest details of factory life, he would be no less directly involved in the activities of his own foundation. The bylaws, for example, provided that there be no more than two gallery attendants and two watchmen at a maximum salary of $2,000 each per year, along with one stenographer clerk at no more than $2,500. The total pay for cleaners and janitorial help was not to exceed $6,000 a year.

Barnes also provided that if the time were ever to arise when the foundation could no longer sustain itself, its assets should be turned over to an "existing and organized institution in Philadelphia or suburbs" with similar aims. Just what institution, he did not specify.

A five-member board of trustees was established to govern the foundation—Albert and Laura Barnes, the Mullen sisters Nelle and Mary, and Captain Wilson, the Barnes's horticulturalist friend. The bylaws specified five-year terms for trustees and stipulated that following the deaths of Albert and Laura Barnes, the Girard Trust Corn Exchange Bank would be empowered to nominate the first successor trustee, who would then serve as corporate treasurer of the foundation. The trustees of the University of Pennsylvania would nominate the second successor trustee; the trustees of the Pennsylvania Academy of the Fine Arts, the third; Penn, the fourth, the Academy, the fifth. Control over the Barnes Foundation would thus be split between these two powerful Philadelphia institutions.

Five months later, in April 1923, Barnes put on his first major exhibition. With the Cret-designed gallery (and an attached home for the Barneses—it would become the administration building after their deaths) barely off the drawing board, the four-week run was scheduled for the Pennsylvania Academy. Among the works shown were some nineteen paintings by Soutine, seven by Modigliani, five each by Matisse (one of them *Joy of Life*) and Derain, two each by Picasso (including *Composition*) and Utrillo, and a single de Chirico.

Barnes, in his introductory essay to the show's catalogue, had asked for a tolerant hearing. The event proved, instead, an unmitigated disaster. Philadelphia newspaper critics, generally hostile to modern art, greeted the show with a mixture of incomprehension, mystification, and anger. Barnes responded in kind, writing bitter replies, often personal, to the critics and equally strongly worded letters to the editor. It was the beginning of a war that would be waged on and off (though mostly on) for the next three decades.

Two years later, greeted by grudging praise from a somewhat less hostile Philadelphia press corps, the Barnes Foundation opened its doors on March 19, 1925. The wonderful gallery that Paul Cret had designed was something that even the most arch-conservative critic could appreciate: a fine, formal, French chateau of twenty-three galleries, connected to the Barnes's new home by a second-story bridge. There to give the dedication address was John Dewey, with President Josiah H. Penniman on hand to represent the University of Pennsylvania and Barnes's friend, maestro Leopold Stokowski, "on behalf of the artists of America."

The same year, the trustees of the Pennsylvania Museum of Art (the Philadelphia Museum of Art or PMA, as it later came to be known) chose as their first director a man as different from Albert Barnes as could have been imagined. Fiske Kimball, a conservative architectural historian, had been chairman of the art history department at New York University. Kimball, a big man who stood well over six feet tall, was arrogant and patronizing. Besides being an academic—seldom a good thing in Barnes's book—Kimball was also a terrible snob. Barnes quickly grew to loathe him.

Kimball aside, it's only fair to point out that Albert Barnes's dislikes were by no means merely personal. The first issue of *The Journal of the Barnes Foundation* (1925), for example, was devoted to an exposé, "The Shame in the Public Schools of Philadelphia." But whether you were Fiske Kimball, the PMA, or the Philadelphia public schools, once Barnes had targeted you, you were there to be blasted.

CHAPTER TWO

DE MEDICI IN MERION

By the mid-1920s, Albert Barnes had become a public figure— in Philadelphia and along the Main Line—with a not inconsiderable persona. Most of his reputation, however, was local—and tarred by his own brush. The philistines among Philadelphia newspaper editors were all too delighted to discover that Dr. Barnes was up to strange stuff, perfectly suited for public ridiculing—like collecting contemporary art that the newspapers' own critics didn't pretend to understand—and that he was eminently quotable, especially when provoked.

If any newspaper in town was likely to give Barnes a break, though, it was the morning *Recorder*. The *Recorder* was the money-losing pet of merchant prince John Wanamaker's aesthete son Rodman and the great rival of the *Inquirer*, the city's other important morning newspaper. (Both were, meanwhile, far distant runners-up to the city's one truly profitable newspaper, *The Evening Bulletin*, which famously claimed, "*Nearly* everyone in

Philadelphia reads the *Bulletin*.") But whereas the *Inquirer* was Republican, the *Recorder* was Democratic and, backed by the immense Wanamaker fortune in those still-flush times, could afford to be allied with the party out of favor.

Among the more energetic members of Rodman Wanamaker's staff was Henry Hart, a young and highly impressionable reporter—just the sort of person likely to be influenced by a cocksure, brilliant, and extremely successful older man. That moment came in 1927, when Hart was told by his city editor to get up and go over to the A. C. Barnes Company factory at Fortieth and Filbert Streets. There was a rumor going around that Dr. Barnes was going to give his art collection to the Metropolitan Museum in New York—and turn his newly opened gallery into an educational institution for Negroes. The reason: Old man Barnes was said to be outraged because an "unscrupulous" building contractor was erecting "a slum" next to the Barnes Foundation in Lower Merion. (Barnes, in fact, helped develop the neighborhood in conjunction with a powerful Republican contractor/developer as his partner.)

Hart did what an enterprising reporter does: He left the city room with a pen, a pad of paper—and an open mind. A good thing, too, because Hart was confounded by almost everything that he saw and heard that day. Some thirty-five years later, Hart could "still remember my surprise when I saw modern paintings on most of the walls and noticed that the offices were furnished more like a home than a place of business." Then there was the supposedly irascible Dr. Barnes, who, it turned out, "couldn't have been more affable."

Not long afterward, Hart was assigned to do a story about conditions in state mental hospitals and was told to find out what was going on at one in nearby Norristown. Before setting out, he called on Barnes and asked for his advice. Barnes, possibly with his own internship at a state insane asylum some three and a half decades ago in mind, offered to accompany him. In the end, the former physician not only went along for the visit, he drove Hart there in his big Packard.

Later that same year, Barnes offered his young friend the editorship of *The Journal of the Barnes Foundation*. And when the ocean liner *Leviathan* left New York harbor for Europe on May 20, 1927, the passengers included not only Mr. and Mrs. Albert Barnes but also Mr. Henry Hart. Barnes paid Hart's way and gave him three hundred dollars a month to spend.

It was a heady time for young Mr. Hart, and never more so than when he accompanied Barnes on his Parisian rounds. Along the way, Hart met Paul Guillaume—who, the reporter estimated, was handling as much as seventy-five percent of Barnes's business—at his gallery at 59, rue la Boetie. More importantly, Hart was given a glimpse into Barnes's character. One night, the older man proposed that they walk over to La Rotonde and have a drink together. Barnes, Hart recalled, "was the kind of heavy-set man who is light on his feet, and he liked to walk at a good clip. He was observant, and interested in everything he saw, no matter how trivial, and when he was walking his conversation was different from what it was at other times." In such moments, Barnes was also, Hart noticed, far less didactic and far more open-minded—more human and likable too.

Barnes's first important brush with nationwide publicity came in September 1928, when Harold Ross's *New Yorker* ran a profile by A. H. Shaw entitled "De Medici in Merion." In the piece, Shaw reported, "Dr. Barnes usually spends his evenings reading and retires early. When he can't sleep, he puts on his dressing gown and walks through a passageway that connects the house and the museum, and in the gallery he studies his pictures and sometimes spends hours arranging one to suit his taste." The doctor, as Shaw called him, was a collector of books as well as art, and he "reads continuously in English, German, or French." Perhaps more to the point: "When [Barnes] finishes reading a book the margins are often black with notes, and

when the author annoys him he writes in the margin a denun-
ciatory epithet."

■

Much of Albert Barnes's time during the decades of the twenties
and thirties was spent writing about art. Apart from the opening
of the Barnes Foundation galleries, the most important event in
Barnes's career was the publication of his *The Art in Painting*
(1925). It was a serious approach to understanding and expli-
cating the roots of art and, as such, was reviewed by the likes of
Leo Stein, Ezra Pound, and A. H. Barr. *The Art in Painting* was
followed by *The French Primitives and Their Forms: From Their
Origin to the End of the Fifteenth Century* (1931), *The Art of Henri
Matisse* (1933), *The Art of Renoir* (1935), and *The Art of Cézanne*
(1939). All but the first were written in collaboration with
Violette de Mazia, a young woman of Franco-Belgian descent
who joined the foundation staff in 1925 and quickly became
Barnes's closest colleague.

The serious student of art who is truly interested in the subject should, of course, read the books. Short of that, John
Lukacs's essay "Albert Coombs Barnes, or the Methodist as
Aesthete" will perhaps suffice. Here, we'll only concern ourselves
with the essence of Barnes's theories—and how they influenced
the way the foundation was run. As the scholar Richard
Wattenmaker has observed, what really set Barnes apart from
other collectors "was his conviction that . . . works of art could
be employed as tools in an educational experiment."

Barnes also rejected the conventional academic scholarship of
his day—and suffered enormously as a result, for just as he dismissed art critics and art historians, many of them, though not
Alfred Barr, casually dismissed Barnes. Not for him dates and
history, or even the lives of the artists. He had no more use for
the academic history of art than he did for the critics. He loved
to cite Degas: "Literature has only done harm to art."

He especially despised the work of the influential aesthete Bernard Berenson: "Mr. Berenson has aided materially in the identification of the works of some of the early Italian painters by means of investigations that are primarily and fundamentally akin to those of handwriting-experts." Critics like Berenson, Barnes believed, "have resurrected the names of a number of early and very bad, Italian painters whose work the picture-dealers sell accompanied by an expert's certificate of authenticity; in other words, antiquity, not aesthetic merit, has become the guide in a traffic in the kind of pictures which George Moore calls 'cock-eyed saints painted on gold backgrounds.'"

Barnes was at his best when he analyzed form and content in painting and when he, the long-ago eager student of Freud, examined the element of psychology in art. In all this, he stressed (though without admitting as much) the subjectivity that exists both in the mind of the painter and that of the viewer. Yet, as Lukacs has pointed out, the basic flaw in Barnes's thought lay in the opposite direction, in his purported need to view art with utter and absolute "objectivity." Or, as Barnes put it: "The conceptions of the artist, in a word, are verified in the same manner as those of the scientist—by experiment, by the production of objective facts which vindicate their standing in the real world." But, of course, they couldn't be, could they? For where line and even form can be measured, the emotive psychology behind them cannot, a point completely obvious to the Romantics, though not to their successors.

In all this, Barnes was what he was: a Victorian, with the Victorian's belief in rationality and science, objectivity and the immutable progress of mankind. As his friend Henry Hart later observed, Barnes seemed to believe that anyone with a brain and the willingness to work as hard as he himself had could master anything.

He was deluding himself. But he was not alone in doing so. Barnes's was the kind of rationality that altogether lacked the ironic detachment that World War I inspired in other, younger men. They had their own primal experience—the war—and it was not his.

A high-minded Victorian Albert Barnes was raised, and a high-minded Victorian he would die.

■

Albert Barnes's timing was often little short of perfect. Barnes chose the summer of 1929—with the stock market at its peak—to sell the company. The buyer, Zonite Products Corporation, it has been reported, paid somewhere between four and six million dollars for the privilege of owning the recipes for Argyrol and Ovoferrin (an organic iron compound for anemia that was the A. C. Barnes Company's other main product). By August 19, Barnes could write Glackens's wife, Edith, that the money was already safely in the bank. When the stock market crashed in October of that year, Barnes was set for life. Yet the Great Crash, provoking as it almost certainly did memories of the Panic of 1893, made Barnes even more cautious with his money.

In September 1930, Henri Matisse was invited to Merion. As the English art historian and former *New York Times* chief art critic John Russell has written in his book *Matisse: Father and Son*, Henri Matisse

> liked and admired the Barnes Foundation. Quite apart
> from the very high quality of much that was on show, he
> was delighted by the candor and the straightforwardness
> with which it was installed. There was no "presentation,"
> no showmanship, no fancy lighting. Matisse even liked the
> promiscuity with which great works of art were shown out
> of context and in company with objects that differed from
> them both in kind and in date. This was—to quote from
> Matisse's pocket diary—"the only sane place" for the dis-
> play of art that Matisse had as yet seen in America.

Barnes wanted to meet with Matisse alone. "Glow[ing] with admiration," Barnes invited the great French artist to paint a mural for the three lunettes that stood above the French windows in the main gallery. It would prove a daunting task, the space being "almost, but not quite" divided into three by broad pendentives— the architectural term for the concave triangular supports of a dome. As Russell notes, "The essential task, therefore, was to ensure that the mural did not seem to start and stop. The action had to be seen to be continuous, irrespective of the pendentives."

The fee that Barnes offered—$30,000, to be paid in three equal installments—was a lot of money in the middle of the Depression. Certainly, Matisse needed the cash. But for Barnes, it was little more than pocket change, the equivalent of about $250,000 in today's dollars. As Russell says, "Barnes drove one of his harder bargains when Henri Matisse agreed to paint [this] enormous and very tricky mural." All the more so as Matisse would learn in February 1932 that he had a "catastrophe of the first order" on his hands. He discovered that the dimensions he'd been working with—the result of his own measurements—were "slightly but irrevocably mistaken," in Russell's words. "The whole thing had to be begun again, all over."

Did Albert Barnes offer to make up for Matisse's mistake? Of course not. As Matisse's son and agent, Pierre, put it at the time: "I'm afraid that he may take a brutal line about what he calls his 'rights' in this matter." Barnes was frugal—and proud of it.

■

During the Depression era, Barnes became an enthusiastic supporter of Franklin D. Roosevelt and the New Deal. Liberal though he was, Barnes did not, however, share Henry Hart's enthusiasm for what Stalin was achieving in the Soviet Union. When news of Stalin's purges became front-page headlines in the West, Hart (who became a political reactionary in his old age) recalled, Barnes just said, "I told you so."

The decade of the thirties—a terrible time for most Americans—brought only more fame and good fortune to the former master of Lauraston. At the big house in Merion, life went on as it had since the gallery first opened in 1925. By day, there were small classes in art appreciation, open only to those whose written requests Barnes chose to grant. (Visiting scholars, generally speaking, need not have applied.) By night, on occasion, there were intimate parties. The guest list was often highly eclectic: not only Leopold Stokowski but also the actress Katharine Cornell, Carl Van Vechten, and Eva Le Gallienne were numbered among the privileged. One of the few Philadelphians whom Barnes chose to have as a regular guest was the brilliant William C. Bullitt, a liberal New Dealer and future ambassador to the U.S.S.R. and, later, to France. Dinners chez Barnes, the *New Yorker*'s Shaw reported, were of a high standard and featured fine vintage wines—oh, how very, very far from the Neck was he by now—and cocktails the good doctor mixed himself, "measuring the amounts carefully, using chemistry beakers."

Fame alone, however, did not guarantee admission to either home or gallery. One would-be visitor who found himself turned away was Alexander Woollcott. In Barnes's eyes, Woollcott had exactly one thing going for him: he was a fellow graduate of Central High. Beyond that, he had just about everything going against him. The former *New York Times* drama critic was a thundering self-promoter: A member of *New Yorker* editor Ross's Algonquin set, he wrote criticism for the magazine and was the host of a popular radio program ("The Town Crier"). He was, in short, oily and obnoxious, corpulent and conceited. But his friends—and they included important people like Ross—tolerated and even liked him.

Another of his friends, George S. Kaufman, wrote an enormously successful Broadway play, *The Man Who Came to Dinner*—it would later be made into a film starring Monte Woolley and Bette Davis—in which a pompous New York theater critic and radio personality named Sheridan Whiteside finds himself the pampered but unwanted guest of a conventional, upper-middle-class Midwestern family. By the time the play opened in Philadelphia in the winter of 1939, Woollcott was, in effect, playing himself. (Some people were surprised that a drama critic with little acting experience would dare to take such a turn on stage. They didn't know Woollcott.)

High-handed as ever, Woollcott sent a telegram to Barnes demanding to be shown the collection "on Thursday or Friday of next week." Barnes immediately fired off a reply telegram:

> *I was alone in the house this morning when a telegraph office employee telephoned that she had a telegram for Dr. Barnes, charges collect. I explained to her that our financial condition made it impossible for us to assume additional responsibility, and I declined to accept the telegram. She said it was from such an important man that I should call Dr. Barnes to the 'phone. . . . My reply was that Dr. Barnes was out on the lawn singing to the birds and that it would cost me my job if I should disturb him at his regular Sunday morning nature worship.*

The reply was signed "Fidèle-de-Port-Manech." Fidèle-de-Port-Manech was, in fact, Barnes's faithful ("Fidèle") dog, the rest of her name taken from the village in Brittany where her master often summered. Barnes sent a copy of the correspondence to the *Evening Bulletin*, together with a note that read: "I haven't seen Mr. Woollcott's play, and I wouldn't dream of doing so, but I understand that he portrays someone who comes somewhere for dinner and stays for weeks. I would be afraid if I let him come to see a dozen of my paintings he might stay to see the more than 1,000 in the collection."

In print and on the air, Woollcott was used to beating up on people. Like Sheridan Whiteside, he not only got away with it, he was applauded for his audacity and pluck. Albert Barnes, though, just plain didn't give a damn.

■

In 1940, the great English mathematician, philosopher, and pacifist Bertrand Russell had left England—about to be engulfed by the Battle of Britain—and come to America to take a chair in mathematics at New York's City College. A Tammany judge, however, revoked the appointment, citing Russell's atheism and advocacy of "free love." Barnes came to the rescue by offering a five-year teaching appointment at the foundation. Unfortunately, Barnes found himself disappointed. The lectures, he felt, were weak and insipid. Worse, he discovered that he couldn't abide the third Lady Russell—nor she him. Barnes tried to fire Russell, who sued in state court for $24,000 in back pay. For once, Barnes's vaunted legal advisors failed him. To Barnes's intense chagrin, the Russells walked away from court winners, to the tune of $20,000.

As he readied himself to enter his seventies, Barnes was starting to think about his legacy—and making preparations for the time when he would no longer be the master of his domain. In 1940, as the war news from Europe went from bad to worse, Barnes began providing for his charges. That year, he granted his great friend Jack Dewey an annual stipend of $5,000 for life, Nelle Mullen $12,000, her sister Mary $5,000, Miss de Mazia $10,000, and three others in the extended Barnes "family" $5,000, $2,800, and $2,400. Laurence Buermeyer, one of the foundation's earliest employees, was given $600 (later increased to $1,800) a year for life. A gifted writer, he also gave lectures at the gallery. But he drank too much, and eventually he suffered a nervous breakdown. There were some who blamed Barnes for the breakdown, though this seems a harsh and probably unfounded judgment.

■

Barnes was seventy years old when he became the subject of a *Saturday Evening Post* profile. Located off Independence Square in Philadelphia's Society Hill area, the red brick Curtis Publishing Company buildings stand to this day, hollow reminders of the power that was the *Post*. Sixty years ago, the power was very real. At the time, the *Post* was probably the most profitable magazine in America—with an enormous million-plus readership. The magazine was—and remains—most famous for its Norman Rockwell covers and middle-America, small-town sensibility. What tends to be forgotten is that the *Post* also paid the highest rates in the country to its writers, and that these included such notables as William Faulkner, F. Scott Fitzgerald, and Ernest Hemingway. None of them had any great respect for the magazine, but they were more than happy to accept its checks. Occasionally, the *Post* managed to run first-rate political and cultural reporting: the young New Orleans newspaperman Hermann B. Deutsch, for example, had brilliantly profiled "The Kingfish" of Louisiana politics, Huey P. Long, in its pages in 1935.

Seven years later, the *Post*'s editors didn't have to go that far to find an equally fascinating subject for a profile. Surprisingly, writer Carl W. McCardle found in Barnes a cooperative subject. But when the four-part profile, "The Terrible-Tempered Dr. Barnes," appeared (March 21, March 28, April 4, and April 11, 1942), Barnes was furious. Though the series was, on balance, mild and even favorable toward him, Barnes felt that he had been duped and, worse, made to look like "a nut." He found himself described by McCardle as a "combination of Peck's Bad Boy and Donald Duck" who was said to get "his greatest personal satisfaction out of writing poison-pen letters." "The Terrible-Tempered Dr. Barnes" reacted as might have been expected: He went on local radio broadcasts to denounce the

Post, published a pamphlet in defense of himself, and drove around the Main Line tearing down *Post* advertising wherever he found it.

He carried on a far more serious feud with his alma mater, the University of Pennsylvania. As we have seen, Barnes had for years intended that Penn and the Pennsylvania Academy of the Fine Arts should share control of his foundation following his and Laura's deaths. The arrival of a new president at the university in 1949 set off the feud. Harold E. Stassen had been the boy wonder of Minnesota Republican politics: Elected governor in 1938 at age thirty-three, he'd made a run for the GOP presidential nomination in 1948, only to be soundly defeated by New York governor Thomas E. Dewey. On the rebound, he'd accepted the presidency of the University of Pennsylvania.

Having been introduced to Barnes at a party, Stassen attempted to insinuate himself with the aging multimillionaire. The effort only served to alienate Barnes. To engage further in continued dialogue, Barnes wrote Stassen, "would be like a Frenchman and a Chinese trying to convey to each other, each in his own language, the essentials of a problem in which both are interested." Stassen was so turned off by Barnes's letter—or so baffled by it—that he waited months to reply. The cost to Penn would be incalculable; for in the meantime, Barnes had changed the terms of the foundation's indenture.

■

Four years before Stassen stepped onto the Penn campus, Horace Mann Bond had assumed the presidency of Lincoln University in 1945. Lincoln had been founded in 1854 by members of the Oxford (Pennsylvania) Presbyterian Church as the Ashmun Institute. Its original purpose: To train young men for missionary work in Africa. It has the distinction of being the oldest black college in America.

Located in bucolic Chester County, Lincoln was a forty-five

minute drive from the nearest railroad station, Wilmington, Delaware—and an hour and a half or more from Philadelphia. "Lincoln was isolated. The people were isolated," is how Horace Bond's widow, Julia, remembers the place. As luck would have it, Albert C. Barnes was also a part-time resident of this rustic backwater. Five years earlier, in 1940, Barnes had bought a pre-revolutionary farmhouse, along with its gardens, and 137 acres of farmland in Chester County. He called it Ker-Feal, Breton for Fidèle's House—after his dog. In the ensuing years, he had restored the place and filled it with early American furniture, glass, pewter, and textiles—everything but paintings. Barnes loved to escape to Ker-Feal and often stayed weekends there.

Barnes and Bond's initial meeting came about by chance, at the October 31, 1946, funeral service of a Lincoln graduate. Niara Sudarkasa, a future Lincoln president, has written about that first meeting. It was, she says, "punctuated by a typical Barnesian quip that he hoped Dr. Bond would not be as 'long-winded' as most 'Negro preachers.'" The story sounds apocryphal. It's not. "Oh, no," says Julia Bond. "That's what my husband told me happened." She pauses, then adds, "Dr. Barnes was a crude man. He liked to shock people."

Dr. Bond, Sudarkasa writes,

disdainfully replied that his remarks would last exactly three minutes, and that he was "not a Negro preacher." This must have piqued Dr. Barnes's interest because after Dr. Bond's brief remarks, he insisted that his new acquaintance join him and his wife for lunch at their residence in Merion. Later, writing to a friend who had introduced him to Dr. Barnes, Dr. Bond recalled lunching on milk and crackers and receiving a personal tour of the Barnes Foundation gallery as well as a lecture by the collector and one of his colleagues on the philosophy of aesthetics.

Her husband, Julia Bond says, "hoped to get money from [Barnes]." Still, she says, "I don't think he had any idea that Dr. Barnes would leave the foundation to Lincoln." Both Julia Bond and her son Julian, the future civil rights leader and current-day chairman of the National Association for the Advancement of Colored People (NAACP), vividly remember a day when Barnes came to visit their house. "The kids," recalls Julian Bond, "were upstairs playing," while his parents were downstairs entertaining Barnes. "And I guess we were making too much noise. Anyhow, Dr. Barnes didn't like it." Julia Bond continues the tale: "Dr. Barnes got irritated, and he asked me, 'Who's making that goddamned racket?' And I said, 'That's my children.' And he kind of frowned at the word *children*, and he said, 'Well, tell them to shut up!'"

Barnes had never ceased tinkering with the terms of the foundation's indenture. Generations of Philadelphia legal talent—from future U.S. Supreme Court associate justice Owen J. Roberts through the then-leader of the city's bar, Robert McCracken—had been instructed to draw its various provisions ever tighter. The death of his old friend, lawyer, and fellow art collector John G. Johnson had particularly energized Barnes. Johnson had, in effect, laid out the blueprint for what Barnes went on to do: Johnson's rambling home had served as an improvised art gallery; and when he'd died childless in 1917, Johnson had left his more than one thousand paintings together with his house to the people of the city of Philadelphia. What the great lawyer could not have known—would not even have suspected—was that under the leadership of Fiske Kimball, the Pennsylvania Museum of Art (PMA) succeeded in 1933 in what has been described as "the legal theft" of the Johnson Collection. The PMA and the city went before an Orphans' Court judge and asked that the beloved house be torn down and the paintings moved to the new Pennsylvania Museum of Art building. Prodded by many of the city's most powerful leaders, the judge granted the petition. As Albert Barnes knew so well, John Johnson would have been appalled. It was a crime—even if it was technically legal.

All too aware of what had happened to Johnson's home and his art, Barnes sought to make his collection ever safer from theft. He couldn't have known that his own best efforts, like Johnson's, would in time lead to near-disaster.

Enraged by the bumbling President Stassen, disgusted with the Penn fine arts department and the academic art professionals at the academy, Barnes on October 20, 1950, once again changed the terms of indenture. This time he granted ultimate control over his foundation to Lincoln University. He just didn't tell anyone at Lincoln that he'd done it.

Under the new provisions of the indenture, following the deaths of Albert and Laura Barnes, a different set of wheels would begin moving. First, the Girard bank would be empowered to nominate a candidate to serve as trustee and treasurer to the foundation. (In practice, this meant that one of the five trustees would always be a banker selected by the Girard Trust, or its successor institutions.)

But from then on, it would be the trustees of Lincoln University who would nominate the trustees of the Barnes Foundation. To add insult to injury, Barnes further stipulated that no trustee ever be named from any of the major local colleges and universities—whether Penn, Temple, Bryn Mawr, Haverford, Swarthmore, or the Pennsylvania Academy of the Fine Arts.

But how serious was all of this? Certainly, Barnes was fond of the Bonds. Moreover, he had begun making efforts to help the college. On May 21, 1951, he wrote Bond, "On Thursday next, I have an engagement with [John] Dewey in New York to lay before him plans to make our resources an integral part of Lincoln's educational program." It was, without doubt, a serious offer coming from a serious man with all the resources to do something about it.

Nevertheless, on June 5, 1951, Barnes was a no-show at the Lincoln commencement where he was to have been awarded an honorary bachelor of science degree. Speculation immediately arose that the college had for some reason dropped out of his favor. Still, Horace Bond reported at the time: "Following Commencement, we delivered [to Barnes] his diploma and hood; and on July 17th, took a party to Merion where we were kindly entertained. . . . We discussed plans for our courses at the Barnes Foundation and had a good visit."

A week later, Albert Barnes was dead.

It was a hot summer day, a Sunday, and Barnes had just dined with Laura at Ker-Feal. Later, she would remember how he seemed unusually pensive and absentminded that day. Following lunch, Barnes and Fidèle hopped into his Packard and sped off in the direction of Merion. When the car reached a crossing stop, Barnes instead blazed through the intersection and into the path of a trailer truck. The old man, so strong-willed and robust even in his late seventies, was thrown from the car. His body was hurled some forty feet, landing in a nearby field, and he died instantly. According to one account, Fidèle, badly mangled and dying, refused to let the troopers near her master and had to be shot.

■

The question hovers in the air: Did Albert Barnes really intend the document dated October 20, 1950, to be his final testament? When I interviewed the ninety-three-year-old Julia Bond, she asked me, "Do you think he intended for Lincoln to have the Barnes?" When I asked her for her opinion, Mrs. Bond replied: "I *think* Dr. Barnes *was* interested in Lincoln. But he'd been interested in all these other places too. Then he got mad at them. He got mad at them and fell out with them and changed his will. So who knows what he wanted to do?"

It's often been speculated—by Penn presidents and trustees,

especially—that this was only a temporary punishment, aimed at making the university and the academy shape up. Perhaps Barnes wanted to get his own way in setting the fine arts agendas at both institutions.

And perhaps not. This is the mystery of Albert Barnes. Perhaps he wanted it just the way he left it: And, oh, the mischief that would ensue!

CHAPTER THREE

THE MYSTERIOUS MISS DE MAZIA

During his lifetime, Barnes was witness to several significant business cycles, including four major depressions (1893, 1907, 1921, and the Great Depression of the 1930s). The Panic of 1893 had come a year after his graduation from medical school, and it coincided exactly with his first—and only—year of practice. One lesson of the crash, the worst of the late nineteenth century, made a strong impression on the young physician. In a severe market collapse, cash and bonds, particularly those backed by the national government, always trumped stocks. It was a point he never forgot.

Albert Barnes knew what it was like not to have money; and, when, at last, he had plenty, he was careful with it. Yes, he spent thousands of dollars building his art collection, but he was neither foolish nor wild when wielding a checkbook. Matisse's *Joy of Life (Le bonheur de vivre)* cost less than $4,000, while the most Barnes ever spent for a painting—and a bargain it was—was only

$100,000, for Cézanne's largest composition of *The Card Players (Les Joueurs de Cartes)*. And, as we've seen, when Barnes finally sold his company, the money was immediately put in the bank, just months in advance of the Black Friday 1929 crash. It turned out to be exactly the right move—and not only in light of the collapse that was soon to follow.

The advent of World War I had led to a rapid inflation of the currency propelled by heavy defense spending and the issuance of war bonds. The raging bull market of the twenties only intensified the inflationary spiral. In contrast, the Great Depression set in motion a deflationary cycle in which the value of money increased by almost a third. The man who had hard cash during those years was a fortunate man indeed. Barnes, of course, had virtually nothing *but* cash.

At his death, Barnes's estate was appraised at $2,123,000, the bulk of which, more than two million dollars, was invested in municipal bonds. Laura inherited most of this. The Barnes Foundation's endowment was, meanwhile, similarly invested in government securities. In 1951, it amounted to $9,000,000. It's worth pausing here, for that nine million is the equivalent of about $62,000,000 in today's dollars—more than sufficient for the foundation's needs for years to come. As we know now, that didn't prove to be the case. But why not?

The answer is simple: Following Albert Barnes's death, the terms of the indenture began to work against the endowment. As long as inflation was low, running more or less in tandem with the return on government securities, the endowment held its own. Given the low rate of return on government securities, the endowment—which now consisted of nothing but federal, state, and municipal bonds—did not grow, but the income was sufficient to cover ordinary expenses. That was the case for at least a decade after Barnes's death. But in the aftermath of the Vietnam War and the Arab oil embargo, inflation soared and the endowment took a beating. By the early 1970s, says former Girard banker and Barnes trustee (1983–1989) David Rawson, the endowment "had lost money. It was down to five and a half or maybe six million dollars." By now, the trustees, says Rawson, had had to invade the principal, just to make ends meet.

Consider: Had returns but mirrored inflation, the $9 million endowment of 1951 would have grown to $14 million in 1971, $19.7 million in 1976, $31.5 million in 1981, $38 million in 1986, and more than $47 million in 1991. Consider too that the approximately $9 million that did constitute the endowment in 1991 was the equivalent of barely $1.7 million in 1951 dollars.

But all that was in the future when, under the terms of the indenture, Laura Barnes succeeded her husband as president of the foundation and director of the arboretum at a minimum salary of $30,000 annually. Her fellow members on the Barnes Foundation leadership team were Nelle Mullen, secretary-treasurer and general manager, and Violette de Mazia, director of education.

■

The first significant challenge to the Barnes trust came less than a year after its founder's death and from a powerful enemy indeed: Philadelphia *Inquirer* publisher Walter Annenberg. Annenberg's father, like Barnes's, had grown up across the tracks. But whereas Barnes was a native Philadelphian, Moses Annenberg was a Chicagoan—and a Jew. As a youngster, Moses had hawked papers during the brutal newspaper wars of the late nineteenth century, when circulation managers thought nothing of sending out gangs to beat up their rivals. Not exactly Norman Rockwell kind of work, but good training for a young tough with brains. Moses Annenberg would later graduate to circulation manager—and go on to make a small fortune as a publisher in Miami. His far greater fortune, though, came as the owner of a racing newswire popular with bookmaking-parlor operators and their clients.

Eventually, Annenberg settled in Philadelphia, where he pur-

chased the morning *Inquirer*. A Republican and a strong opponent of the New Deal, he found himself the target of a federal
probe for income tax evasion in the late thirties. His 1940 plea
bargain—reached after his only son, Walter, had been dropped as
a co-defendant—resulted in a three-year prison sentence and a
then-record fine of $9.5 million. He died of a brain tumor on July
20, 1942, barely a month after being released from prison on
parole. Virtually his entire fortune—including the *Inquirer*—
went to Walter, who was thirty-four at the time. The son would
always believe that his father had been hounded to his death by
Roosevelt's minions—and this, perhaps, accounted for his own
vehemently conservative brand of Republicanism.

Why Walter Annenberg took on the Barnes as an enemy is a
mystery. A knowledgeable observer speculates, "[Albert] Barnes
probably said something nasty about old man Annenberg, and
word got back to Walter." Former Philadelphia Museum of Art
president Robert Mongtomery Scott, who served as chief of staff
to Annenberg when the latter was ambassador to Britain, con-
curs. Annenberg, Scott says, "was obsessed with Dr. Barnes."

Whatever his motives, Walter Annenberg waited a mere seven
months after the death of Albert Barnes to bring suit in state court
in February 1952, arguing that the foundation should be open to
the public. (Limited admission by appointment had always been
possible.) The case was brought in the name of Harold J.
Wiegand, the editorial page editor of the *Inquirer* and
Annenberg's closest associate at the paper. In the end, a
Montgomery County court of common pleas judge found for the
Barnes Foundation, and the state supreme court upheld his ruling. Dissenting was Justice Michael Musmanno. In finding that the
Barnes Foundation was denying the ordinary tax-paying citizens
of the commonwealth their rights, Musmanno, in the words of one
observer, Philadelphia lawyer Gilbert Cantor, gave the *Inquirer*
"the dramatic phraseology, the language of injustice, and the judi-
cial authority with which to rally public opinion and support."

Six years later, in April 1958—egged on by the *Inquirer*—Pennsylvania attorney general Anne Alpern, in her role as custodian of commonwealth charities, filed suit against the Barnes trustees in Montgomery County court. Alpern and deputy attorney general Lois G. Forer, who actually handled the case, asked that the Barnes Foundation be required to show cause why it shouldn't open its doors to the public. The lower court again found in favor of the Barnes. This time, though, the state supreme court overturned the ruling; and, as a result, on December 10, 1960, the foundation signed a consent decree. Henceforth, the public could visit the Barnes Foundation two days a week, on Fridays and Saturdays—though still by appointment only. (Alpern, a Democrat, would soon afterward run for election to the state supreme court—backed by the editorial support of the staunchly Republican *Inquirer*—and Forer would later become a judge of common pleas court in Philadelphia, again with the editorial backing of the *Inquirer.*)

All things considered, 1960 was not the best of years for the Barnes Foundation's Old Guard, as Miss de Mazia and company were often called. That year the first critical biography of Albert Barnes, William Schack's *Art and Argyrol*, appeared in print. It didn't make much of a splash, but, in the course of researching the book, Schack had uncovered some startling information, news that he passed on to another interested party, Lincoln University acting president A. O. Grubb.

In a letter dated December 16, 1959—eight years after Albert Barnes's death and three years after Horace Bond left the Lincoln presidency—Schack wrote Grubb inquiring about the provision in the trust indenture that had conferred on Lincoln "the power of selecting successor trustees to the [Barnes] Foundation." Based on Schack's letter, Grubb made a formal inquiry to the Barnes board regarding Lincoln's future role with the foundation and discovered that Lincoln University ultimately stood to gain control of it. Dr. Barnes's little secret had suddenly popped out of the bag.

The news didn't change the then-current board's practices; nor did a new round of court challenges have much effect. Once again urged on by Annenberg and the *Inquirer*, deputy attorney general Forer went to court in 1962, this time in an attempt to vacate the Barnes board. The trustees, Forer argued, had consistently run the foundation in ways that were eccentric and even bizarre. (Of course, so had Albert Barnes.) Among Forer's other charges: That janitors threatened the safety of the paintings by moving them daily and that guards were constantly harassing visitors. The court, acting in March 1963, ordered the admission fee reduced from two dollars to one. After that, the threat—at least from Annenberg, the *Inquirer*, and Lois Forer—seemed to have been put at bay.

The greater threat, though, came not from without but from within. Mortality was the issue. Laura Barnes was ninety-two years old when she passed away in 1966—her memory living on in the arboretum that she adored. With the provisions of the indenture now kicking in, one might have assumed that her death would have marked the end of the old order at the foundation. Strange to say, it did not. Following her death, the first open vacancy on the board belonged to the Girard Trust (and its successors), and it would be held in perpetuity by a series of bank-appointed representatives. It was with the next vacancy that Lincoln would at last begin to make its mark on the Barnes, or so the college's officials must have thought. When the time came, they were to be sorely disappointed.

Following the death of Nelle Mullen at age eighty-three in 1967, Lincoln finally got to nominate its first trustee, Washington, D.C., lawyer Benjamin Amos. Nelle Mullen, for many years the foundation's secretary-treasurer, had succeeded Laura Barnes as president. Now she was, in turn, to be succeeded as president by Sidney W. Frick, a fifty-two-year-old Main Line patent attorney and Barnes trustee since 1957.

The fact was that as long as Violette de Mazia, Sid Frick, and

Joe Langran—a landscape architect, Langran was a longtime friend of Mrs. Barnes's—remained on the board, the Old Guard would always hold a three-to-two majority. "The 'family representatives,'" says former Girard banker Rawson, "always voted as a block. Before any vote took place, Sid would look in Miss de Mazia's direction, and she'd nod her head yes or shake her head no. And that was that." Even if the bank's representative chose to side with the Lincoln-nominated trustee, Ben Amos, says Rawson, "It wouldn't have mattered anyhow." Not with Miss de Mazia—"an institution unto herself," Rawson calls her—running the show. Not with her 3-2 majority on the board.

■

Violette de Mazia is a figure of considerable mystery. She apparently preferred it that way. According to her obituary in the *Inquirer*, Miss de Mazia was born in 1899 in Paris, the daughter of Jean-Jules de Mazia and Fanny Franquet. Her father was believed to have been born in Russia of Italian parents. Her mother was French.

The young Violette was raised in prewar Brussels and educated there at the Ecole Supérieure de la rue du Marais. During the First World War, the family moved to London, where Violette attended the Priory House School and the Swiss Cottage Conservatory. She seems to have arrived in Philadelphia in either 1921 or 1922 and was said to have lived with wealthy relatives at their home on North Broad Street.

Barnes's early biographer Schack says that Miss de Mazia studied painting in London during the war years and enrolled at the Barnes Foundation as a student in 1925, quickly making "such an impression that Barnes appointed her instructor in 1927." Albert Barnes and Violette de Mazia would eventually collaborate on four books together. Undoubtedly they were traveling companions, as Miss de Mazia frequently accompanied Barnes on his European expeditions from the mid-1920s onward.

Were they more than traveling companions? Main Line gossip had it that they were. The rumor, widely reported at the time, was that Barnes used to drive home from the country—leaving Laura to garden—for Sunday afternoon trysts with de Mazia. The question obviously arises: Was that where Albert Barnes was going the day he sped through the stop sign and barreled into the tractor trailer?

Barnes's other biographer, Howard Greenfeld, has painted a striking group portrait of an uncomfortable *ménage-à-trois*. Laura Barnes, Greenfeld writes,

> *was steadfastly in charge of the doctor's personal life, his hostess in Merion, and his social companion away from the Foundation (though de Mazia often accompanied him on his trips abroad, presumably to assist in the research on their books). She and her husband were both strong-willed people, a fact Mrs. Barnes did well to hide under a mild, polite, genteel manner. . . . Violette de Mazia, however, soon assumed another and perhaps equally important role which inevitably conflicted with that of Mrs. Barnes. The two women were barely on speaking terms. . . . Increasingly the Foundation became [de Mazia's] home and its gallery her salon, where she reigned as hostess throughout the doctor's life.*

Greenfeld had the advantage of having met Miss de Mazia and has described her thus in her old age: "A small, slight woman, her eyes shielded by sunglasses (which she wears because of an allergy), she habitually wears a flower in her hair or on her dress . . . and a ring on her thumb tinkles as she points . . . to a picture she describes."

Lucinda Fleeson also knew Miss de Mazia in her later years. As an *Inquirer* cultural news reporter under the reform regime—Annenberg, on being appointed by President Richard M. Nixon to be ambassador to the Court of St. James's, had sold the paper and its afternoon tabloid-sibling *Daily News* to the more liberal press baron John Knight in 1972—Fleeson was at least mildly welcome at the Barnes.

Students at the Barnes, Fleeson wrote, "recount how Miss de Mazia's lectures were made memorable by her energy and her grace as she moved with a dancer's motions around the gallery, often dressed in clothing that complemented the colors of paintings featured in the lecture of the day."

Violette de Mazia made a striking impression. She was grand, she was exotic, she was mysterious. Maybe she had been Albert Barnes's mistress. Maybe she hadn't. One thing was certain: With the death of Laura Barnes, Violette de Mazia had no rival left at the Barnes Foundation. She was the Barnes, and the Barnes was Miss de Mazia. It was a role she relished and had long since perfected—and one that she would play almost to the day she died.

CHAPTER FOUR

LINCOLN
TAKES COMMAND

When, in 1989, the frail little woman finally breathed her last, she was eighty-nine years old and had been almost completely bedridden for a year. She had outlived Laura Barnes by twenty-two years and Albert Barnes by thirty-eight, and in that time Violette de Mazia had become the living embodiment of the foundation. The "keeper of the Barnes candle" was, of course, a great deal more than that. The petite Frenchwoman with the graceful airs and flirtatious charm had ruled the foundation as an empress, and a very determined empress at that. Miss de Mazia had, after all, managed to hold formidable antagonists—Walter Annenberg and the Commonwealth of Pennsylvania, among them—at bay for decades.

She had not died poor. Court records showed that the former teacher left an estate valued at more than $8.6 million, yielding more than $400,000 a year in income. Childless, like Albert Barnes before her, she left the money to a philanthropy of her own making, the Violette de Mazia Trust. At the time of her death, the size and provenance of the estate—much of it in the form of artworks that were eventually auctioned off by Christie's—were not questioned. Later, when the leadership of the Barnes Foundation fell into very different hands, it would be.

In the meantime, Miss de Mazia's longtime ally, Barnes president Sidney W. Frick, announced, "The Foundation will continue as it has." After all, the paintings on the walls of the chateau on Latches Lane were still hung as they had been the day Albert Barnes died in 1951. Sidney Frick was wrong, however. Within a year and a half, he would be out as both president and trustee. Less than three years later, the paintings would come down. Frick to the contrary, an era ended on Tuesday, September 20, 1988. A friendly obituary in the *Inquirer*—no longer Annenberg's attack dog—lauded Miss de Mazia as an "erudite art scholar and teacher who captivated students for six decades with her lectures at The Barnes Foundation."

Change at the Barnes might well have been expected to come far earlier. Incredibly—actuarial tables to the contrary—during the twenty years following Nelle Mullen's death in 1967, the board had witnessed no turnover, save for a change in bank representatives. Of the other sitting members, Frick and Joseph Langran were well into their seventies. The final two seats were held by banker David Rawson, who'd joined the board in 1983, and the aforementioned Washington, D.C., attorney Benjamin Amos, an African American and Lincoln's sole representative until now.

Two Lincoln members plus Rawson—who had largely allied himself with Amos as opposed to the Old Guard—would mean effective control over the foundation. Franklin L. Williams, the suave and diplomatic chairman of the college's board of trustees, seemed to dismiss the idea out of hand: "I reject the notion that because Lincoln University designates the trustees to be elected that it follows that Lincoln University 'controls' the Foundation. It does not. The board does." It was all semantics, and Williams, a worldly and sophisticated man—a prominent New York lawyer who had previously served as ambassador to Ghana and was currently president of the Phelps-Stokes Fund and a member of the Ford Foundation board—knew as much. Technically, the Barnes board could reject the nominees; but as a practical matter, Lincoln University was now in control of one of the world's richest art collections.

"Once on the board," Frick warned, Miss de Mazia's successor—whoever that might be—would be "obligated to carry out the objectives of the Barnes Foundation" as they had been spelled out in the original indenture of trust. That too was just talk. The fact was that Frick was about to be in the minority on the board.

To have a majority on the Barnes board, though, was one thing. Having a plan of action for the Barnes was another. Rhode Island School of Design president E. Roger Mandle, a member of a short-lived, post-Lincoln Barnes art advisory committee, recalls, "the school was ill-prepared to take control of the Barnes. The Lincoln people didn't know about the condition of the paintings or the condition of the buildings. They could only surmise. And they didn't have a clear notion of a program of what to do with either the paintings or the gallery." On the plus side, says Mandle, Lincoln chairman Williams "was aware—extremely aware—of the awesome responsibility that he and Lincoln had inherited in gaining control of the Barnes." Indeed, the saving grace in the takeover, says Mandle, lay in the character of Franklin Williams himself, a man whose goal "was to get the best possible advice he could get in order to safeguard the collection and to modernize it and the plant." Of Williams, he says, "What you have to recognize, in particular, was the extreme intelligence of the man. Unfortunately, he ran out of time."

■

It was no secret in the closed Philadelphia art world that the banker Rawson had had serious run-ins over the years with the Barnes's ruling triumvirate—Miss de Mazia, Frick, and Langran. Rawson and Lincoln representative Ben Amos had favored running a shuttle between the university's campus in Chester County and the Barnes in Lower Merion to enable students to make use of the galleries and perhaps even take classes there. They'd also proposed endowing a chair at Lincoln, where the art department consisted of exactly one full-time employee. Neither proposal had been adopted. Rawson, in particular, was worried that Miss de Mazia, in her desire to maintain the status quo, had allowed the collection to deteriorate physically.

It was an opinion shared by Robert Montgomery Scott, an heir to the Pennsylvania Railroad fortune and the then-president of the Philadelphia Museum of Art. In Scott's view, Miss de Mazia had been "very reluctant to do much conservation work which might in any way alter existing tones of an object. She was very, very conservative, more so than we, because we recognize that with the passage of time and the arrival of grime, conservation is something we view as very ongoing."

Rawson had pressed hard for more conservation. What he got was a report and the usual delays from Miss de Mazia. At Rawson's urging, the Barnes board had retained the conservator of the Pennsylvania Academy of the Fine Arts in 1985 to study the condition of the paintings in the collection. The conservator found that fifty-seven paintings needed "urgent care." Those paintings were, in fact, subjected to modest conservation techniques. In the three years since, none of the other paintings had been touched.

The banker and the board majority had also clashed over the management of the Barnes' endowment, Rawson favoring a move to petition Orphans' Court to allow the board a more liberal interpretation of investment policies. As we have seen, Dr. Barnes's trust indenture obligated the board to invest the endowment one hundred percent in government securities. With inflation rampant during the early 1970s, the real value of the endowment had therefore plummeted.

While the value of the Barnes collection was now estimated at well over one billion dollars, the endowment's value—unadjusted for inflation—was about what it had been at the time of Barnes's death: nine million dollars. This, in real dollars, however, amounted to less than a fifth of the 1951 total. The major damage to the Barnes endowment, Rawson explains, had come in the late 1960s and early 1970s, "when some idiot had actually bought tax-frees! Can you imagine? Buying tax-free bonds when you're a tax-free institution."

Fortunately, Rawson says, his predecessor as Barnes trustee-treasurer, Girard banker Richard Nenneman, had "stacked up the highest-yielding bonds—taxable, of course—at a time when bonds were getting very high yields." Given that it held taxable bonds yielding 13 percent interest, "the Barnes was getting over a million dollars a year in income," says Rawson, "and using up only seven hundred thousand dollars." The result: "We were capitalizing three hundred thousand dollars a year."

That, however, didn't keep Rawson from arguing that the Barnes board be allowed to spread its endowment over a more diversified portfolio, one with investments in both stocks and bonds. Rawson proposed going to Montgomery County Orphans' Court and explaining to a judge there that the investment restrictions Dr. Barnes had put in place in 1922 made no sense in a world where financial conditions were so vastly different. Rawson made motions at various Barnes board meetings to do just that—and was repeatedly voted down. Of course, Rawson was also voted down whenever he brought up the most taboo subject of all at the Barnes: the employment of a full-time director. The terms of Dr. Barnes's trust agreement had provided that the foundation

board "shall after the death of the Donor, employ an art director
. . . whose function shall be to supervise the gallery to see that the
paintings are properly cared for." Miss de Mazia, needless to say,
saw no need to employ any such potential rival.

Now, though, with Miss de Mazia finally out of the way,
Rawson went public with his litany of complaints, telling
reporters that her death inevitably spelled "tremendous change"
for the Barnes. "Her passing from the scene is going to just really
change the whole equation. The last living link to Dr. Barnes
himself has been broken." Rawson didn't stop there, though: "As
far as interaction with the Philadelphia community, there is no
question that Miss de Mazia herself was involved in the estrange-
ment between the Barnes Foundation and the community."

Rawson predicted that future Barnes board members would
have "an orientation that is broader than just a Barnes orientation." Rawson went on to spell out a manifesto for change at the
Barnes: "These people [the Lincoln-nominated board members]
are going to have a very different view of what Barnes means,
and about taking such a hard line about never granting inter-
views, never lending pieces to museums, never publishing a book
about Barnes." In particular, Rawson suggested that the new
board should consider publishing a color catalogue of the Barnes
collection, "possibly with profits and credit" going, not to the
Barnes, but to Lincoln.

■

Lincoln certainly needed the money. It had 1,200 students, virtually all of them undergraduates—there was but a single graduate program (social welfare)—and an endowment of just $4.7
million as it began academic year 1988–1989. In the recent past,
the condition of Lincoln's finances had careened from the per-
ilous to the brink of disaster. If you were an officer or a trustee of
Lincoln, you had to hope that the treasures of the Barnes
Foundation would somehow provide a measure of financial relief

for the college. Lincoln board chairman Williams, for all his measured words, acknowledged as much. Assuming control over the Barnes, Williams told reporters, would amount to "a big obligation" but also one that would help in "developing Lincoln into an excellent education institution."

But what exactly to do with the Barnes and how to help out Lincoln?

David Rawson perceived the situation acutely: "What Lincoln is going to do," he told a reporter, "is up for speculation. Lincoln's board itself is factionalized into different schools of thought, their attitude towards [the Barnes Foundation], how they perceive Lincoln and [the] Barnes and what they will ultimately mean to each other." How it would all shake out was anyone's guess. "It depends," Rawson thought, "on who wins the political infighting at Lincoln."

By 1988, Lincoln's glory had come and gone, but the decades of the twenties, thirties, and forties had been good ones for the college. Among the graduates from those days: the writer Langston Hughes; lawyer, civil rights advocate, and U.S. Supreme Court Justice Thurgood Marshall; Benjamin Nnamdi Azikiwe, first president of Nigeria; Kwame Nkrumah, first president of Ghana; and U.S. Representative Robert N. C. Nix, Sr., Pennsylvania's first African American congressman. Back then, the college had the reputation of producing "Lincoln men"—much as the Ivies produced "Yale men" and "Princeton men"—who were doctors, lawyers, ministers, the cream of the African American elite. Thanksgiving Day had once featured a fierce football rivalry pitting Lincoln against Howard University that attracted as many as 20,000 fans to the game.

Once upon a time, too, there had been a medical school—and a law school—but now there was money for neither. By 1971, when the formerly private school became state-affiliated, Lincoln's enrollment and reputation had both hit rock bottom. For a time in the mid-1970s, enrollment dropped beneath a thousand.

The university's then-current president, Niara Sudarkasa, was born Gloria Marshall, in Fort Lauderdale, Florida, in 1939. She'd entered Fisk University at age fifteen and graduated from Oberlin College in 1957 at age eighteen in the top ten percent of her class. Later, she'd earned a master's degree and a doctorate in anthropology from Columbia University. Her research interests centered on the lives of African women, with an emphasis on those of Nigeria's Yoruba tribe.

Following graduation from Columbia, Sudarkasa's career path had been straight and quick: assistant professor at New York University for three years, and after that, assistant to associate to full professor at the University of Michigan at Ann Arbor. Along the way, she'd become a university-level administrator, rising eventually to be director of the Center for Afro American and African Studies (1980–1984) and associate vice-president for academic affairs (1984–1987) at Michigan.

On October 6, 1986, Sudarkasa had been appointed to a five-year term as Lincoln president. She was installed four days later and officially started her new job in February of the following year. At her October 10 installation ceremony, Sudarkasa wore a blue and orange robe decorated with academic stripes made of traditional African material. Among those in attendance that day were her husband, John L. Clark, described by the *Inquirer* as a Michigan building contractor, and her son Michael, a second-year student at Harvard Law School. Later, John Clark would play a role in her eventual undoing as president of Lincoln. That, however, would lie more than a decade ahead, at a time when the affairs at Lincoln and those at the Barnes had become hopelessly, disastrously enmeshed.

Not that the future at Lincoln looked all that rosy in 1987, either. Nothing at prosperous Ann Arbor had prepared Sudarkasa for running—not to mention saving—such a desperately poor, strife-ridden semi-public university. To her credit, Sudarkasa was dogged and hardworking. But she was also in many ways the antithesis of Franklin Williams. Where he was smooth, she was sharp-edged; where he was articulate, she was awkward. A diplomat she was not. Still, Sudarkasa was shrewd—and, certainly, she was tough: "A very strong woman," in the words of former Lincoln trustee Cuyler Walker.

Sudarkasa had her work cut out for her. She was somehow expected to drive up enrollments, squeeze money out of the turnip that was the commonwealth appropriations process, and maintain the peace. The latter task was all but impossible given the nature of the Lincoln board. Once the state had come to the financial rescue of the university, Lincoln's status shifted from private to semi-public. The university's board of trustees had been reconstituted in the process. The result was a large, fractious body of thirty-five trustees, among them the governor; the secretary of education; ten others variously appointed by the governor, the state senate, and the state house of representatives; six elected alumni members; and a further seventeen members, supposedly nonpolitical appointees chosen to serve staggered terms. Presiding over this unwieldy body was Franklin Williams.

Williams had told reporters that he expected to convene a search committee to find a successor to Miss de Mazia on the Barnes board sometime soon, in the weeks following her death. But then, according to a contemporary newspaper account, Williams went on "to express an interest in serving on the Barnes board" himself. Williams, the newspaper reported, theorized "that the foundation could undergo a process that has happened at other foundations as their benefactors' influence lessens over time: They become professionalized, hired accomplished personnel in the foundation field."

Together with Mellon Bank East vice-president for corporate affairs Richard Torbert (the successor to David Rawson), Franklin Williams began a five-year term on the Barnes board on December 9, 1988. Williams, the former diplomat, began his tenure in ways calculated to calm the fears of the Barnes Old

Guard. To a newspaper reporter, he explained, "The plan is to administer the [Barnes Foundation] along the lines Dr. Barnes established and to be true to the trust."

Frick and Langran probably couldn't have expected much better, especially at a time when an anonymous Lincoln board member was quoted as telling an *Inquirer* reporter, "It's unclear whether or not there could be a sale of art, whether we would want to endow a chair at the university. It's not even clear whether we have to keep the art in the building or not." The *Inquirer* went on to note, "Lincoln officials have asked the school's general counsel to determine exactly what the university's obligations are and what latitude exists for change."

The university's general counsel at the time was Philadelphia lawyer Richard H. Glanton, who also happened to be one of the more outspoken Lincoln trustees. A non-alumnus, Glanton was a political appointee on the board. Glanton, says former Girard banker and Barnes trustee Rawson, had had his eyes on the Barnes for the past couple of years, at least. Rawson vividly recalls the day in 1986 when he got a call

> *from my boss, Bill Eagleson, the president of the Girard. Bill said, "Come up to my office. I have a fellow here who wants to talk to me about the Barnes. I told him I don't know much about it, but you do." So I went up to his office, and, lo and behold, there's Richard Glanton. And he was here to tell us that he and his client, Franklin Williams, had taken control of the Lincoln board, and they wanted us to get Ben Amos off the Barnes Foundation board. I explained to Glanton that no one had the right to kick any individual board member off. I took him through the [trust of indenture] provision by provision. It was clear to me even then that Glanton intended to be the power behind the throne.*

Although it would be two years before Glanton—with Franklin Williams out of the way—made an overt move on the Barnes, he was already beginning to position himself for that moment. A series of articles in the *Inquirer* didn't hurt his cause.

■

"The Art World Is Banging at the Barnes Foundation's Door" was the headline of one such story. The author of the piece: Lucinda Fleeson, whose beat was Philadelphia culture and the arts. The *Inquirer* reporter and the Reed Smith lawyer were old friends. Fleeson had first met Glanton when she was "covering the labor beat" and he was deputy counsel to Republican governor Richard Thornburgh (1979–1987). Glanton, Fleeson recalls, "helped me many, many times. He was helpful to a lot of reporters. We called him 'Killer.' Dan Biddle gave him that nickname." An *Inquirer* investigative reporter and Pulitzer Prize winner, Daniel Biddle was the grandson of former U.S. Attorney General Francis Biddle. Fleeson continues: "I always felt that Richard was on the side of right. When he helped a reporter out, when he fed you a story, it was usually to get the truth out. I once asked him why, when it often caused him so much trouble, and he said it was fun."

Fleeson says she felt like she'd "fallen into a pot of honey" when legendary *Inquirer* executive editor Eugene L. Roberts, Jr., stopped by her desk and told her that he was "interested in the Barnes and wanted me to look into it." An undergraduate art history minor at Boston University, Fleeson promptly signed up for coursework at the Barnes. At the time, the Old Guard was still in charge. "I can't tell you how bewildering and boring those sessions were," Fleeson recalls. "I couldn't make sense of it."

Fleeson says that she and Gene Roberts heard—she doesn't say from whom—that the Barnes paintings were in bad shape. They decided to investigate, hiring three noted conservators to go "under cover" at the Barnes. To Fleesons's surprise, the conservators—among them Joseph Rishel of the Philadelphia Museum of Art—agreed that the paintings not only "weren't ruined, they were in the *most* pristine condition."

During the first few years of Glanton's ascendancy at the Barnes, Fleeson would come to be looked upon as his favorite reporter. "The Art World Is Banging at the Barnes Foundation's Door" has all the earmarks of the later stories. While the prose is typical Fleeson—staccato and punchy—the first few paragraphs are a virtual Glanton campaign platform:

> *Last fall, as news of a change of regime at the reclusive Barnes Foundation spread through the art world, scholars, curators, and museum officials excitedly speculated that many of the foundation's restrictive policies might be lifted. Curators dreamed that the strict no-loan policy . . . might be relaxed. Scholars hoped that a catalogue of color reproductions of the collection would be published for the first time. Or that the foundation might open its doors to the public for more than just 2 1/2 days a week. It has now been six months since representatives from Lincoln University, a small black school in Chester County, have held two of the five seats on the Barnes governing board; they eventually will hold four. But so far, nothing has changed.*

Having noted that the Barnes still had no administrative director despite the terms of the indenture, Fleeson went on to quote trustee Langran describing the work of president Frick: "He is there every day, taking care of the day-to-day work. Mr. Frick has grown up in the foundation. His father was attorney for the foundation, and a trustee. He really has acted as almost 'the manager.' We can't expect anyone to carry on like he does."

Indeed not. In a single paragraph, Fleeson had drawn a nice little picture of paternalism, and the most damning words had come from the lips of one of the plantation owners. Equally damning were the comments from outside experts. One of these was Charles Stuckey, curator of modern art at the Art Institute of Chicago, who opined, "Supposing I was interested in a study of a Manet [painting] and went to the Barnes Foundation. I couldn't get an X-ray of it, couldn't look at the back of a painting for exhibition labels, couldn't look at records of provenance—a lot of things I could pretty much wangle anyplace else. So there are little chapters in lives and work of many wonderful artists that remain unwritten."

Deaccessioning—selling off art in the collection—had been specifically forbidden by Dr. Barnes in the indenture of trust. Yet here was Fleeson quoting a former Barnes trustee, *Christian Science Monitor* editor-in-chief Richard Nenneman, calling for dramatic action. Nenneman, who had served as the Girard Bank's representative on the Barnes board from 1978 to 1983, told Fleeson that the Barnes should "consider selling a painting in order to ensure the institution's future financial survival."

But which institution's survival? The Barnes's—or Lincoln's?

And just who was really behind the movement to deaccession?

Board member Joseph Langran retired in June 1989 at the age of seventy-six. After thirty-three years on the board—he had succeeded Mary Mullen on her death in 1956—Langran "decided that was long enough." He was, he told reporter Fleeson, too old to be driving up from his retirement home in Crisfield, Maryland, just to deal with Barnes business. Besides, Langran said, the Barnes was in good hands. His replacement: Yet another septuagenarian white male, multimillionaire Sears Roebuck heir Julius Rosenwald 2d. The seventy-five-year-old Rosenwald had served on the Lincoln board for the past thirty-eight years and was a retired director of Sears and the Pennsylvania Savings Fund Society (PSFS), a Philadelphia banking powerhouse. His other trusteeships included that of the University Science Center and the local public radio and television station WHYY.

Like Rosenwald, Williams had come to the table in 1988 with a c.v. brimming with distinguished corporate and civic organization titles: governor of the American Stock Exchange, director of the Council on Foreign Relations, trustee of the New York City Center Opera, and membership on the corporate boards of Consolidated Edison, Chemical Bank, and Borden.

Williams was, in the words of the New York art dealer Richard Feigen, "an impressive man, lean, craggy, and lined of face, serious, cultivated, someone clearly to be reckoned with, a 'man of stature.'" He looked the part of the diplomat too; he was always stylishly attired, emanating in equal measure charm and intelligence. Ambassador Williams, as he was usually referred to in the press, didn't ruffle feathers, either. To the *Inquirer*'s Fleeson, used to dealing with the labor leaders and politicians, Williams seemed "very inaccessible." She "wasn't impressed." And former Barnes trustee Rawson worried that "Williams was the front man and Glanton the power behind the throne." But Fleeson and Rawson were in the minority. Williams, just about everyone else agreed, said the right things. He paid homage to the memories of Dr. Barnes and Miss de Mazia. He promised gentle and thoughtful change. He talked about bringing in a professional art historian-administrator to give stability to the foundation. More importantly, Williams took pains to assure the holdover trustees that he would honor the provisions of Dr. Barnes's trust indenture.

At the September 23, 1989, Lincoln board meeting, Williams announced that Frick and fellow trustee Ben Amos had both chosen to resign, opening two more seats on the Barnes board. He also announced that, in one of its last actions, the old Barnes board had elected him to succeed Frick as president of the foundation. Williams's appointment would be effective September 26, 1989.

Eight months later, Franklin Williams was dead, the victim of a ravenously aggressive throat cancer. What Williams's agenda for the Barnes would have been may never be known. Cuyler Walker, a Lincoln trustee from 1986 to 1994, is today a partner in the Philadelphia law firm of Pepper Hamilton & Sheetz. Williams, he recalls, was one of "the most impressive people I ever knew. He was a man of the greatest possible wisdom and natural authority." There was, Walker believes, "this kind of Gandhi-like presence to him." Walker would himself serve on the Barnes board from 1990 to 1995, and he recalls that though Williams "never sat down and articulated a grand vision," he "did try very hard to identify what had to be done and in what order. You could say that he was on a fact-finding mission. And that was a sensible first step for someone who was coming to the Barnes as an outsider. That's how I perceived it."

Rather than attempt radical change, Williams in his very short tenure had favored cautious moves, beginning with a basic survey of the gallery and its collection. The paintings at the Barnes, says Richard Feigen, who served as a consultant, were found to be in generally "fine condition." The more serious problems included a leak in the roof of the main gallery and the lack of an adequate climate-control system. Money would have to be found to fix these problems, the most expensive of which would be a state-of-the-art climate-control system. All this, Feigen claims, would have required money that the Barnes simply didn't have.

Believing that there was much that had to be done at the Barnes, and knowing that it was going to cost money, Williams took great pains not to alienate Esther van Sant, Miss de Mazia's close friend in the education department. Van Sant had not only succeeded de Mazia as acting administrator of the foundation, she was also one of the trustees of the $8.5 million Violette de Mazia Trust, which was helping to fund activities at the Barnes.

Williams, Walker says, had as his early goals "to put the Barnes on a sound financial footing, to make sure that it was run professionally, by twenty-first century standards—not nineteenth-century standards—and to safeguard and preserve the collection." Like his fellow former Lincoln trustee Richard Feigen, Cuyler Walker believes, "Franklin Williams intended to carry on the Barnes program as Dr. Barnes intended it to be carried on. Now, exactly what that meant, I'm not sure that any of us knew at the time."

The best *Inquirer* reporter Fleeson could get out of Williams at the time was a couple of ambiguous statements: "Any changes [at the Barnes] will result from consultation that will be done over a period of time," Williams was quoted as saying. "I don't see anything happening unless and until the board, having reviewed the circumstances of the Barnes Foundation, decided to institute these changes." As for those interested in the future of the Barnes, Williams advised, "Let them watch."

It would have been an apt motto for his successor, a man wholly unlike Franklin Williams, save for his love of sartorial splendor: Richard H. Glanton.

CHAPTER FIVE

MEET RICHARD GLANTON

A mutual friend, New Orleans neurosurgeon and art collector Richard Levy, introduced Franklin Williams to Richard Feigen in 1988. Lincoln was on the cusp of gaining control of the Barnes, and Williams was looking for an art advisor. Feigen, the owner of an important gallery in New York, seemed perfect for the role. Later that year, Feigen, at Williams's behest, joined the Lincoln board.

Since both men were New York–based, they often traveled together on university business. Feigen recalls how, on those Saturday mornings when there was a Lincoln board meeting, "I found myself rising at five-thirty to meet [Williams] at Penn Station for the monthly trip to Wilmington." A car would meet them at the train station and carry them on to the Lincoln campus, about forty-five minutes away. Feigen says that the frequent trips together made for a formidable bonding experience.

But while he grew closer to Williams, Feigen says, he was also

aware that others on the Lincoln board viewed him with suspi-
cion. "I was an art dealer, and I was a white man," he says. To
put it another way, as Feigen does in his memoirs, *Tales from the
Art Crypt*, "I was the new white boy on the Lincoln block." The
mistrust grew exponentially, Feigen adds, after he apprised the
Lincoln board of the estimated value of the collection as of 1989:
between three and four billion dollars. After that, Feigen adds,
"certain other board members began to develop their own agendas for how to use the Barnes."

■

Lincoln trustee and general counsel Richard H. Glanton, at age
forty-three, was a partner at the venerable downtown law firm
of Reed, Shaw, Smith & McClay—with a history as a political
operator.

Glanton had been born on November 21, 1946, in Georgia's
Appalachian country. The place of his birth was a small town
called Villa Rica, located some forty-five minutes west of Atlanta.
The fourth child and second son, he was one of eleven children
born to a poor farming family. His future law partner David
Marston has said of him, "Richard was born happy. He was one
of eleven kids, you know; and I once asked him if they were all
as happy as he is. And he said, no, only three or four of them
were. The rest were kinda sad actually."

A 1968 graduate of West Georgia College, Glanton attended
the University of Virginia Law School, graduating in 1972. It was
there that he met his future wife, Scheryl Williams. Seven years
younger than Glanton, she had at age eight been—along with her
fifth-grade sister—a plaintiff in the case that finally forced the
Charlottesville school system to open its doors to African
Americans. Married on August 17, 1974, the Glantons would
have two children, a daughter, Morgan, and a son, David.

After working in Washington in the Nixon and Ford administrations—"What reason did I have for being a Democrat?"

Glanton once said to me. "Growing up where I did, you think the local Democrats cared a rat's ass about me and my folks?"—he eventually left for Philadelphia and a job with Conrail. By the mid-1970s, Glanton was a partner at one of the top law firms in town, Wolf, Block, Schorr and Solis-Cohen. It was while working there that he became active in Republican Richard Thornburgh's run for governor.

Murray Dickman, who went on to become the president of the Pennsylvania Manufacturers' Association, met Glanton in 1978 at a time when they were both involved in the Thornburgh campaign. When Thornburgh upset the incumbent Democrat, Milton Schapp, Dickman found himself secretary of administration in the cabinet of the incoming governor. Glanton, meanwhile, was offered a job as deputy counsel to the governor. Over the next four years, the two men would work closely together—though not always in harmony. "Richard, even then," says Dickman, "was a wheeler-dealer."

Today, there is no love lost between the two former political allies. Eventually, Glanton's maneuverings set him squarely against administration stalwarts like Dickman. The point is worth making because it's a pattern that courses through Glanton's career. As he has bulled his way forward into ever grander legal, political, and cultural circles, he has racked up a host of friends—and enemies—in the process. And he has never shied away from controversy. As Dickman says, "I've never met anybody in politics or life who behaves the way he does. The guy is sui generis."

Prior to Thornburgh's reelection in 1982, Glanton had already given notice that he intended to return to private practice in Philadelphia. Scheryl was pregnant with Morgan, Glanton recalls, "and I needed to make some money." It was in the interim following Thornburgh's reelection victory and the beginning of his second term, says Dickman, "that Richard's problems with the governor and his people began." Glanton, Dickman and others say, wanted a "going-away gift." There was a vacancy on the board of the powerful, patronage-laden Southeastern Pennsylvania Transportation Authority (SEPTA); and Glanton had a candidate in mind for the post: former U.S. attorney David Marston. It was an odd choice; Marston had been Thornburgh's Republican party primary opponent in 1978. Nevertheless, says Dickman, "We ran it by the governor, and he said, 'Okay. Marston's a good guy.'"

The story might well have ended there, with David Marston joining the SEPTA board, and Richard Glanton leaving the Thornburgh administration in a spirit of goodwill all around. But it didn't. The next thing Dickman knew, he was getting phone calls from other SEPTA board members "wanting to know what the governor had against Lew Gould." Lewis Gould was the incumbent chairman of the SEPTA board—and an important player in state Republican politics.

A rumor, Dickman learned, was being fanned to the effect that Thornburgh not only wanted to put Marston on the board, he wanted to make Marston its chairman. Someone high up in the governor's office was, in fact, busy rounding up votes for Marston to be chairman. That someone, Dickman discovered, was none other than Glanton.

When Thornburgh called Marston to congratulate him on his appointment to the SEPTA board, the governor, Dickman recalls, made a point of saying, "David, I am calling to let you know that I'm proud to name you as my member. But, David, I do *not* want you to be chairman. I don't care, David, if you *have* the votes to be chairman. You are *not* going to be chairman, and that's it."

Then, says Dickman, "The governor picked up the phone and called every member of that board and said, 'Hi, I'm calling to tell you that I support Lew Gould. I know what Richard told you, but I'm telling you that.'" The next day, Dickman says, Glanton showed up at his office, grinning. Dickman wasn't grinning, though, when he said to Glanton, "Richard, I'm told you're in collusion with Marston. We can't work that way." Glanton, Dickman says, called the charges, "Bullshit, bullshit." But just then—"literally, at that very moment," says Dickman—Glanton's secretary walked in the door and said, "Richard, Commissioner So-and-So from the SEPTA board is on the phone for you."

Dickman recalls shaking his head and saying: "Please, Richard, I do have ears." What was it all about? Dickman thinks he knows: "The chairman of the SEPTA board controls just a hell of a lot of legal business. This was about where SEPTA's legal business was gonna go."

It was "a vintage Glanton performance," says Cuyler Walker, who was himself a junior member of the Thornburgh team. "It's typical of how Richard got things done. He'd go around telling people that he had the votes: 'I've got four out of the five votes I need,' that sort of thing—when he really only had two or three. That's just how he did things at the Barnes, too." Walker pauses, then adds that, "He was even sloppier at the Barnes."

Remembering their days together in the first Thornburgh administration, Murray Dickman sighs: "One thing you have to remember about Richard: Glanton was Glanton long before the Barnes."

■

On the evening of September 23, 1989, Glanton found himself at a reception for Lincoln University trustees at Philadelphia's Franklin Institute. It had already been a busy—and, indeed, momentous—day. That morning, at the regular monthly Lincoln board meeting, chairman Williams had summarized the current state of affairs at the Barnes. Foundation trustees Frick and Amos had both turned in their resignations; Sears Roebuck heir Julius Rosenwald had assumed the seat formerly held by Joseph Langran; and Williams had announced that, as of September 26, he would himself take on the Barnes presidency. That left two seats on the Barnes board to be filled. The question was: Who would be chosen to fill them? There were, of course, a number of possible candidates.

One was Lincoln trustee Richard Feigen. In *Tales from the Art Crypt*, Feigen recalls how Williams, on the train ride down from New York earlier that morning, had "raised the question" of the art gallery owner's going on the Barnes board. Feigen claims that he "advised against it." His profession as a dealer would have left him "vulnerable to criticism," Feigen worried.

At least one other candidate was, however, eager to go where Feigen feared to tread. That night at the institute, the art dealer was chatting with Ambassador Williams when Richard Glanton approached them. The university's general counsel soon got to the point: "Franklin, I'd like that seat on the Barnes board."

Williams, Feigen says, didn't beat around the bush, either, replying, "Richard, I don't think that would be a good idea. We want to keep Lincoln and [the] Barnes separate. You're general counsel of Lincoln. You shouldn't serve on the Barnes board." That, Feigen says, seemed to end the matter: "No one argued with Franklin Williams."

The first new Lincoln nominee for the Barnes board—one nobody could afford to object to—was president Niara Sudarkasa. That, however, still left the other seat to be filled. Whatever Franklin Williams may have thought about his candidacy, Glanton went right ahead and threw his hat into the ring.

Running against Glanton was fellow former Thornburgh administration aide Cuyler Walker, a Lincoln trustee since 1986. Walker's credentials for a seat on the Barnes were not entirely dissimilar from Glanton's, though there were also some distinct differences. Walker was, like Glanton, a creature of Pennsylvania Republican party politics. For more than a year now, he had been working in Washington, D.C., as a political appointee in the first Bush administration. If anything, though, Walker was even better connected than Glanton. His new job: assistant to the attorney general of the United States, Richard Thornburgh.

Walker was graduated from Yale in 1981 and had since taken both his J.D. and M.B.A. degrees from the University of Pennsylvania. None of this necessarily worked against his candidacy; but Walker was, like Feigen, white. With Julius Rosenwald already on the board, that made his choice at this point in the game distinctly problematic. Franklin Williams temporarily solved the problem by putting off the vote. Walker, meanwhile, went off to Europe on vacation.

When he got back to the States in October, Walker discovered that Williams had once again stage-managed a Barnes trustee election. Rather than face a possibly divisive Glanton/Walker election, Williams had settled on a compromise candidate. His choice: Lincoln trustee Shirley Jackson, a physics professor at Rutgers University. Jackson had the advantage of being an African American, a woman, and someone without any discernible agenda when it came to the Barnes. She was, in the words of Richard Feigen, "utterly nonthreatening."

Williams now had a Barnes board in place that presumably would have proven malleable to almost anything he proposed over the course of the next four to five years. But, as we have seen, that was not to be the case. In early 1990, Williams discovered he had throat cancer. At about the same time, the elderly Rosenwald asked to be excused from the Barnes board. The earlier problem resurfaced: Who was going to fill the vacant seat? And, again, the same two candidates presented themselves for the position.

"I was like a son to Franklin Williams," Richard Glanton once told me. "He and I were this close," he added, putting his hands together. Shirley Williams, the ambassador's widow, has a different point of view: "Like a son? I never heard him talk like that about Glanton. But if he ever did, then I think he would have been sorely disappointed in his 'son.' I don't think Franklin ever intended to hand over the Barnes to Richard Glanton."

We don't know who Williams would have chosen to succeed

himself as president of the Barnes, but one thing we do know: When push came to shove in February 1990, Williams chose Walker over Glanton.

It was about this time that former Barnes trustee David Rawson received a phone call from Richard Glanton. "Dave," Rawson recalls Glanton saying, "I remember meeting you in Bill Eagleson's office a couple of years back, and I want to invite you to lunch and pick your brain." The two men met shortly afterward at that bastion of the Philadelphia business and political elite, the Union League on Broad Street. "We must have spent two hours over lunch," says Rawson. "And almost the first thing that Glanton said to me was, 'I run this place now.'" Ambassador Williams was going to die, Glanton told him, "and when he does, I'm moving in." Glanton had some goals in mind for the Barnes: "I'm going to build this institution into a big institution." When Rawson cited the many restrictions in the indenture trust, Glanton cut him off: "I can go to court and get all that changed."

Rawson remembers vividly how Glanton told him, "I'm going to make a big deal of this. I'm going to build up an endowment of fifty million dollars. We're going to put the Barnes on the map, and I'm going to hire all these important people to help us put it on the map." When Rawson asked what kind of important people he had in mind hiring, Glanton replied without hesitation, "Important people with important political connections." It was, Rawson says in retrospect, "a breathtaking performance. I thought, but didn't say, 'Who are you working for? The Barnes? Or Richard Glanton?'"

Glanton wasn't through: "He said, 'David, I'm going to control four of the five votes on the board. Your replacement Richard Torbert, he's not getting on board with what I want to do. How do I get him off the Barnes board?'"

Dick Torbert, Rawson told Glanton, "is a friend of mine. He used to be my boss at the Girard bank. He's highly intelligent, socially committed, and he has good judgment. Princeton under-

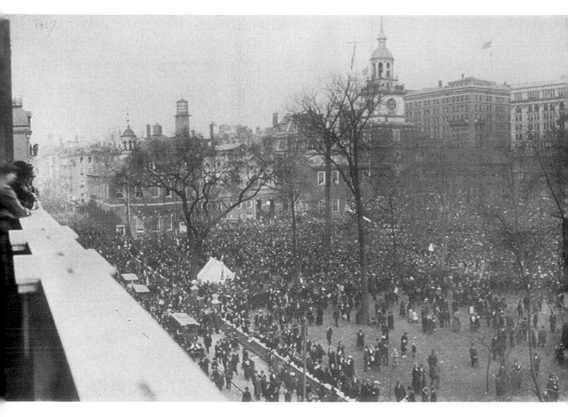

Panoramic view of Independence Square, 1917. With a population of 1.3 million inhabitants, turn-of-the-century Philadelphia was America's third largest city. (Library of Congress, © George Prince)

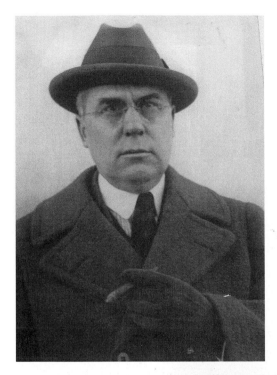

Dr. Albert C. Barnes (1872–1951), at age fifty. Barnes became rich thanks to the drug Argyrol. By 1910, he was a millionaire. By 1920, he had become one of the world's leading art collectors. (Temple University Libraries Urban Archives)

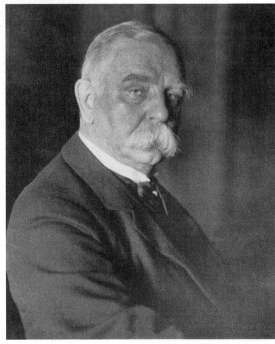

John G. Johnson. The greatest corporate lawyer of his day, Johnson helped Barnes win the legal battle over Argyrol. Johnson was also an important art collector, in many ways Barnes's role model. (Temple University Libraries Urban Archives)

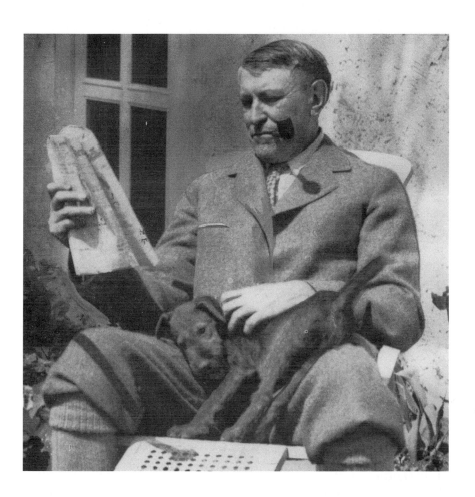

Future U.S. Supreme Court
Justice Owen J. Roberts succeeded Johnson as Barnes's
personal lawyer. It was he
who wrote the 1922 trust
indenture setting up the
Barnes Foundation. (Temple
University Libraries Urban
Archives)

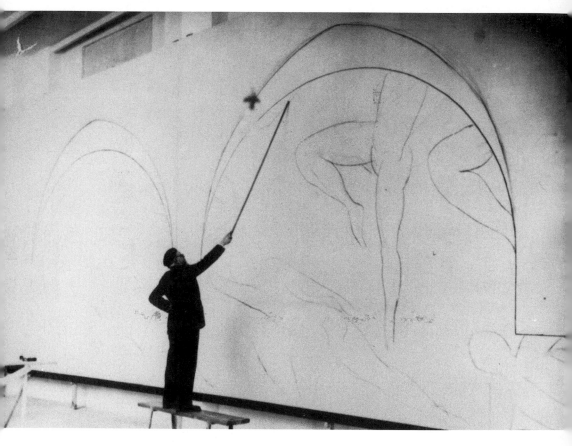

Henri Matisse at work on the great
Barnes mural. Matisse knew he had a
"catastrophe of the first order" on his
hands when in February 1932 he realized that his measurements for the
mural were "slightly but irrevocably
mistaken." (The Barnes Foundation)

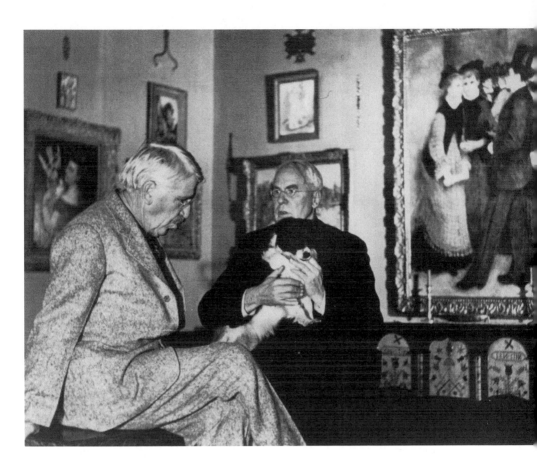

The philosopher John Dewey was for
many years Barnes's closest confidant.
They are here seen together, along
with Barnes's dog, Fidèle-de-Port-
Manech, in the main gallery of the
foundation. Dewey's *Democracy and
Education* (1916) gave a focus and
framework to Barnes's innately liberal
sentiments. (John Dewey Photograph
Collection, Special Collections/Morris
Library, Southern Illinois University
at Carbondale)

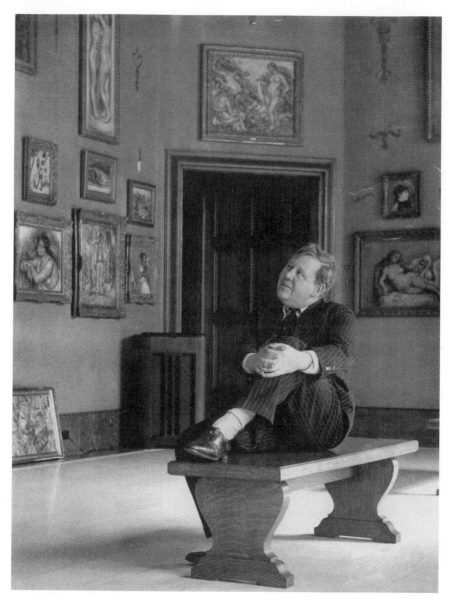

During Barnes's lifetime, visits to the Barnes Foundation were by invitation only. In this October 1940 photograph, English actor Charles Laughton can be seen studying a wall full of Renoirs and Cézannes in the main gallery. (Temple University Libraries Urban Archives)

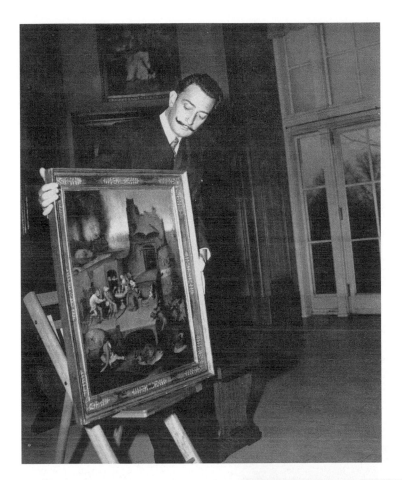

(Above) Another notable visitor to the Barnes Foundation, this time in 1945, was the surrealist painter Salvador Dali. (Temple University Libraries Urban Archives)

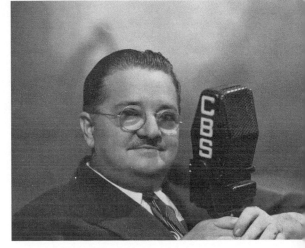

(Right) Not all would-be guests were welcomed at the Barnes. When critic and radio personality Alexander Woollcott sought to visit the Barnes, the doctor's "secretary," Fidèle-de-Port-Manech, replied via telegram that Dr. Barnes was "out on the lawn singing to the birds" and could not be disturbed. (Bettmann/Corbis)

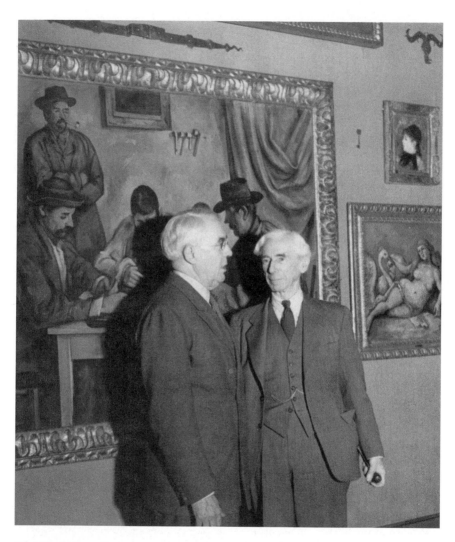

The English mathematician and philosopher Bertrand Russell (seen here with Barnes in front of Cézanne's *The Card Players*) sued—and won $20,000—when Barnes fired him from his job as foundation lecturer. (Temple University Libraries Urban Archives)

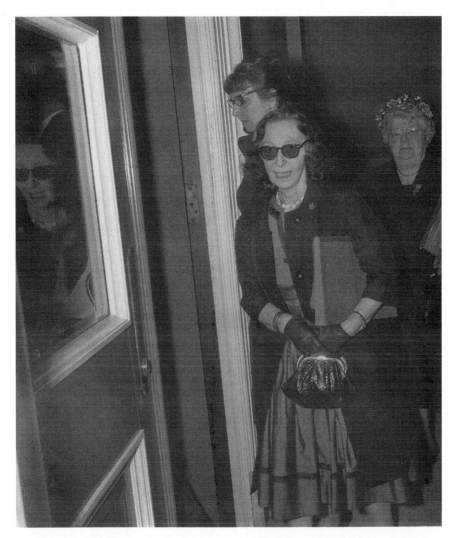

Violette de Mazia (wearing dark glasses in this 1962 photograph) was for many years the education director of the Barnes Foundation. Main Line gossip had it that she was also Albert Barnes's lover. (Temple University Libraries Urban Archives)

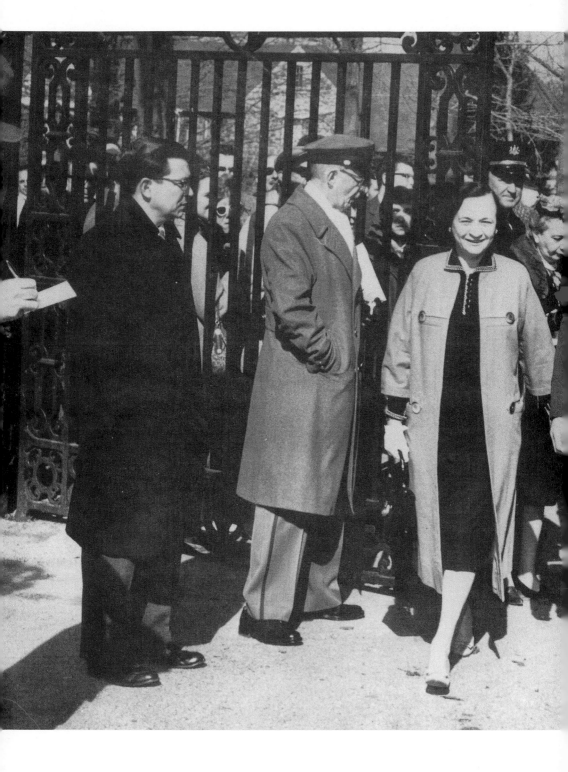

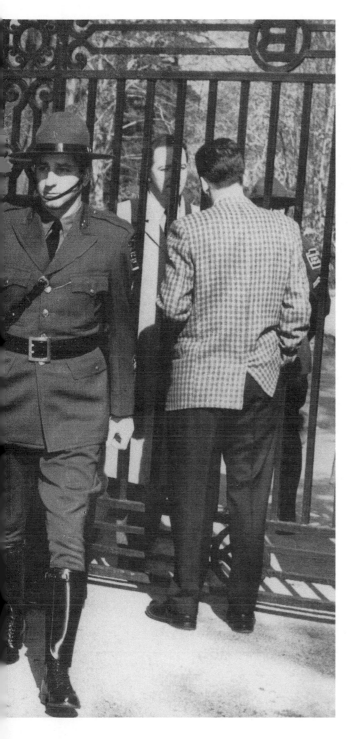

Throughout the decades of the fifties and sixties, the Barnes Foundation found itself under almost constant attack from the Pennsylvania Attorney General's office and from *Philadelphia Inquirer* publisher Walter Annenberg. In this March 1961 photograph, Pennsylvania Attorney General Anne Alpern is accompanied by a state trooper as she enters the grounds of the foundation. (Temple University Libraries Urban Archives)

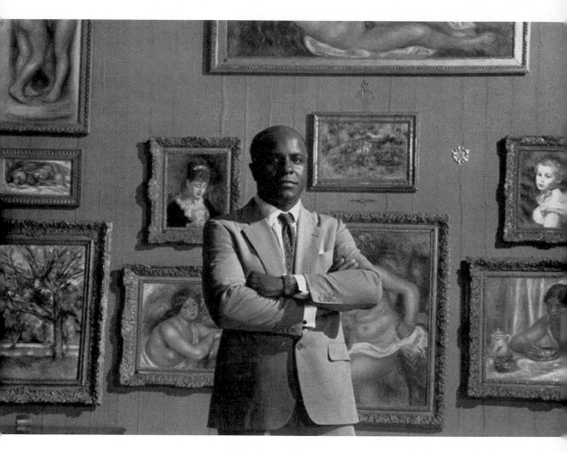

After the death of Miss de Mazia, leadership at the Barnes passed to Philadelphia lawyer Richard H. Glanton (here seen in the gallery), who was soon installed as foundation president. It was Glanton who oversaw the triumphant 1993–1995 tour of Barnes art. But it was also Glanton who presided over the Barnes's losing Ku Klux Klan Act suit against its neighbors. (Associated Press/AP)

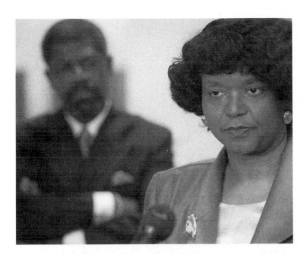

Former Lincoln University president Niara Sudarkasa was, for almost a decade, Glanton's closest ally on the Barnes board. All that changed after the Barnes lost the Ku Klux Klan case. Eventually he lost the Barnes presidency, and she was driven from the presidency of Lincoln. (*Philadelphia Daily News*/George Miller III)

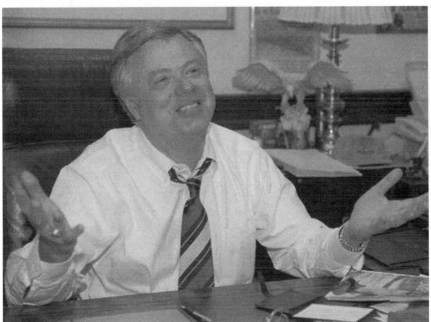

A Glanton ally, Pennsylvania State Senator Vincent J. Fumo launched an investigation into alleged financial improprieties at Lincoln University that led to Sudarkasa's forced resignation. (Associated Press/AP)

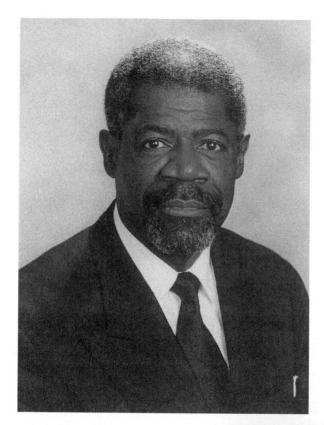

Carl Singley was the lawyer Sudarkasa finally turned to in her dispute with Glanton. His advice to her: Apologize to the Barnes's neighbors and sue Glanton. (Blank Rome Cominsky & McAuley)

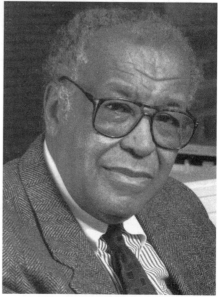

The late former U.S. Circuit Court of Appeals Chief Judge Leon Higginbotham was brought in to help the Barnes Foundation in its appeal of the Ku Klux Klan case decision. (Martha Stewart, *The Almanac*, University of Pennsylvania).

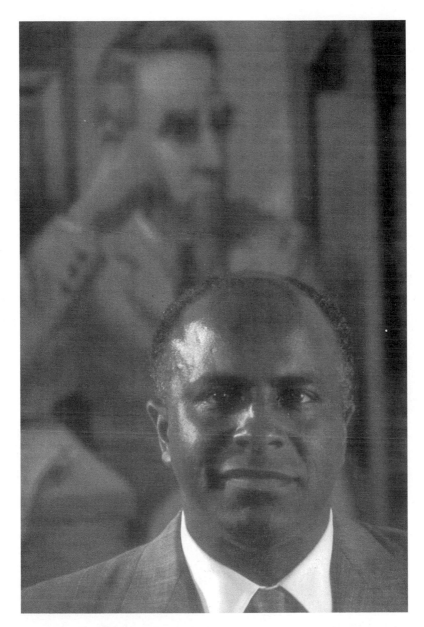

Richard Glanton (shown beneath the de Chirico portrait of Dr. Barnes) eventually found himself confronted in court by his erstwhile ally Sudarkasa. (Sal Dimarco, Jr./Timepix)

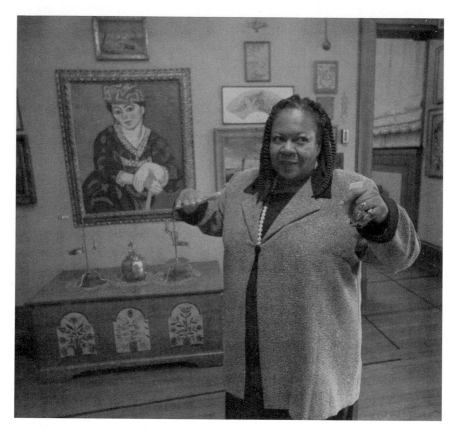

Kimberly Camp, the professional art museum curator who is the new CEO and executive director of the Barnes. The endowment, she says, is "zip." (Librado Romero/*New York Times*)

graduate, Harvard Law School. And he's got a five-year term. You can't get him off the board." (Within less than a year, Torbert was off the board.)

After they'd finished lunch at the Union League, Glanton, Rawson says, took the banker to see his Reed Smith office: "And I'll never forget that great big, corner office. Windows on two sides. Every single inch of wall space covered with celebrity photos: Reagan, Thornburgh, all these important Republican politicians. Looking at those photographs, wandering around that big office, I realized just how ambitious, how extremely politically motivated this guy was. And it was clear to me that Richard Glanton had engineered a coup."

Franklin Williams was by now so sick that he couldn't even manage the train ride into Philadelphia. When the ailing Barnes president convened the first meeting of the foundation's art advisory committee, it was by speakerphone from New York, where he was confined to his bed. Not long afterward, on May 20, Williams succumbed to cancer. Four days later, a notice went out to university trustees informing them of a special board meeting to be held on Saturday, June 2. The purpose of the meeting would be the election of a new Lincoln chairman.

Feigen, who was scheduled to appear on a panel at the Los Angeles County Museum that day, says he called president Sudarkasa's office "not once but twice" to "make absolutely certain" that the Barnes vacancy wouldn't be voted on at the same meeting. He was, Feigen says, "assured" that it was not on the agenda and would not be discussed.

When Feigen returned from Los Angeles on the following Monday, he discovered that "Bernie" Anderson—Bernard Anderson, an urban sociologist and Democratic party activist— had been elected to succeed Williams as Lincoln chairman. Anderson had by no means been the obvious choice to follow Williams. That would have been board vice-chairman Shirley Jackson, who was, in contrast, considered nonpolitical.

"That was Shirley's problem," says Cuyler Walker. "She *didn't* have an agenda." But, by now, Sudarkasa did. "Niara," Walker thinks, "wanted someone on her side as chairman. So, in company of Richard [Glanton], she helped shoot down Shirley." With his candidacy abetted by both Sudarkasa and general counsel (and fellow trustee) Glanton, Anderson was elected.

The new Lincoln chairman quickly appointed a nominating committee to consider the open Barnes trusteeship. The committee did its work in a hurry. That very week ballots went out in the mail to Lincoln trustees with one name on them: Richard H. Glanton.

Later in the week, says Feigen, he received two "curious" phone calls. The first was from Glanton, who told him, "Richard, I want your vote. I don't need it, but I want it." Feigen wouldn't be swayed. "Richard," he replied to Glanton, "I'm sorry. It's nothing personal. I can't give it to you. I think we should have one art person on the Barnes board." It wasn't the answer Glanton wanted to hear, and he didn't mind letting Feigen know it: "I've got enough votes without you. The train is leaving the station."

The second and far more curious phone call came from Glanton's recent ally, Niara Sudarkasa. She was calling, Sudarkasa told Feigen, "to rally opposition to Glanton." Feigen still doesn't know what her reasons were. "She didn't tell me," he says.

Sudarkasa's hopes to the contrary, the train had, in fact, left the station. The Lincoln board—with only scant opposition (Feigen voted for fellow trustee David Driskell, an African American who taught art history at the University of Maryland)—quickly made Glanton's nomination official. The Philadelphia lawyer had finally gained his toehold at the Barnes. Shortly thereafter, on July 20, 1990, Glanton was elected by the Barnes board to succeed Franklin Williams as president of the foundation.

Feigen's assessment of the event is revealing.

No sooner did Glanton force himself onto the Barnes board than he had himself elected [president] by his four captive colleagues. Charles Frank [Torbert's successor as the statutory bank representative] of course wanted to keep the Barnes-de Mazia account[s] at the Mellon Bank. With Anderson under Glanton's thumb, Sudarkasa wanted to keep her job as Lincoln president. Shirley Jackson . . . had only accepted the Barnes seat reluctantly and with the warning that she could not give it any time, always seemed to depend on Sudarkasa, and not really to care what was going on. As for Cuyler Walker, I never could figure him out.

Frank assuredly had to do a highwire act when it came to the Barnes. However, it seems highly unlikely that the de Mazia account could possibly have been threatened by Frank's non-cooperation with Glanton. Similarly, it's hard to imagine why Anderson would have considered himself "under Glanton's thumb." He wasn't being paid to be Lincoln chairman, and Glanton, as general counsel to the university, was, if anything, under *his* thumb. It would probably be more accurate to say that the two men were allies engaged in a tit-for-tat. Glanton had helped Anderson become chairman of Lincoln, and Anderson had helped Glanton get onto the Barnes board. Once Glanton had gotten there, it behooved Sudarkasa to cooperate with him, for he was, if not at this point her ally, then certainly her new chairman's ally.

As for Shirley Jackson, the subsequent history of the Barnes would suggest that Feigen sketched her role in the saga accurately enough. Cuyler Walker is another matter. Over the next five years, he and—increasingly—banker Charles Frank would come to form a minority of two on the board. Eventually, they would prove to be, in Glanton's words, "a couple of royal pains in the ass."

All that would lie in the future. Meanwhile, Richard Glanton's big adventure was just beginning.

CHAPTER SIX

INTO THE
BRIGHTNESS OF
THE FUTURE

Back at Lincoln, Niara Sudarkasa was in trouble. In its August 21, 1990, editions, the afternoon tabloid *Daily News* (which bills itself as "The People Paper") reported that state auditors had found that Lincoln physical plant director John Clark had made more than a quarter of a million dollars in unauthorized purchases. Clark, of course, was the former Michigan building contractor who was married to Sudarkasa. Among the alleged unauthorized purchases cited by the state auditor was Sudarkasa's own 1988 model white Lincoln Continental, "a luxury car," in the words of "The People Paper," that cost more than $26,000. Questioned by reporters, Lincoln vice-president Lloyd Asparagus said that the school's fiscal policies were being revised. Lincoln board chairman Anderson said he was "unaware" of the audit. General counsel Glanton had no comment.

Sudarkasa's problem did not go away, however. Little more than a week later, she was again skewered, this time in the morning *Inquirer*. The story began on a clever—and damning—note:

> *The way Lincoln president Niara Sudarkasa described it, her $26,000 Lincoln Continental was just basic wheels, transportation to and from work—college administrators don't drive jalopies. And Sudarkasa said the decision to set up a university-funded checking account with about $100,000 for purchases by her husband, John L. Clark— who is Lincoln's physical plant director and [who] picked out the car—was a money-saving measure implemented to cut the school's deficit.*

The *Inquirer* went on to quote from a state auditor general's report that criticized Sudarkasa not only for the no-bid purchase of her Lincoln Continental but also for similar no-bid purchases of nine other vehicles "and an array of products ranging from pastel-colored toilets to cleaning equipment."

While the state auditors stressed that they had uncovered no criminal wrongdoing, an anonymous spokesperson for the office went on to say that Sudarkasa's "'highly unusual' management style may have cost the taxpayers money because there was no competitive bidding on items Clark bought." Among the no-bid purchases cited by the auditor general's "routine compliance audit" were heavy machinery, radio communications equipment, and auto repair shop supplies. Sudarkasa told the *Inquirer* that Clark had purchased the Continental only after doing "comparative shopping," by telephoning Philadelphia-area dealerships. Sudarkasa defended Clark's actions: "There's nothing unusual about that. Other university presidents use comparable vehicles. It's not a car that anyone bought for a quote 'wife.'"

The *Inquirer* found that none of Sudarkasa's fellow

Philadelphia-area university college presidents drove Lincoln Continentals. Temple's Peter Liacouras drove an '89 Buick; Penn State's Bryce Jordan, an '88 Buick; and the Ivy League's Sheldon Hackney, president of the University of Pennsylvania, a plain old '87 Ford station wagon.

The way Sudarkasa saw it, the blame for this mess lay with a recently departed Lincoln vice-president. The former Lincoln official, Sudarkasa told the *Inquirer*, had set up Clark's checking account without informing the president (which assumes that John Clark hadn't informed the president, either). What's more, Sudarkasa claimed, there had been proper accounting for "each and every penny that was spent. This was something discussed between the vice president for fiscal affairs and the plant director." It was unfortunate, Sudarkasa said, that the story had "been sensationalized." After all, "This was not a slush fund."

The *Inquirer* account concluded with Sudarkasa's claim that she had reduced Lincoln's longstanding debt to less than $500,000 as "a result of careful management and prudent spending"—her own words. As for John Clark's special account, the university's current vice-president for fiscal affairs, Lloyd Asparagus, said it had since been closed on the advice of auditors. Exactly which auditors—the state's or Lincoln's—Asparagus did not say.

■

At much the same time that Niara Sudarkasa was being pummeled in the press, Richard Glanton was beginning to bask in its praise. A long and laudatory *Inquirer Sunday Magazine* story dated November 11, 1990, was entitled, "Rebirth of the Barnes. The Country's Most Secretive Museum Is Opening Up." The author: *Inquirer* cultural reporter Lucinda Fleeson.

The story would be pivotal in the history of Barnes, and, as such, it's worth studying closely. In a telling comment, Glanton told Fleeson, "I never purported to know anything about art, but

I can lead." Glanton was interviewed in his twenty-fifth-floor corner Reed Smith office—"befitting his position as the firm's biggest rainmaker"—in the then-new Liberty Place tower.

The Barnes president was full of ideas, his principal goal being to transform "this most private of institutions into a major cultural presence." One project that Glanton specifically cited was the conversion of Albert Barnes's country retreat Ker-Feal "into an artists' residence for lectures, courses, [and] even fundraising events." Glanton also announced that he was interviewing publishers for a color catalogue of the Barnes's art. Of course, all these projects—as Fleeson was quick to add—"would take money and plenty of it."

Where, though, would the money come from? The endowment, as Fleeson pointed out, generated "$1 million a year, just barely enough to support 40 or 50 employees." On the other hand, the assets of Dr. Barnes's art collection were "mind-boggling."

"Many people," Glanton told Fleeson, "both inside and outside the foundation," had suggested selling "some less glamorous holdings like Ker-Feal." Glanton said he was opposed to so radical a step as that. However, for the first time publicly, he broached deaccessioning the collection, confessing that he had "no fanatical commitment to following those aspects of the indenture that don't make sense." After all, as Fleeson herself commented, "Just selling a few Renoirs could make the Barnes one of this country's most richly endowed institutions." A sale, Fleeson added, "is obviously under discussion."

Interviewed more than a decade later for this book, Fleeson recalled how she first learned of Glanton's bid to deaccession Barnes art: "One of Richard's associates got drunk at an *Inquirer* party and [told her] about how they were going to sell some art. So I got on that story right away." The day the story came out, Fleeson says, she was coming from the gym when "this big black Mercedes pulls up. It was Richard, and he was grinning."

There you had it. Richard Glanton, via the reporter Lucinda

Fleeson and the pages of the *Inquirer*, was floating his game plan for the Barnes, a game plan that called for selling off some of the collection's paintings—fifteen is the number that's been most often cited—in order to build up an equally significant endowment. Or, as Glanton put it: "My goal is to see that the board does not become Hamlet in the process of grappling with the question of how to build up the endowment."

When Albert Barnes died, Glanton told Fleeson, "the lights went out" at the foundation. The implication was obvious: Miss de Mazia and company had turned the Barnes into a palace of obscurantism. Glanton was, however, quick to add, "I am resolved and resolute that I would not, in any way, shape, or form, criticize those who had gone before me." Curiously, it was not Laura Barnes or Violette de Mazia that Glanton saved his kindest words for. No, it was Dr. Barnes's old antagonist Walter Annenberg, whom Glanton "commend[ed] . . . for his role in forcing the Foundation to hold public hours." No timid, hermit-like curator, the new Barnes president saw himself as "an agent for change."

On November 11, 1990, Glanton appeared before a judge in Montgomery County Orphans' Court and formally requested permission to increase the admission fee to the Barnes; to "permit modern investment" (to allow, in other words, for investment in securities other than government bonds); and to "request a one-time authority to empower the Barnes board to make a decision regarding deaccessioning to enhance the endowment." The figure Glanton had in mind, the Barnes's lawyers told the court, was $15 to $18 million in paintings. The judge agreed to take matters under advisement.

By mid-1991, organized opposition to Glanton's various plans had begun to galvanize. On February 28, 1991, the Barnes's art advisory committee met for only the second time. The committee had been chosen by Franklin Williams, well before the advent of Glanton. Its membership was made up of a veritable Who's Who of the American art world, not only Feigen but also, among others, Philadelphia Museum of Art director Anne d'Harnoncourt, Smithsonian Institution assistant secretary for museums Tom Freudenheim, National Gallery deputy director E. Roger Mandle, and Metropolitan Museum of Art associate curator of European paintings Gary Tinterow.

Glanton began the meeting, held at the Barnes headquarters in Lower Merion, with a state of the foundation address, detailing his plans to deaccession paintings in order to build up the endowment. According to Feigen, Glanton privately "boasted to committee member Roger Mandle that this was only the first stage of a bigger plan to sell not $15 million worth of pictures but $200 million worth, ostensibly to make the Lincoln-Barnes combination a 'force' in the Philadelphia educational scene."

Mandle thinks the comments might have been made over lunch but confirms that Glanton told him that he intended to sell some $200 million worth of art. "To my memory, yes, that's what he said," recalls Mandle. "It was," he adds, "a staggering amount—one that curled my toenails."

As the committee members listened—"sitting there speechless," Feigen says—Glanton assured them that Montgomery County Orphans' Court would rule in his favor based not on the rule of law but because "his power with the state attorney general and the court ensured that his petition would be granted." Next, he announced that Walter Annenberg was to be honorary chairman of the art advisory committee. Annenberg had accepted the post; and he supported Glanton's plan to deaccession. Glanton also informed the committee members that he was "inclined" to give the contract for a color catalogue of the Barnes collection to the publishers Alfred A. Knopf, Inc.

PMA president Robert Montgomery Scott was not a member of the committee, but he knew Walter Annenberg well. Scott—a man who is "smart, sophisticated, but not warm and fuzzy," in the words of former *Inquirer* editorial page editor Michael Pakenham—had served as Annenberg's chief of staff at the Court of St. James's back in the early 1970s.

He and Annenberg, Scott says, "had had many discussions about the Barnes." Annenberg's own collecting days began in earnest just about the time Barnes died, says Scott, who adds, "I don't think Walter liked rivals." Scott speculates that "Walter led Glanton to think that he might support him in a bid for public office. Governor, perhaps. Senator, perhaps. Senator Glanton—that would sound good."

Not to Richard Feigen, it wouldn't have. By now Feigen was incensed—and ready to go public with his concerns. The museum officials on the Barnes advisory committee, Feigen recalls, had planned to draft an open letter of protest, "which they intended to publish but then called off." Annenberg had yet to decide which museum or museums would eventually inherit his magnificent collection of impressionist paintings—and no director or curator anywhere dared risk his displeasure, says Feigen. After Glanton filed a petition with Orphans' Court on March 18, seeking to sell paintings, Feigen took the matter up at a subsequent Lincoln board meeting. Chairman Bernard Anderson, Feigen says, "gaveled me down. He said, 'If you have any questions about the Barnes Foundation, ask Richard Glanton after the meeting.'" From then on, Feigen says, he was a pariah both at the Barnes and at Lincoln.

Feigen promptly fed the story to Grace Glueck, the art news reporter of *The New York Times*. Her story ran on March 29, 1991. A few months later, Feigen received a letter signed "Board of Trustees The Barnes Foundation," dated July 22, terminating his services as a member of the advisory committee "effective immediately." The letter continued, "The Board firmly believes your service on the Committee has not been constructive." Less than a year later, on February 11, 1992, Feigen, having decided that "I had no credibility left," resigned as a trustee of Lincoln

University. Feigen really didn't have much choice, says Cuyler Walker. "Richard [Glanton] had accused him of deceit, disloyalty, etc." As a result, concludes Walker, "He was drummed out of the universe."

■

In the spring of 1991, the Samuel I. Newhouse Foundation suddenly donated two million dollars to Lincoln University. A record gift, the money came from a heretofore untapped source: the charitable trust set up by the late newspaper and magazine publishing magnate Sam Newhouse and controlled by his billionaire sons, S.I. and Donald. The Newhouses were the owners of dozens of newspapers (such as the New Orleans *Times-Picayune* and the Newark *Star-Ledger*), the Condé Nast stable of glossy magazines (*Vogue, Vanity Fair,* and the like)—and Random House, Inc., the venerable book publishing empire. A few months later, in June 1991, Random House's Alfred A. Knopf, Inc., subsidiary agreed to pay $800,000 to the Barnes Foundation as an advance against royalties for the rights to publish a lavish color catalogue of mostly French paintings in the collection. The two events, Richard Glanton told me (winking broadly), "were totally unconnected."

Only days before the Knopf deal was announced, Glanton had taken *Inquirer* reporter Fleeson "Into the Back Rooms of the Barnes to See a Museum in Sore Disrepair," as the headline had it. Standing on the steps to the Barnes, Glanton enumerated "everything that was wrong" with the physical plant. By the time he had finished ticking off all the problems, Fleeson was seemingly in shock. "Basically," she reported, "the structure that holds one of the world's great art collections needs to have all of the major systems—heating, cooling, electric, plumbing, and security—ripped out and replaced." There was no fire protection system or sprinkler system. Metal frames had "turned to mush." When "an assistant" told Fleeson that filters were to be installed on windows to block ultraviolet rays and allow in more natural light, Glanton quipped, "Yeah, so it won't look like a mortuary all the time."

Glanton made a special point of taking Fleeson down into the bowels of the main gallery, past the two ancient boilers. The one, he noted, dated from 1926; the other, from 1928. In 1981, Glanton said, canvases had been warped by the humidity, and in 1984, steam had escaped. "What happened to the paintings?" Fleeson wanted to know. "They got wet," Glanton told her.

"I just laughed when Glanton got in there and started screaming about how the Barnes was sinking," recalls former trustee David Rawson. "Not only was the Barnes solvent when Glanton 'inherited' it, the physical plant was in good shape. We'd replaced the roof. The place was watertight."

Earlier, Glanton had estimated that the cost of repairs to the Barnes would be in the neighborhood of ten to twelve million dollars. Now, after a meeting with building consultants the week before, he told Fleeson that the cost might be as high as eighteen million dollars.

■

All that spring and early summer, opposition to Glanton's plan grew steadily louder. First, and predictably, a collection of former Barnes students and staff began making themselves heard at protests and in print. (They produced a newsletter, "Barnes Watch," and eventually an internet site as well.) Next, the foundation's own art advisory committee registered its disapproval. After that, the Association of Museums Directors announced plans to file a brief in opposition—they had a longstanding, frequently stated position against deaccessioning art. Meanwhile, Richard Feigen was personally keeping up the drumbeat. "Richard Glanton's objective," he told Fleeson, "is pure and unadulterated lust for power—to advance him in the political arena. Once he opens the door, I think he plans to decimate the collection."

On June 21, 1991, the Barnes board voted to drop its plans to deaccession. Trustees Cuyler Walker and banker Charles Frank had opposed the plan from the beginning. According to Walker, Shirley Jackson was on the fence, while Niara Sudarkasa was inclined to back Glanton. But then, adds Walker, "Richard being Richard, [the Barnes president began] making statements, being confrontational. Niara got furious at Richard's public comments—we'd all agreed not to comment publicly." As a result, Sudarkasa faxed around a resolution that, if passed, would end all talk of deaccessioning. Jackson and Walker voted for it, and that was that. According to Walker—and his is an opinion shared by former Lincoln vice-president Eugene Cliett—"No one could put Richard in his place the way she could." Confronted by an angry Sudarkasa—"She's a powerful person," says Walker—Glanton "would quake."

The vote to withdraw the petition to deaccession was unanimous.

"Cut off at the knees," in Walker's words, Glanton retreated—for the time being. According to at least three sources in a position to know, two of them trustees Sudarkasa and Walker, Glanton never completely gave up his goal of selling some of the Barnes art. A third person who was once close to the former Barnes president agrees. "Richard," this person says, "never really worried about raising money because—I believe—he always intended to deaccession. With a hundred-million-dollar endowment—you sell just one *good* painting, and you can get that—he could preside over years and years of spending."

The same person adds, "Richard makes three hundred fifty, five hundred [thousand] a year [at] Reed Smith for 'development,' being a big rainmaker, bringing in clients like PECO [the main supplier of electricity in the Philadelphia area whose parent, Exelon Corporation, is another of the companies that Glanton is a director of]. He doesn't do any real lawyering at all. He *thinks* he does, but he doesn't."

A similar view is held today by Niara Sudarkasa. "Richard,"

she says, "wanted to walk with the big boys." There was nothing that her erstwhile ally wanted more, the Lincoln president claims, than "the ability to command resources that can open doors. The Barnes was the validation of Richard Glanton."

According to Sudarkasa, Glanton continued to negotiate with the Getty Museum for a long-term lease on what may be the Barnes's most valuable work of art, Matisse's *Joy of Life*. "Richard," says Sudarkasa, "spoke many times of how [the] Getty wanted us to let them have it." The deal, as it was presented to Sudarkasa, in at least one incarnation: a 100-year lease at one million dollars per year, or $100 million over the course of the contract. "I told him we'd be crucified if we did that," Sudarkasa recalls. "But he kept on pushing it. Finally, I just said, 'No.'"

As we've seen, Glanton had earlier told the *Inquirer* that the Barnes was facing an $18 million fix-up. At the time, Glanton, of course, believed he had a solution to the problem that would have covered virtually all the costs. The question now was: Where was the money going to come from?

Readers of a July 22, 1991, Fleeson piece ("At the Barnes: From Crisis to Dilemma, The Art-Sale Plan Was Doomed and Dashed. So What's Next for the Foundation and Its Pursuit of Funding?") might have noticed a curious reference to the de Mazia Trust: "Government bonds," Fleeson wrote, "yield . . . a steady income of $900,000 a year" for the Barnes Foundation's endowment, while Miss de Mazia's $8.6 million estate "yields $400,000 more in annual income to the foundation budget." Little wonder, then, that one of the subheads in the story referred to Glanton as "A Man with Vision."

On January 17, 1992, the trustees of the Violette de Mazia Trust announced to the press, through their lawyer, that they had reason to believe that the Barnes Foundation trustees had "improperly diverted" the two-million-dollar gift from the Samuel I. Newhouse Foundation. The money, they argued, should have gone to the Barnes Foundation—and not to Lincoln. Now, the de Mazia Trust was filing suit against Lincoln and the Barnes trustees in an effort to force them to transfer the money to the Barnes endowment. Glanton's response: "They are saying black institutions shouldn't be allowed to benefit from relationships which exist."

Those were the first salvos in what soon became open warfare between the trustees of the two foundations. Slightly over a month later, on February 20, Esther van Sant, one of the de Mazia trustees, turned in her resignation as education director of the Barnes. Van Sant told the press that her position had become "untenable" and that she had, in effect, been forced out. Glanton, she claimed, had had her locked out of the buildings. In her letter of resignation to Glanton, van Sant complained, "You called to berate me angrily and state that, 'No one who fights me goes into the Gallery.'" Glanton denied the charges and said that the locks had been changed as part of the promised security upgrade.

Three months later, the Barnes Foundation's lawyers went before a judge in Montgomery County Orphans' Court and alleged that "many of the works of art [liquidated at a Christie's auction following Miss de Mazia's death] to create the corpus of the de Mazia Trust were the property of the Foundation." Dilworth, Paxson, Kalish & Kauffman partner Bruce W. Kauffman argued the case for the Barnes. Kauffman—a former Pennsylvania supreme court judge, protégé of Republican U.S. Senator Arlen Specter, and future federal district judge—would be the first of many high-flying, high-paid attorneys to serve the Barnes's interests over the next decade. His argument: Miss de Mazia had stolen approximately $8.6 million in art from the Barnes.

CHAPTER SEVEN

THE SUBJECT WAS CHEST HAIR

Not quite two weeks after the *Inquirer* first reported that the de Mazia Trust had filed suit against the Barnes Foundation, Philadelphia newspapers had a heyday, the likes of which were unusual even by scandal-ridden City of Brotherly Love standards. That's when Kathleen Frederick, a Reed Smith associate from November 1987 until February 1990, filed a federal sex discrimination suit against the firm and Glanton. A 1983 cum laude graduate of Villanova University Law School, Frederick charged that Glanton had promised to help her gain partnership at the firm in return for sex. In her late thirties at the time, Frederick was not only married but the mother of two children. The afternoon tabloid *Daily News* quoted Glanton as saying that Frederick and her lawyers had been making demands on him for the past couple of years. Her lawyers, Glanton said, first asked for $100,000, then eventually escalated their demands up to a million dollars. Neither he nor the law firm intended to pay

Frederick a dime, Glanton told reporters. The former Reed Smith associate's claims were, he contended, "a total and complete fabrication. She was terminated for poor performance."

Jury selection in the case didn't begin until early August of 1993. In the meantime, a number of events had taken place at Lincoln and at the Barnes. On April 22, 1992, Niara Sudarkasa was given a second five-year term as president of Lincoln University. Despite her problems with the state auditor general's office, Sudarkasa was now seemingly in a much stronger position both at the university and at the foundation. A few months later, on August 21, 1992, Judge Louis J. Stefan of Montgomery County Orphans' gave the Barnes permission to take approximately eighty of its most prized works on a one-time tour to Washington, D.C., Paris, Tokyo, and then back to Philadelphia (for a showing at Dr. Barnes's nemesis, the PMA). Subsequently, on February 23, 1993, the Barnes gallery closed for renovation work under the guidance of the famed architect Robert Venturi.

The Kathleen Frederick sex discrimination trial opened in federal court on August 10, 1993. When the former Reed Smith associate—described in one account as "thin, [with] blond hair, [a] sweet smile, [and] bitter eyes"—took the stand three days later, she was, the *Daily News* reported, "often in tears." By having sex with Glanton, Frederick told the court, "I lost my dignity and self-respect. I basically prostituted myself to save my job." In her six hours on the stand in U.S. District Judge Robert F. Kelly's courtroom, Frederick testified that Glanton "pawed her breasts on occasion, [and] told her on another [occasion] that he liked her dress because he could 'see her tits.'" He also, Frederick said, invited her to a client's toga party.

Glanton, Kathy Frederick told the jury, used to ask her questions like, "Are you sleeping with anybody?" and would then volunteer, "You need someone else." He told her, Frederick testified, that she was in her "sexual prime" and that he "would be good for me." When the firm began an evaluation of her work,

Frederick told the court, Glanton took her to the piano bar of a local restaurant, where he let her know that he'd given her the highest rating—and then offered to give her "a deep, whole body massage." Another time, Frederick said, Glanton had stopped by her office at Reed Smith with a bottle of wine, told her he loved her, and said, "I want you to be my mistress. I can help you."

Continuing with her testimony, Frederick recalled how Glanton, on another occasion, had taken her to an expensive restaurant at the Four Seasons Hotel. After dinner, he'd offered to drive her home, but instead pulled off West River Drive into a parking area where he "hugged me and pressed himself against me and unzipped his pants." When she refused to have sex with him, Glanton angrily drove her home, Frederick told jurors. At work the next day, he was cold; and Frederick feared that she would lose her job. The next time he stopped by her office, though, Glanton was his old self. When he again offered to drive her home, she took him up on it. But instead of driving her home, Glanton once again pulled off the road and parked his car, this time alongside the Schuylkill River. He told her that he wanted to have sex with her. "We did," Frederick told jurors. On another occasion, after having dinner at a restaurant in suburban Haverford, Glanton drove back to the same spot—and, again, the two had sex.

Probably the most titillating of Frederick's tales concerned an event that allegedly took place the Sunday after Thanksgiving 1989. With her husband out of town, Frederick agreed to have sex with Glanton in her own bed. Afterward, Frederick said, she felt "degraded."

Frederick, however, also admitted that she broke off the relationship because she believed that Glanton was seeing another female associate at the firm. She reacted to the news, Frederick told the court, by leaving an anonymous phone call on the other woman's home answering machine—a call that the woman's husband listened to. Frederick eventually confessed to having left a whole series of calls on the answering machine.

Glanton, meanwhile, had given a deposition dated March 29, 1993, which was entered into the court record. In it, he referred to Frederick as a "nut" and "completely crazy." Frederick, Glanton claimed, "was purporting to be my friend, setting me up, sucking up to me."

On the stand, Glanton described Frederick as, "sick and [in] need of help." Her tale of sex in the Mercedes, he told jurors, was nothing but "a despicable, damnable lie." Following him on the witness stand was his wife Scheryl, who testified that Frederick phoned their house "excessively" following her evaluation at the firm. When Glanton's lawyer asked if she could imagine anything wrong with her husband taking Frederick out to such places as the Swan Lounge at the Four Seasons Hotel, Scheryl Glanton replied, "No." The Swan Lounge, she added, was like "an extension of our home."

On August 3, as the *Daily News* reported, "The subject was chest hair. . . . When asked if Glanton had chest hair, Frederick gave the wrong answers. . . . Glanton has a hairy chest, and the hair color is white, testified Dr. Charles R. Clark, a forensic pathologist from Ann Arbor, Michigan."

On August 7, 1993, after two days of deliberation, the jury of five men and five women ruled in favor of Reed Smith and Glanton on the sexual harassment charges. Frederick, the jurors found, had not suffered permanent damage to her reputation. But they did award her $125,000 for a separate libel action against Glanton, $100,000 of it in compensatory damages and another $25,000 in punitive damage. Kathleen Frederick's case, Glanton had told a reporter, was nothing but "an extortionist lawsuit brought by a disturbed woman."

Lucinda Fleeson had left the Barnes beat at the *Inquirer* earlier that year to work in the home design section of the newspaper. While she didn't cover the Frederick trial, she—like almost everyone else in Philadelphia—did keep up with what was happening in the courtroom: "It was a slow news summer, and I couldn't believe the coverage it got. I think it ruined Richard's career, or at least his political career. If not for that, who knows what he'd have become in the [second] Bush administration?"

■

Gene Cliett had been a friend of Glanton's for well over a decade when he first met Niara Sudarkasa in the fall of 1992. Forty-seven years old at the time, Eugene L. Cliett, Jr., was already a well-known figure in Philadelphia business and political circles. A native Philadelphian, Cliett had attended the University of Bridgeport and graduated from Clark University with a bachelor's degree in accounting. After that, he'd taken graduate school classes at Temple and Drexel Universities. For four years (1968–1972), Cliett, a certified public accountant, had worked at Deloitte & Touche. From there, he'd gone on to work for CIGNA, the large insurance company headquartered in Philadelphia; and, in 1974, he'd joined the administration of Mayor Frank Rizzo as deputy city controller, briefly serving as acting city controller.

Cliett's big break, though, had come six years later, thanks to W. Wilson Goode. Under Rizzo's successor as mayor, William J. Green, Jr.—a moderately liberal former U.S. Representative whose father had been the longtime boss of the city's Democratic party machine—Goode had been the city's first African American managing director. When Green declined to seek reelection in 1984, Goode had succeeded him as mayor. Widely perceived as a workaholic, Goode had a well-earned reputation as the bureaucrat's bureaucrat. But as mayor, he quickly proved himself to be politically inept. And in his eight years in office, Goode managed to lead the city far along the path toward financial insolvency.

Cliett had served in both the Green and Goode administrations as city revenue commissioner, a cabinet-level position. From there, he'd gone on to be executive director of the city-owned Philadelphia Computing Center (1985–1993), his tenure more or less overlapping with that of Mayor Goode (1984–1992). In the fall of 1992, Cliett was approached by Sudarkasa to be her vice-president for fiscal affairs at Lincoln. It was only after he'd accepted the post in October 1992, Cliett says, that Sudarkasa first showed him the critical state auditor general's report. What he read there, Cliett recalls, was "a virtual indictment of her and her husband. I said, 'My god, why wasn't I shown this before?'" Stunned, Cliett backed out of the job. Later, in early 1993, he did agree to work as a consultant to the university, but only after Sudarkasa had come back to him, he says, and "painted a very, very sorrowful and bad picture" of Lincoln's financial situation. The situation, as Cliett explains it today, was indeed shocking. Lincoln, he says, had accumulated a two-and-a-half-million-dollar deficit the previous year on a total budget of only $27 million. Worse, there wasn't anywhere to go to make up for the deficit. A third of the university's money came from the state, 20 percent from the federal government, and the rest from tuition and fees. The endowment contributed "maybe one or two percent" of the university's annual needs, says Cliett. The bottom line was that Lincoln had to spend less money to make up for the continuing deficits. The university, Cliett says, had no choice in the matter. It "was in significantly bad shape."

Cliett's plan to rein in spending at Lincoln called for cutbacks and layoffs, most of them in the physical plant. "And that," Cliett recalls, "started my problems with [John Clark] and with the president, to some extent. They felt I was picking on the physical plant." Worse, Cliett says, "We were talking about changing the culture [at Lincoln]. And when changing the culture involves making the president's husband behave, now that's a very tender and sensitive situation."

While he may not have made many friends among the Lincoln staff, Cliett did manage to reduce the university's 1993 deficit to $200,000. The Lincoln board rewarded Cliett with a two-year appointment as vice-president for fiscal affairs. But when he came aboard full-time in August, Cliett found that his problems with the president and her physical plant director had not gone away: "It was just very, very difficult [to deal with John Clark]. The way he had been allowed to operate was the way he intended to keep on operating." Sudarkasa, says Cliett, "made it clear to everyone" that she and John Clark were "a package deal." The Lincoln president, Cliett claims, "even said that on one occasion at a staff meeting. She just went on a tirade about it." Furious, Cliett turned to his fellow administrators and said, "To those of you who don't know, Mr. Clark and I are having a disagreement." Cliett still simmers about the relationship to this day: "She always came down on his side," he adds.

General counsel Glanton's role in all of this? "He was very supportive of the president," says old friend Gene Cliett. "She had problems. He had problems." And as long as Sudarkasa was supportive of his dealings at the Barnes, Glanton "was part of Madame President's team."

■

Richard Glanton faced reelection as president of the Barnes in December 1993. He would not be unopposed. Charles Frank had had run-ins with Glanton as far back as October 1992, when Glanton had proposed that the Barnes publish a glossy color newsletter. After Frank questioned the financing of the project, Glanton phoned the Mellon banker and accused him of "acting in a racist manner." Frank, fellow former trustee Cuyler Walker recalls, "was extremely upset about it and told me that he had indicated that to Richard in the strongest possible terms."

Frank wasn't the only Barnes trustee who was angered by Glanton's tactics. Says Walker, "Richard was encouraged at various times while I was on the Barnes board to involve the trustees in any public statements that were made on behalf of the Barnes." And while Glanton's chief critics remained Walker and Frank, Walker claims that "at one time or another, each of the other board members expressed that preference too."

At the December 1, 1993, meeting of the Barnes board, Walker proposed replacing Glanton as president with Shirley Jackson. But while the Rutgers physicist "said she thought Mr. Glanton was out of line," recalls Walker, she also refused to run against him. Walker's desire to see him removed from office, Glanton insisted, was racially motivated. Recalling the scene some years later, Walker noted, "The discussion was very heated." Then again, he admitted, "I'm not sure I was shocked by anything at that point."

CHAPTER EIGHT

TRYING TO REFORM
RICHARD

Strange as it might seem, in late December 1993, the Barnes Foundation board found itself enmeshed in the politics of prison reform. Two days before Christmas, trustee Cuyler Walker discovered that one of the Barnes's longtime providers, Security Guard Systems, had been fired without warning. They were replaced by Foulke Associates, Inc. Walker was incensed. He could not, Walker complained to Glanton, "conceive of any justification for your taking this unilateral action." Not forty-eight hours before Glanton had terminated the company, "The Board [had] assembled for our annual meeting. You did not mention one word about the security contract."

Years later, one of Glanton's bitterest opponents, Philadelphia attorney Paul Rosen, theorized that the firing had more to do with "deal-making" than with increased security at the Barnes. Foulke Associates, Rosen explains, was controlled by Charles Sexton, a powerful figure in suburban Republican politics. The head of the Delaware County prison board, Sexton had recently led a successful effort to privatize the jail system there. As a result, the prison board was now in the process of trying to choose an appropriate for-profit operator for the system. The leading such "private prison-provider" nationwide, Rosen points out, is Wackenhut Corrections Corporation. Rosen continues: "Well, Wackenhut is a Glanton client [at Reed Smith]; and they've made a bid [to operate] the Delaware County prison system. So they get the DelCo prison contract from Sexton [and] Sexton gets the Barnes [security] contract [for Foulke Associates]. Ever heard of 'influence peddling'?" It's a charge that Glanton vehemently denies.

The facts in the matter are these. In 1993, Charles P. Sexton, Jr., was a fifty-five-year-old former Lower Merion police officer, who had founded Foulke Associates, Inc., in suburban Media, Pennsylvania, in 1971. The Barnes contract would be worth a good deal to Foulke: $282,792 in 1994 and $262,433 in 1995, according to the foundation's federal tax filings for those years. By 1998, Sexton was chairman of the Springfield Township, Delaware County, Republican party and a top fundraiser for Governor Tom Ridge. That was also the year that Foulke received a no-bid emergency contract at the Haverford State Hospital—a four-and-a-half-month contract worth $114,000. In October of the year before, Foulke received a contract to guard Philadelphia State Hospital at Byberry—a state-run mental institution— which would be worth $1.5 million by the time of its expiration in June 1999. And, as attorney Rosen observed, Sexton was also the chairman of the Delaware County prison board. In August of 1998, the county's expensive—$53,000,000—state-of-the-art prison opened for business. It would be staffed by privately contracted correctional officers—supplied by the Florida-based Wackenhut Corrections Corporation, which today counts among its outside directors Richard Glanton.

As Murray Dickman, the former Thornburgh administration

official, had discerned many years earlier, Richard Glanton had a definite modus operandi. "Richard," claims Niara Sudarkasa, long his closest supporter on the board, "would just go off and do something without consulting anyone." Years later, her friendship with Glanton turned to bitterness, Sudarkasa concludes that what happened with the security contract "was typical Richard."

■

January 1994 opened with Sudarkasa in trouble—again. Her problems this time lay with the Internal Revenue Service. The IRS had informed the Lincoln president that it intended to perform an audit on her taxes from 1990 to 1993. Of particular interest to the IRS were perquisites provided by the university that Sudarkasa had not paid taxes on: She believed them, she says, to be nontaxable. The IRS took a different view. Sudarkasa went to Glanton for help. Glanton told her that Reed Smith couldn't represent her: That might be a conflict of interest.

The prior December, art conservator Paul R. Himmelstein had appeared before Montgomery County Orphans' Court judge Stefan in opposition to the Barnes's request to add two venues to the tour. Himmelstein testified that Matisse's 30-foot mural *La Danse* had suffered "permanent irreparable damage" from the wear and tear of having been carted about during the first phase of the tour.

Judge Stefan nevertheless found for the Barnes, granting the foundation's request to add Toronto and Fort Worth to the tour. The judge, however, coupled that decision with one denying the Barnes Foundation permission to spend the money generated by these additional venues without express approval from the court to do so. The judge particularly noted his concern about "the apparent attitude of the trustees that any funds generated by allowing additional venues may be used by them . . . as they see fit." Maintaining an ongoing building fund, Judge Stefan wrote, might help avoid "a repetition of the emergency atmosphere"

previously prevailing at the Barnes. Gordon Elkins, a lawyer for
the de Mazia Trust, told reporters, "What [the judge is] really
saying is, 'We don't want you coming back here for another
tour.'" Court papers disclosed that the Kimbell Art Museum in
Fort Worth had paid three million dollars for its part of the tour,
April 24 to August 14, while the Art Gallery of Ontario (the
AGO) had paid $3.2 million for its early September through
December show.

Little more than ten days later, the Barnes Foundation board
met. Prior to the meeting, banker Charles Frank sent around a
memo to his fellow trustees in which he spelled out matters that
should in the future "be submitted to the Board for approval at
regularly scheduled meetings or at special meetings called for
such purpose following adequate notice describing the proposed
action:

1. entering into any contract or agreement . . . involving payments of $10,000 or over . . .
2. retaining professionals;
3. decisions to institute, appeal, or settle litigation where the
   amount in controversy exceeds $10,000 . . ."

No single issue demanding board approval would prove more
important in the subsequent history of the Barnes than item
three. Other points on Charles Frank's list included: "5. hiring of
employees and consultants at annual rates of $30,000, or more;
and, 6. any other matter out of the ordinary course."

Frank's memo also called for the regular scheduling of board
meetings, the preparation of minutes "reflecting all actions taken
at any meeting," annual "meetings with auditors to review management," and an "undertaking to provide any Board member
any information concerning the Foundation, including financial
information, that is requested."

The list was concise, to the point—and obviously applicable

to exactly one Barnes board member, the only one who really counted, President Richard Glanton. Surprisingly, Frank's list, entered as a formal motion, was unanimously approved by the board at its March 9, 1994, meeting. According to the minutes, "Mr. Glanton and Mr. Walker agreed that they were all excellent suggestions and should be adopted and implemented." Charles Frank's resolutions might have been adopted; they would never be carried out in practice.

Glanton, it might be noted—like his ally Sudarkasa—was usually on his best behavior when having to fight battles on two separate fronts. Kathy Frederick's attorneys had filed an appeal, arguing that the trial judge had erred by excluding evidence that showed that Glanton had sexually harassed another female associate, had a romantic relationship with another, and that the alleged romance with the unnamed attorney could be supported by Glanton's telephone records and "records of Mr. Glanton's frequent renting of hotel rooms for single nights in the Philadelphia area."

Two months later, though, with the Frederick appeal temporarily on the back burner and out of the daily press, Glanton struck again. Cuyler Walker discovered that Glanton had acted unilaterally—forget the resolution of March 9—to move the Barnes's checking account to the United Bank. Walker let Glanton know that he didn't approve of the action:

> *I object to your depositing funds in any bank which has not been approved by the Board of Trustees. . . . I object in the strongest possible terms to the proposed deposit. Furthermore, if you proceed to make such a deposit without the Board's approval, you will be violating the By-Laws of the Foundation.*

Glanton's reply, via fax and dated June 8, read, "This acknowledges your memorandum objecting to the Foundation's funds being deposited in the United Bank, the only African-American bank in Philadelphia."

Charles Frank wasn't happy either, but he took a more diplomatic approach than his colleague Walker—at least at first. "I have no objection per se to the investment of Foundation funds in government securities through United Bank," Frank wrote to Glanton, but "I would recommend that the Board vote [on the proposal]."

When the Barnes board met to reconsider Glanton's action, Frank lost his cool entirely. As Glanton recalled in a later deposition, "Mr. Frank vigorously and vehemently objected to the African-American bank receiving a deposit [and] I told him I didn't understand that, and it had implications that were, in my view, based on prejudice." Asked what Frank's reaction was, Glanton said, "He became, as best I can recall, crimson."

"You mean flushed red?" the attorney questioning him interjected.

"No," Glanton replied. "I meant crimson."

Walker too was by now in high dudgeon. It was clear that Glanton was going to have his way, in any case; but in the meantime, Walker felt that he'd been slandered: "Your most recent memorandum is offensive. . . . You know full well that I have never objected to the Foundation's funds being deposited in an African-American bank." His objection, Walker added, had nothing to do with race and everything to do with correct procedures. After all, he says, "We were trying hard to reform Richard. Back then, maybe, we thought we could."

Walker, says his fellow former Thornburgh administration colleague Murray Dickman, "is a pleasant fellow [and] smart. [He] tried to keep Richard Glanton in check, but he was playing with a tarantula, and Cuyler Walker is a gentleman. These are guys who play by very, very different rules."

In retrospect, it's clear that Glanton had no intention of being reformed, by Walker or by anyone else, especially not at a time when he was riding high. For one thing, the specter of Kathy Frederick was now past him. During the first week of January 1995—a mere seventeen months after the trial had ended—the case was quietly settled out of court. Having reached a confidential settlement, both parties filed a joint motion in federal court to end their appeals. The size of Frederick's settlement was reported to be a half-million dollars.

A week later, the Barnes Foundation and the de Mazia Trust also announced a settlement. The de Mazia Trust would drop its court case to remove the Barnes Foundation's trustees, and the Barnes would drop its case to recover the whole of the de Mazia Trust's endowment of $9 million. In return, the de Mazia Trust would hand over $2.75 million to the Barnes: $1.5 million within sixty days, and the remaining $1.25 million in seven annual installments.

The Barnes Foundation's lawyer in the de Mazia Trust case, as it turned out, was David W. Marston, whom Richard Glanton had tried to make chairman of the SEPTA board, whose wife he would later hire to administer the Barnes, and who would himself eventually be Glanton's partner and staunch supporter at Reed Smith.

Court records show that Buchanan Ingersoll—Marston's firm at the time of the de Mazia Trust challenge—earned $448,127.01 in legal fees from the Barnes Foundation.

■

The great Barnes Foundation art tour had, from the start, been an ingenious gambit. In the course of any kind of serious renovation, the Barnes would be forced to close its doors, and the de Chiricos, the Seurats, the van Goghs, and the rest would have to come down off the walls for a couple of years at least. Why not then put the paintings on tour—and charge a lot of money for the privilege of showing them? That, in turn, would pay for Robert Venturi's costly renovation yet presumably leave at least some money in the kitty.

Why not, indeed? "Because the physical condition of many of those paintings was poor," says art critic Hilton Kramer. "And every time you crate and uncrate [paintings], there's wear and tear." There's no question in his mind, Kramer says, that the Barnes's touring paintings "should never have been put through the international travel schedule they were put through."

National Gallery deputy director Roger Mandle had been in charge of organizing the original tour. Mandle, says a well-known American art historian, "was at the time an eager beaver, a big fan of the tour. Carter Brown may have been the driving force, but Roger was the one whose career was really riding on it." In retrospect, Mandle, who is today president of the Rhode Island School of Design, says he thinks the tour "was a good thing to do at the time. I still do. The question in most professional curators' minds, though, would be how much is enough. Glanton decided to put the pedal to the metal and keep going. I wouldn't have." The problem, Mandle explains, is that "traveling art is almost inevitably subject to damage, usually minor in nature. But damage nevertheless."

Glanton had no such qualms. The upside of a tour, in his mind, far outweighed the downside. And, as we have seen, a judge in Orphans' Court agreed. Thus the tour began. Almost alone among the trustees, Glanton went everywhere the paintings went. And virtually everywhere, he was honored for bringing the paintings with him. His crowning moment came in Paris, where President François Mitterrand made him a commander of the Order of Arts and Letters. He was treated, Glanton says proudly, "like a king in France. Mitterrand himself pinned the medal on me."

Niara Sudarkasa's recollection is somewhat different: "To let Richard tell it, all credit goes to himself. Everyone was embarrassed by the way Richard hogged the spotlight. [All the Barnes trustees] went to Paris. And we were all shocked. Richard wanted Mitterand by himself." She pauses: "It was *so* childish."

One venue where Glanton would not be honored was the Eternal City of Rome. In early February 1995 Glanton had flown to Italy to have talks with civic and museum officials anxious that Rome be added as a seventh stop on the Barnes tour. By the time he left three days later—having been royally wined and dined, not to mention put up in a luxury hotel—the Italians thought they had a done deal. They soon found that they were sorely mistaken.

Antonio Guizzetti was the man who thought he'd put Rome on the Barnes's map. An international financial consultant with offices in Washington, D.C., Guizzetti, who held a doctorate in economics from the University of Paris, had first met Glanton several years earlier at an Italian embassy black-tie dinner in honor of the National Gallery's trustees. At the dinner, Glanton had held Guizzetti spellbound with his tales of the Barnes collection—scheduled to open at the National Gallery on May 2, 1993—and the Italian had come away determined that his country should be added to the tour.

Not long afterward, Guizzetti accompanied Glanton to Venice, where they met with officials of the Palazzo Grassi and the Fiat motor works, the proposed sponsor of the Italian segment of the tour. Fiat refused to put up the three million dollars Glanton demanded; and that seemed to put an end to the possibility of an Italian venue. A year or so later, though, Guizzetti got a phone call from Glanton: There was still a chance, he was told, that Italy could be added to the tour—for the right price.

The mandatory conditions, Glanton wrote Guizzetti on December 2, 1994, included "a minimum of $3 million in cash payments to be made in three equal installments prior to the opening of the exhibition." By early February of 1995, Guizzetti believed that the city of Rome was prepared to meet all Glanton's demands—the full three million dollars plus the cost of transportation, insurance, and security, all of it guaranteed by ENI, the national energy company and one of the world's largest oil suppliers—and he and the Barnes president flew to Italy to seal the deal. Over the next three days, Glanton, having been lodged in the exclusive Hotel Bernini Bristol with a car and chauffeur at his disposal, met with business, cultural, and poltical leaders. Wherever Glanton went, Guizzetti tagged along, acting as host and interpreter.

Among the places they went was the Museo Capitolino on the Piazza del Campidoglio, the proposed setting for the tour. Home to the oldest public art collection in the world, begun by Pope Sixtus IV in 1471, the Museo Capitolino was built in 1644–1655 on a site, the Campidoglio, designed by Michelangelo. Having inspected it carefully, Glanton seemed to come away impressed. So much so, that, according to Guizzetti, Glanton told him that he was prepared to guarantee the deal. All he needed, Guizzetti recalled Glanton saying, was the receipt of a letter of confirmation from Francesco Rutelli, the mayor of Rome. On February 8, while still in Rome, Glanton received just such a letter, which read in part:

> *This will confirm our discussions of today in which it was agreed that the city of Rome would enter in an Agreement with The Barnes Foundation, subject to the approval of the Orphans' Court . . . for the exhibition of 'Great French Paintings' from The Barnes Foundation, to be held in Rome beginning in April 1995.*

When Glanton left for home, the Italians believed they had a commitment. Three weeks later, Glanton was in Munich courting officials at the Haus der Kunst (the "House of Art"), built during the Nazi era of the thirties. He pitched the same spring and summer 1995 dates to them.

By mid-March, the Italian officials were beginning to get nervous. After all, they had yet to see a formal contract offer from the Barnes. They never would. On March 20, the Barnes trustees approved the Haus der Kunst as the final venue on the tour. The price tag agreed to by the Munich museum officials was $2,225,000—$750,000 less than the Italians had earlier agreed to pay. Guizzetti, Rutelli, and company were understandably furious when they got the news.

The story broke in America only on October 23—one day after the Munich exhibition closed its doors. Asked by *Inquirer* reporter Leonard W. Boasberg if he had made promises to the city of Rome officials, Glanton replied, "I never promised you a rose garden, and you can quote me." Asked what he meant by that, "Glanton declined to clarify further. 'That's my answer,' he said."

Asked why he chose the Haus der Kunst over the Museo Capitolino, he told Boasberg, "I was not comfortable with what I experienced" in Rome. The Romans, Glanton said, "were very nice and courteous, [but] they spoke in Italian. I didn't have a translator. I didn't even know what they were saying." But, as Boasberg pointed out, Guizzetti, who went virtually everywhere Glanton went, "is fluent in English."

The Haus der Kunst, Glanton added, "had more prestige 'in terms of its being an exhibition hall'" than the Museo Capitolino. Years later, in a conversation with the author, Glanton told about his feelings on first experiencing the Museo Capitolino: "It was old and decrepit, and there were pigeons everywhere. I wasn't going to put the Barnes collection in a place like that!"

When the Italian ambassador to the United States protested the Barnes board action, Glanton failed to reply. Ambassadors, he told the *Inquirer*, "represent the interests of their country but I don't have to respond because they call." As for the *Inquirer*, Glanton told reporter Boasberg, the newspaper was only interested in the city of Rome story "because you want to damage the reputation of a black person."

Former Barnes trustee Cuyler Walker has his own take on the city of Rome imbroglio: "Did Richard Glanton lie? Yes. Did he treat them [the Italians] in the most despicable way? Yes. Did they have a sound legal basis for a suit? No." Still, says Walker, "there's no doubt in my mind that something was going on when Richard diverted the tour to Munich. He'd been pushing Rome for so long." Walker adds his own best guess: "It probably had something to do with rainmaking. Reed Smith had a huge gala reception in Munich." Then again, Walker thinks, "I could always be wrong. With Richard, you just never know. It's so hard to figure out his motives. They're always so self-serving."

■

Whether it was Paris or Toronto, Munich or Fort Worth, Richard Glanton didn't often go alone. Accompanying Glanton on many of his trips was the head of Reed Smith's Philadelphia office, Michael Browne. The two men made for an odd couple, for Browne was as white shoe as they came—"a two-syllable Southerner," in the words of another Philadelphia lawyer—having graduated from Princeton (Class of '68) and the University of Pennsylvania Law School. Theirs was a friendship that had begun when both men were serving as members of the Thornburgh administration, Glanton as deputy counsel to the governor and Browne as commissioner of insurance. For a time, the two were roommates in Harrisburg, commuting back and forth together from their homes in Philadelphia. Later, it was Browne who recruited both Glanton and their mutual friend former U.S. attorney and SEPTA board member David Marston for the firm. When Glanton joined the firm, Reed Smith's Delaware Valley office numbered fewer than twenty lawyers. Today the total is more like two hundred, and in the decade of the nineties, Michael Browne grew to be an influential figure within the far-flung Reed Smith empire. Browne, says Cuyler Walker, "was Richard's protector in the firm."

Years later, deposed by Niara Sudarkasa's lawyer Carl Singley, Browne recalled that he and Reed Smith managing partner Daniel Booker—the firm was headquartered in Pittsburgh, where Booker had his office—had occasionally had discussions about Glanton's usefulness to the firm. Booker and Browne, though, were "like two peas in a pod," in the words of the Philadelphia lawyer who also called Browne "a two-syllable Southerner." The two powerful Reed Smith managers agreed, Browne testified, that "Richard would be more productive for us if he was spending—the time that he was spending at the Barnes, if he was spending it representing clients."

Wasn't it true, asked Singley, that Reed Smith had thrown lavish receptions for clients almost everywhere the Barnes art tour went? Well, Browne replied that there were receptions in Munich and Paris, maybe even Toronto—he couldn't remember for sure—and, yes, he flew to Paris with Glanton. But "rainmaking" was out of the question. "Reed Smith," Browne testified, "never got any business out of the Barnes."

"I can tell you what I got out of it," Glanton told the *Inquirer*'s Lucinda Fleeson, "headaches, grief, accusations, scorn, contempt, praise, recognition, friendship, acclaim, enemies." Glanton, Fleeson reported, had only recently "ended a brief flirtation with running for mayor." The mayoralty was, no doubt, too trivial a position for one who "has been toasted around the world as the visionary who brought the Barnes Foundation out of the closet." Glanton went on to tick off his most recent honors. In Paris there had been "a reception fit for a king." In Tokyo, a member of the royal family cut the ribbon. In Fort Worth, Texas governor Ann Richards presented Glanton with a pair of cowboy boots, a ten-gallon Stetson, and a sheriff's badge. In Canada, it was the Ontario Medal of Distinction.

In Philadelphia, though, said Glanton, "They treated me like they would have Dr. Barnes." The PMA's opening party for twelve hundred had counted Glanton as an honored guest. Afterward there had been a private dinner at the Rittenhouse Hotel for corporate partners who'd given $2,500 or more to the museum. Glanton hadn't been invited. When he found out, he was furious.

And he'd even given the PMA a break, charging them only a half-million dollars rather than the full freight of one million plus that he'd charged the other museums on the tour! Compared to his reception in Philadelphia, Glanton said, what had come before—Tokyo, Paris, Toronto, and Fort Worth—"would cause one to think he should dream himself among the Caesars."

Alas, even Caesar had to worry about the exchequer now and again. With the tour at an end that spring of 1995, Glanton was faced with a more mundane concern: Where was the Barnes's operating income going to come from in the future? Orphans' Court had made it clear that the tour was a "one-time event." No question, though, the Barnes was facing a financial crunch. "Just do the arithmetic," says Cuyler Walker. The renovation had cost over $12 million—Richard Feigen remains convinced that a reasonable job could have been done for as little as $7 million—almost twice the amount originally projected. The tour, meanwhile, had netted more than $16 million. That left four million dollars, but that money was a set-aside, under the direct supervision of Orphans' Court, for maintenance. The Barnes's endowment of $9 million, on the other hand, had been drained of more than two million dollars in legal fees between 1990 and 1995, the result of a string of costly but mostly successful courtroom battles fought against a wide range of foes. Yet, according to court papers, the Barnes needed in excess of one million dollars annually just to operate as it had in 1992—before the renovations began.

Fundraising for the Barnes had never taken off—not even with a full-time director of development, Laura Linton. Formerly an administrator in Republican district attorney Ronald Castille's office, Linton was many things at the Barnes during her tenure there: development officer, public relations woman, and, in the words of Cuyler Walker, "Richard's eyes and ears." Unfortunately, she had an almost impossible task. Says Walker,

In the beginning [when Lincoln took control over the Barnes board] there was an immense well of goodwill out there. The Philadelphia art community—the brie and chablis crowd—would have loved to have given [money] to the Barnes, particularly as it was controlled by this poor, historically black school. That's just the opposite of what Richard says. The problem is that he blew it. Once the newspapers got wind of his plans to sell the paintings, he immediately lost their goodwill. It was never the same.

Glanton's solution to the problem: change the closed-door admissions policy at the Barnes. He proposed to board members that when the Barnes reopened, it should begin charging a ten-dollar admission fee. He also projected more than 120,000 visitors a year—more than three times the number previously allowed. Way more than the wealthy neighbors on Latches Lane were willing to tolerate. Indeed, Glanton had been explicitly warned of that threat by Tom Massaro, the consultant he'd recently hired to help smooth over potential zoning board difficulties. In a memo to Glanton dated July 17, 1995, Massaro wrote, "I continue to believe that the prospect of a 'parking problem' could be the instigation for a legal assault against the Foundation by irritated, well-counseled neighbors who are undaunted by the notion of extensive and expensive litigation." Glanton, for his part, wasn't deterred in the least.

In September 1995, Glanton told a judge in Orphans' Court, "Frankly, what we can do is, with the resources we have and with the collection as important as it is, we can say—look what the Louvre has done with the Mona Lisa—we can have four Mona Lisas."

Court records show that the Barnes's lawyers in this latest court battle were being paid handsomely for their services. A single firm, Dilworth, Paxon, Kalish & Kauffman, collected

$1,593,414.14 from the Barnes Foundation in legal fees over the course of just four years, 1992–1996.

■

Glanton was busy all that summer and fall. No small part of his time was being devoted to Niara Sudarkasa's unfortunate problems with the IRS, which wanted to tax her on the value of her university-owned house, car (the ill-fated Lincoln Continental), her chauffeur, and her housekeeper—in addition to her $130,000 a year salary. Worse, the IRS wanted back taxes with penalties and interest: a total of more than $163,000.

Sudarkasa once again appealed to Richard Glanton to take on her tax problem himself. Years later, Sudarkasa's lawyer Carl Singley would ask Glanton on the witness stand: "You think she came to you twice and didn't trust you?" No, Glanton replied, Sudarkasa came to him because "I was competent."

Sudarkasa "insisted" that Reed Smith take her case; again, Glanton demurred: "I said, 'We can't represent you.'" Eventually, though, he claims, the business affairs committee of the Lincoln University board of trustees authorized the action. "Was [there ever] a board resolution?" Singley wondered. No, Glanton replied, but "there was a scribbled sentence from Earle Bradford," the committee chairman. "Where?" Singley asked.

"On a piece of paper sent to me by Gene Cliett."

What is clear is that the business affairs committee approved an expenditure of $10,000 to help defray the president's legal fees. On May 4, 1995, Sudarkasa conveyed her tax information to Richard Glanton at his Reed Smith offices. Glanton, in turn, referred the case to two tax law specialists at the firm, Wendi Kotzen and Ted Marascuilo. Kotzen recommended that Sudarkasa also hire the suburban Jenkintown-based Goldenberg Rosenthal accounting firm, where her father was a partner. Sudarkasa did, and eventually the Reed Smith team managed to reduce her IRS debt to $28,000. "I was very happy with the savings" and with the tax work done by Reed Smith, Sudarkasa would say years later. What she wasn't happy with, Sudarkasa also testified, was the unwanted exposure of the details of her tax problems. For now, both Richard Glanton and the Goldenberg firm—we haven't heard the last of them in this saga—were privy to the exact nature of Sudarkasa's finances.

Bedeviled from the outside by the IRS, Sudarkasa was also having her troubles internally at Lincoln. Her physical plant director, husband John Clark, and her vice-president for fiscal affairs, Gene Cliett, couldn't stand one another. Cliett's own account of the matter is instructive—and not only for what it says about Sudarkasa and Clark: "I come from a pretty formal background. I've run organizations larger than that university, had staffs reporting to me [that were] head and shoulders above the v.p.s out at Lincoln. I would even have to say that I never even reported to a board [of trustees] that was so junior in their experience."

Sudarkasa, says Cliett, "was difficult. She'd say, 'You're a problem, Gene. You've been running your own organizations for so long.' I'd say, 'Madame President, I give you the best advice I can give you.'" President Sudarkasa, claims Cliett, "was someone absolutist [and] autocratic." Lincoln's trustees, Cliett felt at the time, "wanted me to do their job. They wanted me to control [Sudarkasa] and her husband." But Sudarkasa, Cliett says, didn't want to be controlled: "She'd say, 'I don't want anyone to interfere with my house.' I'd say, 'We're not gonna play a game of Twenty Questions.' She'd say, 'You'd never talk this way to any of the mayors you worked for.' I'd say, 'None of the mayors would ever have put their wives in my shop.'"

John Clark, Cliett insists, was impossible to work with: "In my twenty-five years' experience in supervising people, I've never had anyone as disrespectful and insubordinate as him." The bigger problem, as Cliett saw it, was that "he reported to her." In other words, Clark went over his ostensible boss Cliett's head and reported directly to the president. When Cliett "mentioned to [Sudarkasa] that some of the things [Clark] was doing were improper and illegal," he says, "her comment to me was, you know, 'I'm not going to allow you to walk into my office and make a comment that my husband is doing something improper and illegal without me taking issue with it. I said, 'Then, fine.'"

Life became a lot easier, says Cliett, after Clark left as physical plant director. That came only after Cliett offered his own resignation in July 1995. Cliett continues his account: "That was the year the students had shut down the school. We"—Cliett and Sudarkasa—"got into a screaming match, a vicious argument. In so many words, she called me a liar." At issue, Cliett says, was an automobile that Sudarkasa wanted to buy, but had been denied her by the business affairs committee. "And I guess she blamed me and went into a tirade, and I told she [*sic*] and her husband I had had enough and she told me I know what I could do, and I said, 'You're right, and I intend to do it.'" Cliett adds that he also told Sudarkasa, "I've had enough of you, your husband, your car, you know, the board too. I'm leaving."

Cliett says he then "reached down, picked up my papers, [and] said, 'I won't have you question my integrity for a darned second.'" Cliett stormed out of Sudarkasa's office, went to his own, and dictated his resignation. By the time he got home there was a fax waiting for him from Sudarkasa that began, "We share the vision." As he recalls today, the fax continued, "We agree on the big things, it's just the small matters. Why don't you and I meet in Philadelphia at some neutral place."

The neutral place: the Reed Smith offices of Richard Glanton.

■

Chief Barnes factotum Laura Linton sent out a press release dated September 5 announcing the gallery's grand reopening on November 15. The renovation had taken thirty months, and more than 4.5 million people had seen the masterpieces of the

Barnes collection. Linton went on to announce the Barnes board's decision to seek the higher $10 admission fee and to project an annual rate of visitation above 120,000.

As consultant Massaro had predicted, this latest news turned the Latches Lane neighbors apoplectic. Glanton also wasn't winning any friends among the township officialdom. By early November, Glanton and township manager David Latshaw were engaged in an increasingly heated correspondence—Latshaw because he learned only three days before the Barnes's grand reopening just what the foundation's plans were; and Glanton, complaining that getting permits from the Merion authorities was like getting emigration visas "from the Soviet Union before the fall of the iron curtain."

As luck would have it, the reopening proved something of a disaster. The night of November 15, 1995, was marked by a torrential downpour, and the tent spread across the lawn of the Barnes Foundation grounds became a sort of Noah's ark. Many of the wealthiest people in Philadelphia went home chilled to the bone. For their part, the neighbors on Latches Lane complained about the noise and the music, but, above all, about the additional traffic.

The logical step was to build a parking lot on the Barnes's grounds. Certainly, there was plenty of room for one on the foundation's twelve acres—the only hurdle was getting a permit. But few legal firestorms have started from smaller sparks. As soon as the Barnes applied for a permit, neighborhood opposition galvanized. Their argument: Latches Lane measured a mere twenty-four feet across. It couldn't possibly handle hordes of visitors. Open meetings followed, at least one of them attended by Glanton.

The very night of the gala opening, the Lower Merion commissioners adopted a resolution requesting that the Barnes Foundation postpone indefinitely the reopening of its gallery until the township had time to review its traffic plans.

CHAPTER NINE

■

NO END
OF MISCHIEF

The last two months of 1995 and the first two of 1996 were momentous ones in the Lincoln-era history of the Barnes. In mid-November, the galleries reopened to great acclaim, much of it heaped at the feet of Richard Glanton. The Barnes president, says former trustee Cuyler Walker, was "on a high after all the favorable publicity." Barely a week later, though, frustrated by the zoning board dispute involving the proposed Barnes parking lot, Glanton denounced the Lower Merion Township commissioners in the pages of the *Inquirer* as "racists."

It was the kind of thing that Walker cringed at, but what made Cuyler Walker cringe no longer mattered to Richard Glanton. At Glanton's—and Niara Sudarkasa's—urging, the Lincoln University board of trustees had declined to renominate Walker for the Barnes board. His replacement, handpicked by Glanton, would be an HMO executive named Randolph Kinder. The Connecticut-based Kinder also happened to be Glanton and

Cliett's partner in an incipient Philadelphia health care organization known as Philcare. As of early December 1995, the Barnes board would be the Glanton board. Only banker Charles Frank could be counted on to oppose the wilder schemes of the Glanton regime.

Charles Frank was a white, middle-aged graduate of Yale University and a senior executive at the Mellon Bank. Appointed to the Barnes board as the statutory bank representative in December 1990, Frank had consistently voted with Walker and against Glanton and Sudarkasa. While he and Walker had seldom won on the substantive issues, they'd nevertheless been a corrective force—and, in Glanton's opinion, "a couple of assholes." Without Walker's vote, Frank was effectively isolated on the board. Just how isolated he was would soon be apparent.

On January 11, the Barnes board officially filed an appeal with the Lower Merion Township hearing board, raising as grounds for appeal the contention that the Township was discriminating against it and violating its constitutional rights to equal protection. With that, the writing was on the wall. Glanton wasn't pleased with the opposition to his proposed parking lot— or the long, bureaucratic process that threatened to hold it up. The way Glanton saw it, the Barnes had to have 100,000 visitors a year. To get that number, he needed a parking lot. It was a simple equation. And if it would take a lawsuit to solve it, that's what he would do.

The next day, under orders from Glanton, Blank Rome Comisky & McCauley partner Ann Laupheimer began drafting a federal civil rights complaint against the township. (For reasons that are still unclear, Glanton had chosen Blank Rome rather than Dilworth or Buchanan Ingersoll to shepherd the Barnes's zoning board problems. Former trustee Walker speculates that it was because Glanton wanted to curry favor with Blank Rome's powerful chairman, David Girard-diCarlo, an influential figure in the state's Republican party hierarchy.

Glanton's choice, whatever the reasons behind it, eventually resulted in $449,942.68 in legal fees during the period 1995–1996.)

Three days later, Laupheimer and partner Richard McElroy concluded that there was sufficient factual and legal cause to warrant filing a complaint against the township. Laupheimer accordingly forwarded the draft complaint to Glanton. He rejected it out of hand. According to lawyer Paul Rosen, later to become his courtroom opponent, "As soon as Glanton saw the 'run of the mill' civil rights action, he immediately contacted counsel at Blank Rome and directed them to name the individual commissioners of the township as well as the neighbors as individual defendants."

Twelve hours later, on January 16, Glanton faxed the revised draft complaint to the other Barnes trustees. "Acting under color of state law and in concert and conspiracy with certain neighbors of the Barnes," the township, the complaint read, had acted arbitrarily to deprive the Barnes of its rights. "The neighbors have combined together with the Township to form a conspiracy, the purpose of which is to harass [the] Barnes, to deny [the] Barnes its constitutional rights, and to shut [the] Barnes down."

Earlier in the day, Glanton had called individual trustees with the news. Charles Frank, for one, was stunned by what he heard. Glanton, he testified, "told me there was a deadline [for filing the complaint in federal court]. I listened [to him], and believed that there was a deadline." When he returned to his office on the seventeenth, a fax from Glanton was waiting for Frank at his office in Mellon Independence Center. It was a draft of the proposed complaint. Frank asked for time to study it.

According to his April 17, 1996, deposition, Frank began reading the legal draft on the train home that night. He recalled finishing it later in the evening. The next morning, the eighteenth, Frank returned to his office, "extremely concerned and shocked by what I had read." Frank decided to call his personal lawyer, Samuel Klein of Dechert, Price & Rhoads, for legal advice. In the meantime, Glanton called back, demanding a response.

"What was so shocking about what you read?" Rosen asked Frank at his April 17 deposition. Frank replied:

> *The allegations of racial motivation that [were] being directed at the Township commissioners on an individual basis and the neighbors. . . . specifically had no factual [basis]. So I was very concerned. . . . Was I concerned about putting my name to [such] a filing? Yes, absolutely.*

Under questioning from Rosen, Frank recalled "basically" telling

> *Richard that I could not lend my name to the complaint. . . . And, basically, he told me that it was a done deal, that there was a signature approval document that was on its way over to me. I told him I could not sign that. And then he made some comment about, "Well, I have got three signatures, anyway."*

Asked by Rosen if he'd ever seen those three signatures, Frank replied, "I have not." Frank says he "indicated to [Glanton] that I felt that this type of allegations [*sic*], this type of complaint, required a discussion of the [entire Barnes] board."

"And what did he say?" Rosen asked.

"That didn't seem to matter."

Rosen went on to ask Frank if he knew "of any [Barnes] meeting which you attended in which this issue was . . . discussed?"

"I never attended a board meeting where this issue was discussed," Frank answered. The Barnes board, he recalled, "was never specifically asked in a meeting to approve the filing."

Rosen continued, "And as you understood what was Richard

telling you was mandatory for the 18th? What was so magical that he was pressing you that there was no time?"

"I don't know," Frank said. "I believed him. There was a deadline in response to—I interpreted it as a response to the December 14th 30-day Township issue."

Asked if he would be surprised to learn that there was no deadline on the eighteenth, Frank said, "Yes, I would be surprised."

Glanton, Frank testified, "was only after his parking lot—and nothing else." The mathematics, as presented by the Barnes president, were self-evident, said Frank: "In order for us to achieve our revenue goals of $120,000 per month . . . we were going to need parking."

That same morning, January 18, 1996, Frank received a further fax from Glanton, addressed to all Barnes trustees. The cover note read: "Please return signed; a fully executed copy will be sent to you upon request. Thank you." The second page, on Barnes Foundation stationery, began, "Resolved that the Board of Trustees of the Barnes Foundation authorizes the Foundation to initiate a legal action in the U.S. District Court for the Eastern District of Pennsylvania against the Lower Merion Township Commissioners and several neighbors, based on the unlawful State action by the Township against the Foundation."

Curiously, neither the cover letter nor the board resolution mentioned the fact that the federal court action was going to be taken under the Ku Klux Klan Act; nor did they cite racism on the part of the defendants or the number of defendants or the fact that the Lower Merion Township commissioners were to be sued as individuals.

The only signature on either the cover letter or the resolution was that of Richard H. Glanton.

Charles Frank faxed an immediate reply:

Dear Richard,
This will confirm our telephone conversation this morning

in which I expressed my opposition to filing the draft complaint which you sent to me on January 16. I have serious concerns whether the allegations in the draft complaint are appropriate or accurate.

Glanton, Frank has testified, never responded to his fax.

On January 18, on Barnes Foundation stationery marked for "Immediate Release. Contact Laura Linton," the news went out, in capital letters: "THE BARNES FOUNDATION FILES CIVIL RIGHTS ACTION TO INSURE PUBLIC ACCESS." The release stated that the Barnes

charges that the Lower Merion Township Commissioners have engaged in a pattern of arbitrary, capricious, and racially and otherwise discriminatory conduct by inconsistently imposing parking, police, fire, and zoning requirements. [The] discrimination stems, primarily, from the fact that a majority of the Foundation's trustees are Americans of African descent and because Dr. Barnes entrusted the stewardship of the Foundation to Lincoln University, a historically African American university.

Years later, when she was no longer Richard Glanton's ally—or even his friend—Niara Sudarkasa reflected on what happened that week in January 1996. Yes, she voted with Glanton to bring the Ku Klux Klan suit, Sudarkasa says. But, no, "it didn't have anything to do with race. It had to do with Richard wanting a parking lot. That's all it was ever about: A parking lot that would generate money."

■

As was often the case, Richard Glanton being at his most daring—or outrageous—coincided with Niara Sudarkasa being at her weakest and most vulnerable. In the days leading up to the filing of the Ku Klux Klan suit in federal court, Sudarkasa had been busy campaigning to be reelected president of Lincoln. As late as mid-January, her chances seemed uncertain at best.

Within a week of Gene Cliett's threatened resignation in July 1995, John Clark had surrendered his own job—at least on paper. Clark was allowed to take retirement on a medical disability. But though Cliett had quickly hired a new physical plant director, John Willis, Clark's "presence" was still felt strongly on the Lincoln campus. Cliett says Clark would "come pull men out of the work line-up and have them go over to the president's home and work on it. Half a dozen, [even] ten men at a time. He'd tell them, 'You don't have to take orders from this guy [Willis]. I still run the place.'" Cliett would complain to Clark: "John, are you ready to quit?"

Asked what Clark did after his retirement, Cliett replies, "Nothing. He'd just stay there in that house [the presidential home] and go over to the physical plant and get men to work on that house." There was a leak in the basement, a garage needed to be built, the floors had to be cemented.

Repairs to the president's home were not, however, a major source of contention with Lincoln board members, says Cliett. The more significant problem, he claims, was "that she just wasn't a very good administrator." A core group of influential trustees were constantly questioning Sudarkasa's judgment, Cliett adds, and these included such Lincoln board luminaries as Adrienne Gray Rhone, David Bright, William King, and Earle Bradford, most of them members of the important business affairs committee that Bradford headed.

Sudarkasa's worries came to a head in the weeks immediately following the filing of the Ku Klux Klan suit. Cliett remembers sitting in a hotel room in Philadelphia in February 1996. With him was Sudarkasa, whose reappointment as Lincoln president was being voted on in another room by the university's trustees. "She was shaking," recalls Cliett. "She was saying, 'If they offer me a one-year contract, I won't accept it.'" Instead, she got a five-year renewal. "This was something that was really driven by Richard Glanton; he put the votes together." According to Cliett, it was Glanton who delivered the good news: "When he came into the room and told her she had a five-year contract, she was speechless." Glanton, Cliett says, "walked over to her, and he stuck out his hand, and he said, 'Congratulations, Madame President.' Then she was crying, saying, 'I know I would not have received this contract without the efforts of Gene Cliett, straightening out all the problems we have had.'" Cliett, for his part, was unmoved: "I just sat there."

Back then, says Cliett, Glanton and Sudarkasa were "very, very close, extremely close. It was the two of them against the world. Then [for a brief time, at least], it was the three of us against the world." Both Glanton's close friend and Sudarkasa's right-man at the college, Cliett was in a unique position to witness the relationship. It all began to unravel, that tight trio held together by mutual self-interest, thinks Gene Cliett, long before the Ku Klux Klan litigation blew up in Richard Glanton's face. The source of the problem: "Niara. She had five more years. She got a raise"—to $160,000 a year—"plus house, utilities, furniture, food, and car." The package, Cliett reckons, was worth a quarter of a million dollars a year. Madame President, Cliett adds, "was set."

After that it was all downhill. First, the pebbles began to roll. Then came the rocks. Sudarkasa, Cliett says, came to believe that with her new contract in hand, "She didn't need Richard." The point, Cliett adds, was driven home that same month when Sudarkasa told Glanton and Cliett that she wanted to rid herself of board chairman Kenneth Sadler, the man who had succeeded Bernie Anderson after the latter joined the Clinton administration in Washington, D.C. Unlike Anderson, who was well known in Philadelphia Democratic circles, Sadler was considered relatively apolitical. Gene Cliett's take on him was unflattering, to say the least: "I used to say to the president, 'His kids are going to grow up to be juvenile delinquents. This guy doesn't take a position on anything.'"

Ken Sadler was a dental surgeon and HMO administrator in his hometown of Winston-Salem, North Carolina. He was also too far removed from the Lincoln campus—and too busy with his dental practice—to be the kind of hands-on chairman that Anderson, a professor at the University of Pennsylvania's Wharton School of Business, had been. Sadler wasn't a political wheeler-dealer. Ironically, that's what Sudarkasa held against him. "She didn't like it that Sadler let [dissident] board members run amok," recalls Cliett. "She blamed him for the revolt" against her.

Now, Sudarkasa wanted Sadler out—and, says Gene Cliett, she knew just the man to help her do the job: Richard Glanton.

In the event, Glanton managed to make at least one formidable enemy: Carl Singley, the former dean of the Temple University law school and key ally of Philadelphia's then-city council president (and current mayor) John Street. Singley would also eventually be Sudarkasa's personal lawyer. That he took her on as a client had much to do with what happened between him and Richard Glanton in the spring of 1997.

Singley's account—vehemently denied by Glanton in its particulars—goes like this:

> *I got a frantic call from Richard Glanton. He needed to talk to me, and it was urgent. Now, Richard never bothered to call me back when I called him asking for contributions to John Street's [mayoral] campaign. But now, it was different. He wanted to stop by my office, and I said, "Sure, sure. Come right over." He came over here, and he was sweating. He said, "I got some [Barnes Foundation] legal business for you." I said, "Cut this shit, man." And he said, "I need your vote." And I said, "My vote?"*

As it turns out, Singley's then-junior colleague Roosevelt Hairston happened to be on the Lincoln board of trustees; and, as Glanton soon made it clear, he wanted Singley to persuade Hairston to vote to help unseat Sadler. Singley continues: "I said, 'At a minimum, that is improper.' He said, 'I can get you legal business.' I said, 'Out of respect, as a senior member of the bar, I'll have Roosevelt come talk to you.'" There it might have ended.

Glanton, Singley says, told Hairston that "he would give the [Barnes legal] business direct to Roosevelt, minus me—and criticized me personally. 'Fuck Carl,' he said. 'I'll give the business to you—and he won't get a dime of it.'"

We have but three witnesses to the above events, and only one who was present on both occasions. Two say the story played itself out just as Singley has described it. The third says it didn't. One thing's for sure: Richard Glanton managed to make a serious enemy out of an important Philadelphia political and legal kingpin—a man "with the kind of weight I don't have," says a well-known local African American lawyer, a man "big enough to bring even Richard down."

No one could have guessed how much the dispute over a relatively small parking lot at the Barnes Foundation would eventually cost, either in careers or dollars. And this was especially true in the first months of 1996. Still, Shirley Jackson might well have been forgiven for having second thoughts about ever having joined the Barnes board. Jackson, says former trustee Cuyler Walker, was "an absolute straight shooter," but never very active in the management of the Barnes. She'd declined to run against Glanton for the presidency, and afteward seemed to take, if anything, even less interest in events out in Lower Merion.

Within six weeks of Glanton's filing the federal Ku Klux Klan suit, Jackson resigned from the board after President Bill Clinton appointed her to be chairman of the U.S. Nuclear Regulatory

Commission. Giving up her seat on the Barnes board didn't, however, keep Jackson from being sued.

On March 12, 1996, the Lower Merion Township commis-
sioners, acting as private individuals, filed suit in Montgomery
County court of common pleas against Richard Glanton and the
Barnes Foundation trustees—including Shirley Jackson. The
commissioners' lawyer in both the state court action (styled
"Davis v. Glanton," after commissioner Kenneth E. Davis) and
the federal Ku Klux Klan suit would be the same "pit bull,"
Philadelphia litigator Paul Rosen. A small, compact man of late
middle age, Rosen was chosen, thinks Philadelphia attorney Paul
Diamond (who would come to work with him on the case),
"because the commissioners believed that Rosen could stand up
to Glanton. Paul's loud and abrasive and tough, someone who's
not going to be cowed by Richard." Rosen adds, "My clients
wanted someone just as tenacious as Glanton on their side.
Hiring me was a message to Richard." The state suit filed by
Rosen alleged that Glanton had defamed the commissioners
when he told a reporter that the commissioners were engaged in
"thinly disguised racism" and "that [t]here is no way you cannot
see racism in the way they are treating the Barnes Foundation."

For their part, the foundation's trustees were, for the time
being at least, still represented by counsel from Blank Rome, led
by veteran litigator Richard McElroy. Surprisingly, given the
usual mind-numbing slowness of the legal system, depositions in
the two intertwined cases began almost immediately—a mere one
month after the filing of the suits. Those depositions, spread out
over thousands of pages of court-reported documents, would
together offer an extraordinary insight into the workings of the
Barnes Foundation under Glanton's leadership.

Later, after Glanton and McElroy had come to loggerheads
and Blank Rome retired from the case, the Barnes would come to
be represented by a man as stubborn and voluble—"as out-
landish even," in Diamond's words—as Rosen himself, Robert

Sugarman. The Harvard-educated lawyer had a well-deserved reputation as an old lefty, but by now he was also a well-connected one: State senator Hardy Williams, Lincoln trustee and West Philadelphia ward boss, had been the best man in his wedding; and a close friend and sometime client was the ultimate Philly power broker, state senator Vincent J. Fumo, Democratic chairman of the appropriations committee (on which *his* friend Williams served). Sugarman also had another reputation: "As disputatious as they make them—a guy who will argue anything in court. He will object and object and object. He'll wear you down," in the words of Paul Diamond. And because the principal lawyers employed by the two sides—Rosen and Sugarman—would prove so antagonistic to one another and to the various witnesses, the often day-long sessions would not infrequently turn into shouting matches. Sugarman, says Paul Rosen, "is a guy almost as crazy as I am."

When Charles Frank was first deposed in mid-April 1996, Blank Rome's McElroy was still the Barnes's lawyer. The proceedings went reasonably smoothly—too smoothly for Glanton's taste. Rosen wanted to know if Frank had ever had discussions with any other Barnes trustee regarding "Mr. Glanton's use" of "the race card"?

"Yes," Frank replied. He and Cuyler Walker had had several such conversations. In late 1993, for example, Frank had objected to the publication of a Barnes brochure on financial grounds, only to have "Richard accuse me of being a racist as the motivation for my decision."

Asked if he felt "shocked" by the accusation, Frank said yes.

Rosen went on to ask Frank about the January 29, 1996, Barnes board meeting where discussion centered on the Ku Klux Klan suit that had, by now, already been filed. Frank was shown his own handwritten notes from the meeting and asked to deconstruct them. "RG," he noted, had explained that the lawsuit was "aimed at avoiding protracted hearings RE parking on the

Barnes Foundation grounds." The intent of the suit, said Frank, was to "bring intense pressure on [the other] parties." When Frank asked, "Could this have been done without reference to race?" both Glanton and Sudarkasa pointed out examples of what they believed was racially motivated harassment directed at the Barnes by commissioners and neighbors.

Frank objected: "I wanted them [Glanton and Sudarkasa] to be very clear at the board meeting what my position was. That I had no personal knowledge about the motivation of the neighbors." Frank went on to "raise the question about lawyer fees, where they were going to come from. And Richard's answer was they were coming out of the endowment." Frank continued to object, raising the obvious question: What, he wanted to know, would be the ultimate financial impact on the Barnes if the two interrelated cases proved protracted? Glanton brushed the question aside: "Richard's answer was he didn't think it would be, I guess, significant." Frank knew better. The earlier Barnes litigation, he warned board members, had "had an impact on the budget for many years, and I was concerned about that, yes." Glanton, in contrast, seemed unconcerned: "Richard thought that the process of the [federal] complaint would bring the parties to a conclusion on the parking issue. That was his intent all along."

CHAPTER TEN

THE TICKING OF
THE CLOCKS

The first hint of a problem in the Barnes federal suit came during the early summer of 1996, when Richard Glanton demanded that the foundation's lawyers at Blank Rome ask U.S. District Judge Anita Brody to recuse herself from hearing the case. Glanton's objections centered on Brody's ties to the Delaware and Montgomery County Republican committees and the obvious fact that she and her husband were residents of Lower Merion Township. Blank Rome's Dick McElroy strongly advised against the move. For one thing, McElroy didn't think Glanton had much of an argument. For another, he saw no reason to antagonize the judge—especially if she chose not to recuse herself and insisted on hearing the case. When McElroy refused to ask for recusal, Blank Rome and the Barnes wound up going their separate ways. When Blank Rome was shown the door, Bob Sugarman entered the scene—a crucial choice in the saga that soon began to unfold.

On June 3, 1996, Judge Brody dropped all seventeen of the

Barnes neighbors from the list of defendants on grounds of First
Amendment immunity. At the same time, however, Brody denied
motions to dismiss filed by the township and commissioners. Two
weeks later, those same parties to the dispute filed a tort coun-
terclaim against the Barnes and its trustees in federal court for
abuse of process. That month and the next, the Lower Merion
zoning board held hearings with regard to the proposed Barnes
parking lot.

Meanwhile, in law offices all over town, testimony in the case
continued to be taken—hour after hour of wearying depositions.
On occasion, these reached levels of profound cosmic weirdness.
Take, for example, nuclear physicist Shirley Jackson's July 9 deposition. Seldom has a legal conference room been peopled with
such a quartet: Jackson, who seems to have known nothing and
remembered less; Rosen, her caustic chief antagonist; state senator Williams, her purported advocate (chosen by Glanton, his
fees were paid for by the Barnes); and Williams's longtime friend
and the Barnes' own lawyer, Sugarman. Colliding over proce-
dural issues, the lawyers baited one another relentlessly:

> *Mr. Rosen: "I'm talking law."*
> *Mr. Williams: "What's law is [sic], your action is dis-
> missible."*
> *Mr. Rosen: "Well, then, get it dismissed."*
> *Mr. Williams: "Don't you terminate this with some
> street talk. . . . This lady is not to be a remote nothing."*
> *Mr. Rosen: "All right. She likes being sued."*
> *Mr. Williams: "This is Dr. Shirley Jackson, who you are
> deposing. . . . This woman is very, very denigrated, as far
> as I'm concerned."*

When Rosen showed Jackson a copy of the fax of the resolution that Glanton had sent trustees seeking approval of the federal suit, she couldn't recall ever seeing it. Nor did she recall even

discussing the matter. But then Jackson also said she was unaware that Glanton had called Charles Frank "a racist," that she had "no recollection" of the earlier resolution that made board approval mandatory in the case of litigation in excess of $10,000, and that she couldn't recall any discussion at board meetings of racial animus on the part of Lower Merion Township commissioners. Jackson did not know what court the suit had been filed in, she could not recall having voted on the Barnes presidency in 1995, and she did not know the length of Glanton's terms of office. She also didn't "recall being at very many meetings" of the Barnes board. Shirley Jackson seemed astonishingly unaware of everything she was asked to testify to.

In her defense, the redoubtable Williams objected that "all the questions you're asking are dancing around talking [*sic*] about Richard Glanton. If you are interested in Richard Glanton, go after Richard Glanton."

To which Rosen replied, "I am going after Richard Glanton."

Williams countered with the impenetrable comment: "I'm sixty-five, okay. You're more crooked and more tricky, but I don't do those things."

After that exchange, it was all downhill in the conference room.

> Mr. Rosen: "I just want to get the questions answered."
>
> Mr. Williams: "That's not what this is all about. We come here with procedure. We are talking about lawyers and bar and all that stuff. . . . If that's the way you think, fine, but don't impose it on me when I'm trying to be a gentleman."
>
> Mr. Rosen: I'm not imposing anything on you."
>
> Mr. Williams: "Yes, you are. Boom, that don't count. I'm only talking—"
>
> Mr. Rosen: "I will do what I want to do in this case to protect my clients."

>   Mr. Williams: "You do what you want to do. I am talk-
> ing about attitudes. . . . You can't have enough respect to
> even listen."
>   Mr. Rosen: "Respect? This has nothing to do with
> respect, Senator, nothing to do with it. Has to do with
> harassment and interfering with the deposition."
>   Mr. Williams: "I don't want to hear this garbage. It
> has to do with your liking to hear yourself talk garbage."
>   Mr. Rosen: "I think you like to hear yourself talk."
>   Mr. Williams: "Well, maybe I do, but— "
>   Mr. Rosen: "I think so."
>   Mr. Williams: "I don't like hearing your garbage even
> if it is creative."

Two hundred forty-eight pages into the deposition, at 6:10
P.M., Sugarman (who had been unusually quiet by his standards)
announced that he had to leave. Jackson went ballistic: "I object.
. . . I will sit here till midnight if it takes that. Excuse me. . . .
This is my lawyer. You speak for me. But everyone is talking
around me—and dragging me around. I don't have anything to
do with this. But everybody talks back and forth and talking
around me."

Shirley Jackson, represented as she was by state senator
Hardy Williams, put the hammer to the nail. She just didn't know
how hard.

■

When Cuyler Walker was deposed a week later, the questions
focused on Glanton's style of leadership at the Barnes. Was
Walker concerned about Glanton's propensity to label opponents—including himself and Charles Frank—"racist"? Yes. Did
Walker and Frank ever try to vote Glanton out as president of the
Barnes? Yes, in 1993. (As we've seen, Shirley Jackson was asked
to run, and declined; and when Glanton found out, he denounced

Frank and Walker as acting in a "racially motivated manner," as Walker put it.)

Walker was also asked if board members had ever asked Glanton to "involve them in any public statements that were made on behalf of the Barnes"? Yes, Walker replied, "I believe at one time or another each of the other board members expressed that preference." That, of course, proved as ineffective a plea as the other "sentiment expressed by the board . . . that members should play an active role in the foundation." Early on, Walker testified, the board members had each been assigned a specific role: Sudarkasa, on education and reproduction of the paintings; Charles Frank, on financials; Shirley Jackson, on the renovation work; and Walker, as touring exhibition coordinator. The desire of the board at the time was obvious, said Walker: They wanted "a more limited role for Richard Glanton or any [other] president [of the Barnes]."

While Walker and the trustees were being deposed, attorneys James E. Beasley and Michael A. Smerconish were putting together yet more litigation aimed at the Barnes. Their principal client: the city of Rome. Beasley, then in his late sixties, was a legend in Philadelphia, known far and wide as "The King of Pennsylvania Torts." He had humbled the mighty *Inquirer* and its fabled editor, Eugene L. Roberts, Jr., twice in seven-figure libel actions, once racking up a record $57,000,000 judgment against the Knight Ridder–owned newspaper. Smerconish, his younger colleague, was, like Glanton, active in local Republican party politics. He had succeeded David Marston's wife, Linda—about whom much later—as regional director of the federal department of Housing and Urban Development. And in that role, Smerconish had won laurels as a crusading reformer from the likes of former *Inquirer* reporter and best-selling author Buzz Bissinger. He'd also won the undying enmity of some local Democratic officeholders and ward leaders, one being Hardy Williams.

In the "City of Rome suit," as it was soon labeled in the press, Smerconish would charge that in the winter and spring of 1995, Barnes president Glanton had "repeatedly made verbal and written assurances" to the Roman officials that the city would be the final venue on the tour. It would be a hard case to win. Glanton's promises—if they were promises—were oral.

While the city of Rome suit slowly began to wend its way through the courts, a number of noteworthy events were taking place at the Barnes. Least surprising was Charles Frank resigning from the board "effective immediately," on August 6. His replacement would be Mellon Bank executive vice-president Sherman White. More surprising was that on September 3, the Lower Merion zoning board announced that it had granted the Barnes Foundation's special exception and variance application. Just a tad later than the nine months' time that the Barnes's consultants Tom Massaro and William Wermuth had predicted it would take, the Barnes was now free to construct its parking lot. The news gave Richard Glanton reason to crow: The Barnes Foundation, he told a young *Inquirer* reporter, Anne Barnard, was now "batting .900" in achieving its goals. A more thoughtful gloss was that of Duquesne University land-use law expert Joseph Sabino Mistick, who told Barnard, "It's hard for people to imagine, I suppose, that little zoning boards have awesome powers."

So the Barnes would, after all, have its parking lot. But, meanwhile, it would have to contend with a slew of lawsuits. Deposed by attorney Paul Diamond, who'd been brought in to represent Lower Merion Township, Tom Massaro was asked about his role at the Barnes. Massaro, it turns out, was a Harvard-trained city planner with a political background. He'd been assistant to former Newark, New Jersey, mayor Kenneth Gibson; afterward he'd served as president of the Newark Housing Development Rehabilitation Corporation under Gibson and then as director of housing and community development under former Philadelphia mayor Bill Green. From 1985,

Massaro had been doing consulting work in the Philadelphia area.

He'd known Glanton since 1980 or 1981, said Massaro; and had first been contacted by the Barnes president in the early 1990s about "problems they were having with the boiler [and about] a serious asbestos problem [and] problems with humidification [and] temperature controls."

Besides his consulting practice, Massaro told Diamond, he also had a real estate firm called Terra Firma Associates. No, he testified, Richard Glanton wasn't a partner in Terra Firma Associates. But Glanton was a partner "in a property I manage [at] 6354 Germantown Avenue." Another of the partners in that property: Randolph A. Kinder, the HMO executive from Connecticut who was now both a Lincoln and a Barnes trustee.

Massaro's rate for the consulting at the Barnes, he testified, was $125 an hour. (Court records drawn from the Barnes's 1995 audit would show that Thomas Henry Massaro, described as an "owner's rep," received $99,572 from the foundation that year.)

■

Newly appointed board member Sherman White was deposed on October 17. As part of the deposition, White was shown a letter he'd written to Glanton thanking him for his personal tour of the Barnes on September 26. In it, White used the excuse of a "thank you letter" to raise substantive issues, noting, for example, that in May 1994, "a set of governance resolutions was disseminated [to board members], but no action appears to have been taken regarding their adoption."

In the same letter, White also told Glanton that he believed it "appropriate" for the Barnes board to consider the hiring of an executive director, providing a detailed line item budget, and cutting down on litigation. White recalled that while on their tour of the galleries, he and Glanton had "discussed the status of all outstanding matters of litigation, [but] time did not permit nor did

I pursue with you at the time the Foundation's strategy for resolving these matters." What White wanted, he said, was a detailed "written current status report and resolution strategy from counsel for each legal matter." Glanton's reply: "I propose to dessiminate [*sic*] the resolutions for consideration by the Board" at its next meeting—two months hence.

As it happened, the Barnes board met earlier than that, on October 25, 1996. In the minutes, "Under New Business," we find the following: "the Board resolved to hire an Executive Director. Mr. Glanton will distribute to the Board a job description for this position by November 15." Court documents show that on Sherman White's copy of the minutes, in his hand, he wrote a note to himself: "Where is it?"

White called Glanton's bluff and demanded financial information from the Barnes's business manager, Vivian Cline. She refused to supply what he asked for. White wrote Glanton demanding to see the financials, and the Barnes president responded on December 5: "You stated that [Cline] had informed you that I instructed her not to provide you with any information. I regret this misunderstanding on your part. I never gave Mrs. Cline any such instruction."

White and Cline would both be deposed at length in the new year. White, though, alone among the current Barnes board members, would bring with him his own lawyer, the well-regarded Sam Klein of Dechert Price & Rhoads. Cline would be represented—as Sudarkasa had been—by a lawyer chosen for her by Richard Glanton: Robert Elliott.

In his deposition of February 13, 1997, White was asked why he, of all Mellon Bank executives, was chosen to serve on the Barnes board. His answer: "The reason, one of the reasons they picked me is because of what I do at Mellon Bank. . . . I'm head of the credit recovery department which . . . is responsible for working out problem credit situations." And how would that be useful to the Barnes situation? asked Lower Merion Township

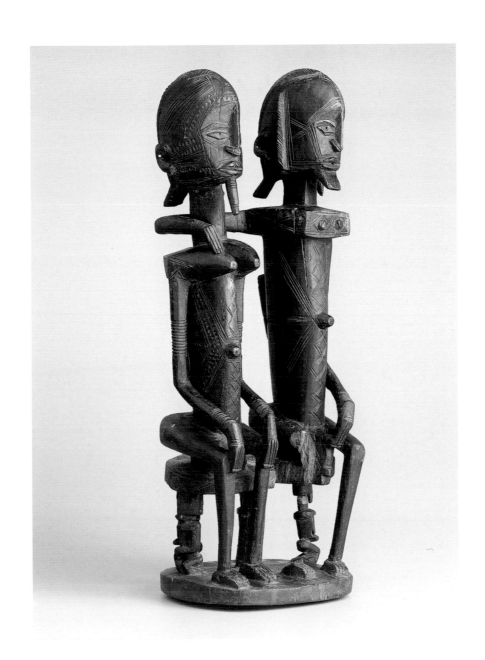

Dogon Couple, Mali Nineteenth Century (BF #A197). © 2003. Reproduced
with the permission of The Barnes Foundation.

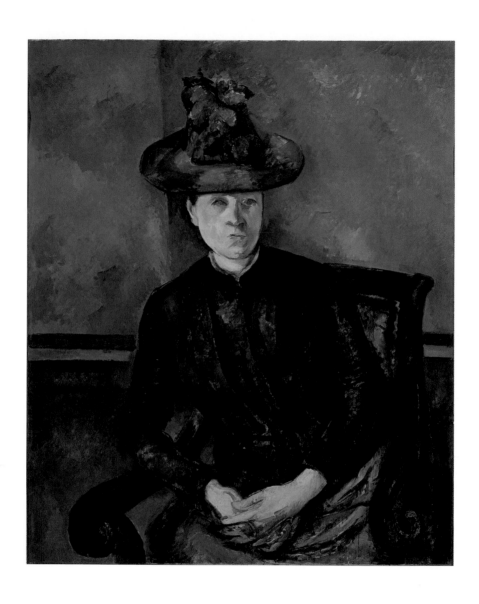

Woman in a Green Hat, Paul Cézanne (BF #141). © 2003.
Reproduced with the permission of The Barnes Foundation.

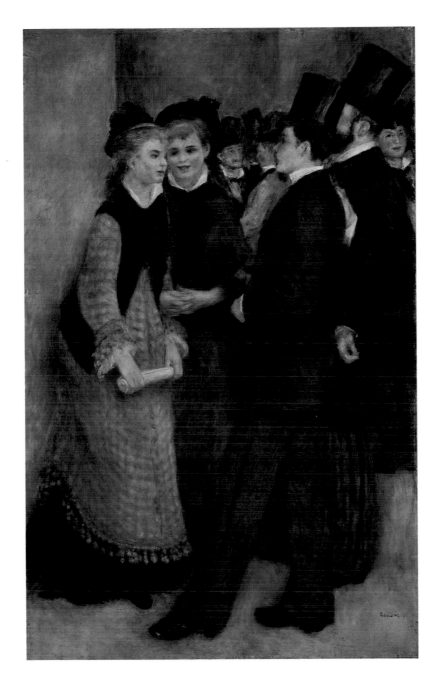

Leaving the Conservatoire, Pierre-Auguste Renoir (BF #862). © 2003.
Reproduced with the permission of The Barnes Foundation.

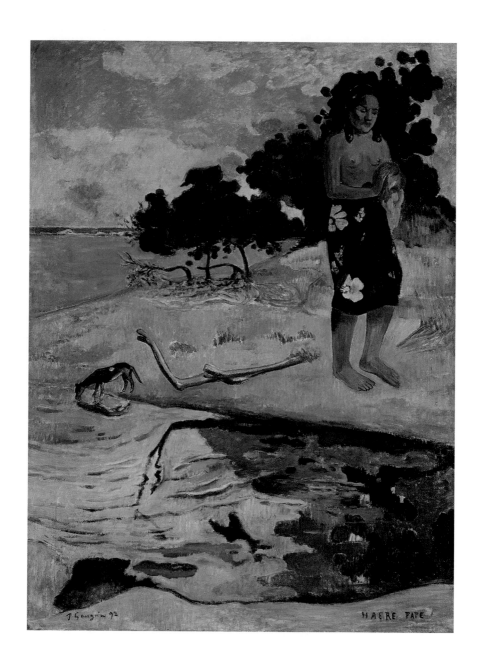

Haere pape, Paul Gauguin (BF #109). © 2003. Reproduced with the permission of The Barnes Foundation.

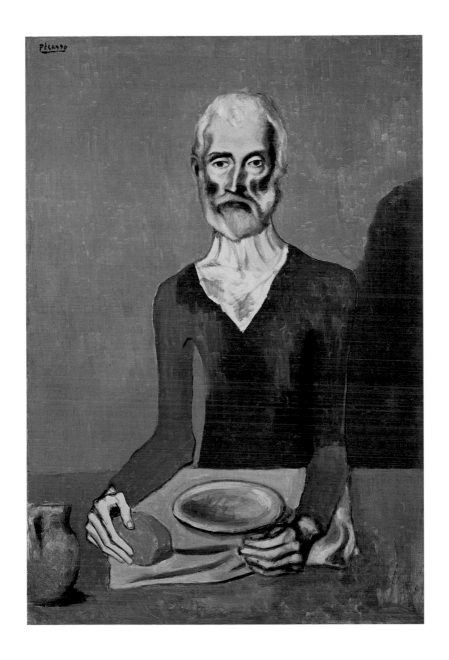

The Ascetic, Pablo Picasso (© 2003 Estate of Pablo Picasso/Artists Rights Society [ARS], New York/BF #115). Photograph © 2003. Reproduced with the permission of The Barnes Foundation.

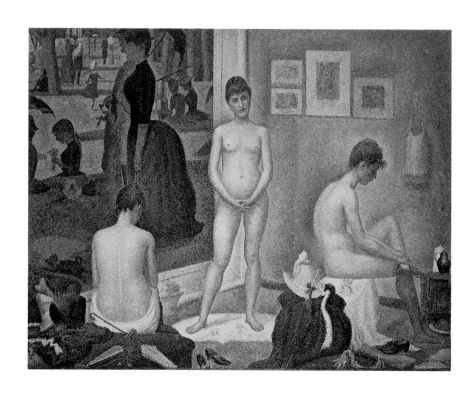

Models, Georges Seurat (BF #811). © 2003. Reproduced with
the permission of The Barnes Foundation.

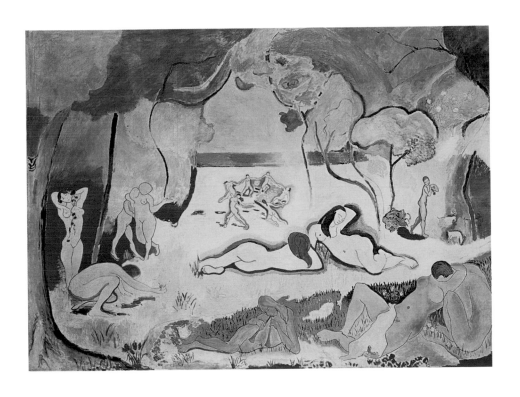

Joy of Life, Henri Matisse (© 2003 Succession H. Matisse, Paris/Artists
Rights Society [ARS], New York/BF #719). Photograph © 2003.
Reproduced with the permission of The Barnes Foundation.

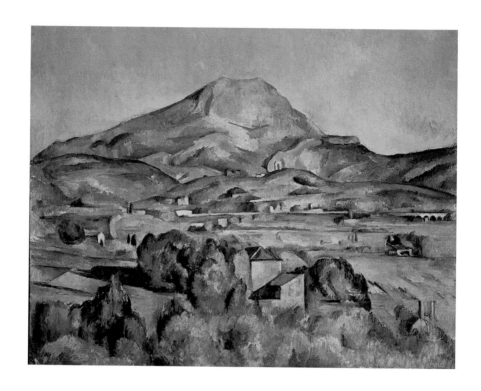

Mont Saint-Victoire, Paul Cezanne (BF #300). © 2003. Reproduced
with the permission of The Barnes Foundation.

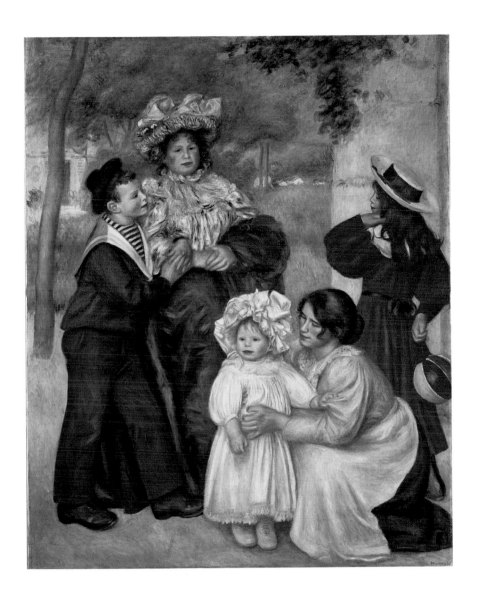

The Artist's Family, Pierre-Auguste Renoir (BF #819). © 2003.
Reproduced with the permission of The Barnes Foundation.

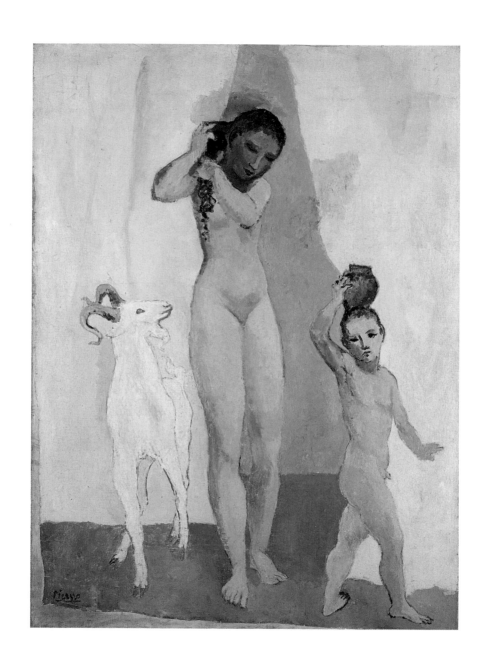

The Girl with a Goat, Pablo Picasso (© 2003 Estate of Pablo Picasso/Artists Rights Society [ARS], New York/The Barnes Foundation, #250)

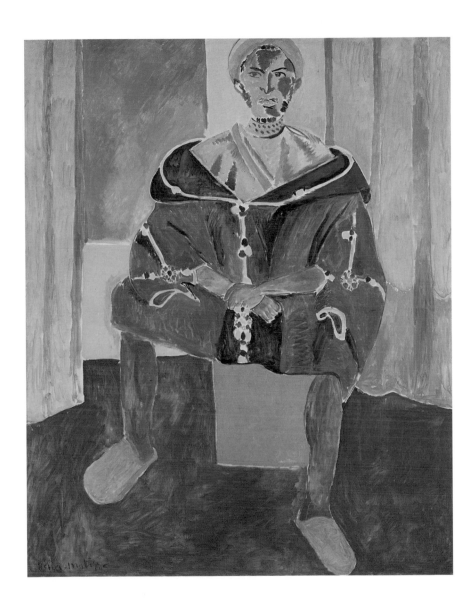

Seated Riffian, Henri Matisse (© 2003 Succession H. Matisse, Paris/Artists Rights Society [ARS], New York/The Barnes Foundation, #264)

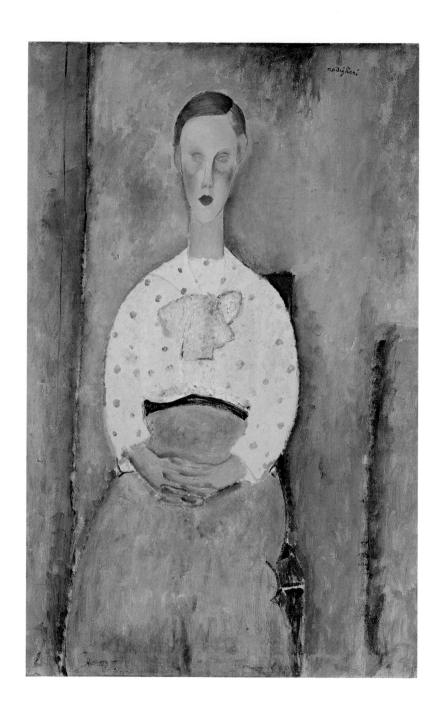

Girl with Polka-Dot Blouse, Amadeo Modigliani (BF #180). © 2003.
Reproduced with the permission of The Barnes Foundation.

lawyer Paul Diamond. "Because generally it involved significant litigation," was White's succinct reply. And were Mellon CEO Bill Stallkamp and trust department head David Officer concerned about the spiraling cost of litigation at the Barnes? "Yes," White admitted. "The fact that they would ask me [to serve on the Barnes board] would have indicated . . . that they thought it was important."

Diamond went on to query White about how the day-to-day business of the Barnes was carried out. White's answer was short and to the point: Vivian Cline handled payments to third-party vendors, but she, like everyone else employed at the foundation, ultimately reported to Richard Glanton.

"Would it surprise you," Diamond asked White, to know that the Barnes had reimbursed Glanton for personal expenses in 1995 totaling almost $57,000? "I'm not aware of the level of expenditures to Mr. Glanton," was White's rather terse reply. Diamond continued in the same vein: "In your experience, do most public charities have any kind of guidelines about expenditures of their officers and trustees or directors?" Yes, said White, they do. But not the Barnes?

"I'm not aware of any."

Vivian Cline had begun work at the Barnes in November 1986 and became business manager there two or three years later. Cline held a degree in economics and business administration from Muskingum College in Ohio, and, in her own words, "I handle everything financially connected [with] the Barnes Foundation . . . all the receivables, all the payables, all the accounting."

Her day-to-day supervisor?

"Mr. Glanton."

One of her other duties, Cline testified, was to keep minutes of the Barnes board meetings. President Glanton, she said, made it a point to review the minutes. She was asked whether he sometimes asked her to make changes in the minutes. "Occasionally, yes," Cline said. Diamond asked her if she made those changes, and she answered yes.

Diamond was also curious as to find out just what happened to Cline's shorthand notes of Barnes board meetings.

"I destroy them once the minutes are completed," Cline told him.

CHAPTER ELEVEN

THIS THING WAS GONNA BE A CAKEWALK

Good news for the Barnes came on April 15, when U.S. District Judge Marvin Katz dismissed the city of Rome's lawsuit. The parties, Judge Katz found, never had a contract. Barely a week later, though, Lower Merion Township and the commissioners filed motions for summary judgment in the Ku Klux Klan case. In court papers, township lawyer Diamond went straight for the jugular—Richard Glanton's jugular. In his memorandum, Diamond argued, "The record shows abundantly that the Barnes' finances are Mr. Glanton's private province," and went on to cite Glanton's Barnes Foundation credit card charges, his well-known propensity to live the high life, and the lack of "written criteria or guidelines as to what is or is not an appropriate expenditure" at the Barnes. Financial affairs at the

Barnes, Diamond concluded, were almost "entirely a matter of Mr. Glanton's 'discretion.'" (And, as we have seen, the depositions of Mellon bankers White and Frank, former trustee Walker, and Barnes business officer Cline all tended to support that thesis.) If the Barnes was indeed "going out of business," Diamond maintained, it was because of Richard Glanton's "litigious, profligate management style and self-dealing." Elsewhere, Diamond made reference to what he described as "the venal and profligate mismanagement of the Barnes by its own President."

The Barnes president was, meanwhile, making yet another run at forcing Judge Brody to recuse herself from the federal Ku Klux Klan suit. The Barnes's lead attorney, Sugarman, had filed the second of what would eventually be three separate petitions for a writ of mandamus asking the Third Circuit Court of Appeals to require Judge Brody to remove herself from the case. In an affadavit, Glanton—who described himself therein as since 1990 having "consistently rendered legal advice to the Board of the Barnes Foundation, in a position as legal advisor as well as President"—complained of Judge Brody's "bias." Glanton went on to cite, in particular, the political aspirations of Brody's daughter Lisa. An attorney, Lisa Brody had been a candidate for the Lower Merion Township Environmental Hearing Board and, after that, had been "promoted by at least three Lower Merion Township Commissioners and Defendants in writing . . . for the hotly contested political vacancy on the SEPTA board." Glanton concluded by arguing, "Judge Brody's support for her daughter's political ambitions has become inextricably intertwined with her ruling involving the Lower Merion political officials who are Defendants in this case."

Judge Brody again refused to recuse herself, and on September 26, 1997, she released an Order of Summary Judgment in the federal suit:

*The vast majority of the Barnes's evidence has nothing to
do with race, but rather only details various aspects of an
ordinary zoning dispute. Moreover, what little evidence
there is in the record that is even remotely related to race
fails to show that any of the Defendants acted with a
racially discriminatory purpose towards the Barnes.*

*The Barnes has produced no evidence whatsoever that
any of the Defendants' actions were motivated by a racially
discriminatory purpose. Indeed, the vast majority of the
Barnes's evidence has nothing to do with race, but merely
details various stages of a run of the mill land dispute.*

Judge Brody not only pitched out the Barnes's federal suit
filed under the Ku Klux Klan Act "for violations of the Equal
Protection and Due Process Clauses of the Fourteenth
Amendment," but she did so "with prejudice," meaning that the
case could not be refiled in any form in U.S. district court.

■

Judge Brody's order of summary judgment instantly changed the
equation at the Barnes, where affairs of state had become
increasingly unstable since midsummer. The seemingly unending
stream of depositions had gone on unabated, while the Barnes's
legal bills mounted astronomically. By granting summary judgment, Brody was also opening the door wide to defendants'
motions for attorneys' fees and sanctions. If the Barnes were to
lose all, the toll now could rise well into the millions.

Faced with such a prospect, and determined to mount an
appeal in the U.S. Court of Appeals for the Third Circuit, the
Barnes board turned to the illustrious historian of race and the
law in America, the former chief judge of that powerful body, A.
Leon Higginbotham, Jr. Retired from the bench, Higginbotham
commuted between New York—where he was of counsel to the
law firm of Paul, Weiss, Rifkind, Wharton & Garrison—and

Cambridge, Massachusetts. He and his wife, Evelyn, were professors of law and history, respectively, at Harvard. Higginbotham was by now an old and tired warrior. He had a heart condition, he wheezed and huffed, and he walked slowly. His mind was still sharp, though, and the veteran civil rights lawyer still had a trick or two up his well-worn sleeve. Higginbotham's reply to the motions for attorneys' fees and/or sanctions stunned even the usually unflappable Paul Diamond, the township's lawyer. Almost 200 pages long, it offered a categorical defense of the use of the Ku Klux Klan Act in the Barnes case—along with a not-so-short history of race in America. More extraordinary still was the accompanying 100-page "supplemental appendix" printed on heavy, oversized paper. The appendix opened with a blown-up photograph of "the remains of Zachariah Walker, burned to death on August 13, 1911." Page two carried another grisly photograph, this time of "the burning of William Brown in Omaha, Nebraska (1919)." Most of the next eighty pages were devoted to photocopied newspaper accounts of the infamous 1944 Motorman's Strike that precipitated race riots in wartime Philadelphia. If Paul Diamond was baffled by all this, Richard Glanton was not. "Only a moron," he argued, "could think that the opposition to the Barnes parking lot wasn't based on race."

President Glanton was, meanwhile, coming under newly focused scrutiny from within. Shirley Jackson had been succeeded by Kenneth Sadler, the North Carolina dentist, whose presence on the Barnes board had introduced a certain tension, given the fact that Glanton and Sudarkasa had earlier plotted to have him removed as chairman of the Lincoln board. Then too there was Sherman White, the Mellon banker, who had begun to rankle Glanton.

A month before Brody ordered summary judgment in the case, the Barnes board—prompted by White—had finally voted to hire an executive director of the foundation. A high-powered search firm, Heidrick & Struggles, was commissioned to identify appropriate candidates. After all these years, it appeared that the Barnes would have as its day-to-day chief operating officer a professionally trained museum director or art historian. It didn't work out that way.

Two days before Judge Brody signed the order, Lincoln president Sudarkasa woke up to learn in her copy of that morning's *Inquirer* that the Barnes had hired as its "administrative manager" Linda Marston. Marston had been regional director of the U.S. Department of Health & Human Services (H&HS) in the Reagan administration—she'd been succeeded in that position by lawyer Michael Smerconish (Glanton's antagonist in the city of Rome suit)—and was married to Glanton's close friend and fellow Reed Smith partner David Marston, the former U.S. attorney and SEPTA board member.

Sudarkasa was livid: "I read this, and I said, '*What!*'"

Glanton's unilateral hiring of Linda Marston was, thinks Gene Cliett, "the straw that broke the camel's back." When that was followed two days later by Judge Brody's decision, even Sudarkasa had had it with Glanton. Says Cliett, "He had promised her this thing [the Ku Klux Klan suit] was gonna be a cakewalk. And then it blows up in her face." After that, adds Cliett, Sudarkasa "really began to lose faith in Richard."

On September 29, Sudarkasa faxed Glanton the draft of a letter she intended to send to Barnes trustees.

No amount of explanation can excuse or justify the fact that Richard Glanton, in his only position at the Barnes, namely that of President, created what is now the seniormost management position at the Foundation, and filled that position without informing, much less consulting or obtaining authorization from, the Board of Trustees. Before now, I would have said it is unthinkable that the Board would learn about such a development by reading in the newspapers.

There followed a long litany of complaints. Glanton, Sudarkasa charged, had "spent Barnes Foundation money recklessly," failed to report adequately those expenses, and had run roughshod over other board members. Perhaps worst of all, he'd exercised questionable judgment "in dealing with our various legal entanglements."

"Where do we go from here?" Sudarkasa asked, then answered her own question: "After the death of our previous President, Ambassador Franklin Williams, the Trustees agreed to have a rotating presidency. I suggest that we activate that model in December when we elect [a new] President."

Cliett had already seen it coming. There'd been "rumblings," he says, all summer long as Sudarkasa complained, "Richard did this, he did that, he's in the paper." The Lincoln president was telling friends that Glanton wasn't as effective as he used to be, especially when it came to helping her deal with the Lincoln board: "She was going around saying, 'He never delivers on this, he never delivers on that.'" In short, Cliett says, Sudarkasa now considered Glanton "a liability." Even before Judge Brody's decision, Sudarkasa had confided in Cliett "that she'd decided to push him out." The reason, Cliett thinks, is that Sudarkasa no longer needed Glanton. With a new contract for a five-year term as president in hand, Sudarkasa, says Cliett, finally concluded that Glanton had "served his purpose." But she wanted, he adds, to find a compromise that would keep Glanton from being completely alienated from her. "She was going to be Queen Solomon," as Cliett puts it, then imitates her saying, "I'll take him off as president of the Barnes, but I'll see that he keeps the Lincoln legal business. And I'll have the best of both worlds."

■

When he received Sudarkasa's draft letter to the Barnes trustees, Glanton insisted on seeing her—that day. The Lincoln president accommodated the Barnes president, driving in from Chester

County to meet with him in a conference room at Reed Smith's One Liberty Place offices. Glanton, Sudarkasa says, "was practically shaking." He told her bluntly, "Niara, you can't do this to me. You're trying to destroy me."

Sudarkasa promised to think it over: "I said, 'Okay, I won't send this [draft] to the [Barnes] board.'" But she also told Glanton, Sudarkasa says, that "it was unthinkable that the [Barnes] board of trustees found out this thing [Linda Marston's hiring] in the newspapers."

Had she asked his advice, Cliett could have told Sudarkasa what to expect. Cliett offers a well-informed explanation of why the Barnes was so important to his friend Glanton: "He makes tons of money [and] sits on these prestige [*sic*] boards, but if you're out with him at dinner, he says, 'Richard Glanton, president of the Barnes.'"

The Barnes presidency, agrees former trustee Cuyler Walker, was "a platform for Richard Glanton. Secondarily, it was [about] legal business." Still, he adds: "The bottom line," for Glanton, "was all ego. He loved the spotlight." Walker vividly remembers that when S.I. Newhouse, Jr., "landed his helicopter at the Barnes, Richard's tongue was hanging out. Richard clearly steered the [Barnes book] contract to Knopf. It was full-court press after seeing Si in his helicopter." According to Walker, "Richard is part celebrity hound, part ambulance chaser. He loves to sit up in First Class. [And] he really misses the luster and excitement of the [Barnes] tour."

The Barnes, Cliett explains, "catapults you into high society. You're running with people who are art afficionadoes, cultural bigwigs." When Princess Diana died, Cliett recalls, "Richard called Channel 6 to come to his house and interview him because he 'knew her.' I said, 'Oh, my God.'"

Such were the opportunities offered by the Barnes presidency, says Cliett, who adds, "He couldn't get that at Reed Smith. But with the Barnes, well, this was what was taken from him, and this is what he had felt was his." Glanton, Cliett continues, is "very much an elitist. More than you could know." Madame President, by contrast, "is an autocrat. But Richard thought she was sort of a plebe. For him to be shot down by a pedestrian [*sic*] like Sudarkasa has hurt him more than you could know." Sudarkasa, Cliett says, "was counting on [the fact] that she could keep him in line." Counting, in other words, on the importance to Glanton of maintaining the more than $200,000 in legal business that Reed Smith got every year from Lincoln.

But if she *couldn't* control him . . . A Lincoln trustee—a man who spent years on the other side of the table from Glanton, Sudarkasa, *and* Cliett—describes Glanton as "certainly the most confrontational person I've ever worked with. And, as it turns out, he's dangerously eccentric. It's too bad. The guy's brilliant and articulate and a great personality." But, the anonymous trustee adds, "Combine those characteristics, and that makes for chaos; and we've suffered a lot of chaos working with Richard." There was, he says, "implicitly a great conflict of interest from day one [with Glanton serving as Lincoln trustee, Lincoln general counsel, and Barnes president] . . . an inherent conflict that Richard was quite comfortable with—and it turns out that was his style."

When she'd first contemplated taking the Barnes presidency from Glanton, Sudarkasa had worried aloud, Cliett recalls that, "Richard is vindictive and vicious, and he's gonna do something to me." Cliett remembers what happened next: "I paused and said, 'Madame President, he's afraid of you.'" She didn't believe him, but as Cliett explains, Glanton was indeed "frightened of her. She was the swing vote he could count on [on the Barnes board]." And that, Cliett says, worked both ways. Sudarkasa also needed Glanton "to cover her tracks at Lincoln." If, as Cliett says, "there was little control or reporting [that] Richard did to the Barnes board—it was after the fact, fire then aim—[the] same [was true] with Niara Sudarkasa. She did pretty much as she wanted at Lincoln." Cliett explains: "At Lincoln, she would lie, and he would swear to it; and at the Barnes, he would lie, and she would swear to it."

But when Sudarkasa threatened to take the Barnes away from Glanton, the coalition collapsed. Richard Glanton might well once have feared Niara Sudarkasa, but that was before September 29, 1997. Afterward, fear did not enter that side of the equation. On the other side, the fear factor rose precipitously, and with just cause: As Gene Cliett recalls, "She said he would try to get her."

CHAPTER TWELVE

THE PURSUIT OF JUSTICE

With the new school year about to begin, the *Inquirer* sent columnist Annette John-Hall and a photographer out to visit Niara Sudarkasa at her home on the Lincoln campus. The resulting story was little more than a puff piece—"Sudarkasa and Lincoln seemed a perfect fit," wrote John-Hall. "If they can learn to say Gorbachev, they can learn to say Su-DAR-kasa," said the Lincoln president. "A Shared Pride," as the story was called, occupied half the front page of the September 7, 1997, real estate section and another half-page inside.

Color interior shots—of the foyer and of Sudarkasa in her living room—made no doubt that the Lincoln president's house had been spiffed up. It had had to be, Sudarkasa told the *Inquirer* columnist. Her predecessor, she said, had taken the furniture with him, "leaving the house looking much like a grand old hostess who hadn't a stitch to wear." But as a photograph of the exterior showed, the Lincoln president did not live in opulence. "A stately Victorian with a wraparound front porch," was how John-Hall described it. A big old sprawling pile of red brick might be a better description. But a mansion? No.

Not, that is, unless your name was Vincent J. Fumo.

By the fall of 1998, Senator Fumo was arguably the most important Democrat in the state of Pennsylvania. Within the boundaries of Philadelphia itself, Fumo's only possible rival was Mayor Edward G. Rendell, and even Ed Rendell didn't have the senator's clout statewide or within the local party apparatus. Fumo was a throwback to the days of the big city ward bosses—years ago, he'd been indicted on federal corruption charges and found guilty, only to have his conviction overturned on appeal—a pol who much preferred operating behind the scenes to being in the spotlight.

There was nothing ideological about Fumo. He certainly wasn't a liberal, but he wasn't really a conservative, either. He was, instead, a porkbarreler in the great Philadelphia tradition that goes back to the late-nineteenth-century Republican crowd who built City Hall. He was a tough-minded, tough-talking politician who took care of friends and enemies with considerable zeal. As Democratic chairman of the state senate appropriations committee, Fumo wielded a mighty gavel. Locally, he had connections to just about every tentacle of the party—including county chairman and U.S. Representative Bob Brady. But Brady was merely one of the many friends of Vince Fumo: Other notables on the list included Senator Hardy Williams and State Auditor-General Robert Casey, Jr. (the son of the conservative, anti-abortion rights, anti-Clinton Pennsylvania governor, he would be Fumo's choice to run against Rendell in the 2002 Democratic primary for the same office). The senator knew everyone, and everyone knew him. And everyone in politics knew that Vince Fumo was someone you didn't want to cross.

Niara Sudarkasa wasn't aware that she'd ever done anything to earn Senator Fumo's wrath. No wonder she was perplexed,

then, when she received a letter from Fumo dated October 15.
The letter, on the stationery of the state senate appropriations
committee, read in part:

> *My office has received inquiries from members of the*
> *Lincoln University Board of Directors [sic], faculty, and*
> *administrators concerning expenditures for improvements*
> *to the President's residence [House # 26, as it was also*
> *styled]. I became particularly disconcerted after reading*
> *the September 7 article in* The Philadelphia Inquirer
> *which references the transformation of the house. I am*
> *hereby requesting that the University supply my office*
> *with all expenditures and costs in connection with this*
> *residence for the period 1993 to the present.*

Reading Fumo's letter made her feel, Sudarkasa says, like
she'd been "struck by a bolt from the blue."

Cliett's initial response, he says, was: "Fumo? Why Fumo?"
Soon his thoughts turned to Glanton. Glanton, Cliett knew, was
unhappy about the way events were unfolding at the Barnes. In
fact, it was just about all he could talk about. "Richard," Cliett
remembers, "would come back like a broken record with the
same thing—he was stuck on this authority thing" at the Barnes.
For his part, Cliett says he "was getting annoyed" with Glanton.
In Cliett's opinion, Sudarkasa shouldn't have threatened Glanton
with removal as president, "but I was annoyed with Richard.
He'd say he understood, then ask the same damn things."

Cliett, however, was no fool. The timing of the Fumo letter
came two weeks after Sudarkasa had faxed an abbreviated and
toned-down version of her September 29 memorandum to Barnes
board members calling for rotating the Barnes presidency. (Trying
to calm Glanton, Sudarkasa had advised him to show the memo
to his wife Scheryl. Glanton told her that he already had, and that
Scheryl had told him, "She's trying to *kill* you, Richard.")

Remembering how Sudarkasa had warned him that Glanton was vindictive and would "get her" for attempting to take away the Barnes presidency, Cliett turned to his boss and said, "You *told* me." Her response surprised him: "She said, 'Oh, no, no, no.'" Asked later why she didn't put Glanton and Fumo together at the time, Sudarkasa replied, "Well, Mr. Glanton is a Republican; and Senator Fumo is a Democrat."

A man in Harrisburg who knows both Glanton and Fumo well—"a highly placed lawyer in Pennsylvania legal circles," as he agreed to be referred to in print—explained to me, "Fumo, well, he and Richard are a lot alike. They're both big shots and they're both very, very Machiavellian. Knowing them both, I would say that neither guy would have the slightest, would have no qualms about crossing party lines to do a deal that was strongly in his interest." He paused, then added—this was in mid-August 1998—"Of course, we don't know where Fumo will land in the end, do we?"

Sudarkasa didn't get it, but the man in Harrisburg did. Had they been friends—they weren't—he might have advised the Lincoln president to read a relevant passage in the late historian T. Harry Williams's classic study of politics, *Huey Long*:

The ease with which [Huey] Long and [his sometime ally, sometime foe, Public Service Commissioner Shelby] Taylor formed their alliance illustrated one of the strangest aspects of Louisiana politics, one that has always puzzled outside observers who do not understand the conditions that produce it. Louisiana politicians were and are much like feudal barons. They operate as rulers of geographical principalities or personal followings, independently, calculatingly, and sometimes irresponsibly or petulantly. Two barons may seem to be friends and allies, and then suddenly, because one or the other senses an advantage to be gained or is seized by a whim, they break and

become enemies, and just as suddenly and for similar rea-
sons, they will come together as allies. Over a stretch of
years the pattern can become bewilderingly complex, as
leaders break, ally, and rebreak, in an endless chain of
combinations.

Williams ascribed this phenomenon to his adopted state's
"exaggerated devotion to professional politics." Louisiana, however, was not unique in this respect. Gene Cliett had been around
Pennsylvania and Philadelphia politics far longer than
Sudarkasa. His advice: "Madame President, let's go up to
Harrisburg and sit across the table" from Senator Fumo. Cliett
also advised her to "reach out" to Glanton. "Richard," Cliett
explained, "is AC/DC. He cuts across political lines." Sudarkasa
wouldn't budge: "She didn't want [Glanton] involved."

■

Three weeks after Sudarkasa received the letter from Senator
Fumo, the *Inquirer*'s front page was filled with the first in a
multi-part series entitled "The Girard Legacy" by investigative
reporters Marc Kauffman and Dan Stets. Their tale, spread over
the next week's worth of *Inquirer* front pages, was the result of a
year-long investigation into one of the more obscure corners of
Philadelphia politics.

The Girard Trust was a Philadelphia institution, one of the
oldest and once one of the richest nonprofit foundations in
America. Early nineteenth-century banker Stephen Girard, the
wealthiest man of his day and age, had left his money in keeping
for the orphans and indigent youth of Philadelphia. That, at
least, had been his intention. More than a century later, the
Girard Trust, Stets and Kauffman found, was little more than a
patronage machine for the politically connected.

As the two reporters discovered, between 1988 and 1997, the
$300 million Girard Trust had cut spending by 28 percent while

its assets rose 43 percent. At much the same time, spending at trust-owned Girard College, which had only been integrated in 1968 on orders of the U.S. Supreme Court and which now had an 85 percent minority enrollment, had declined 31 percent, from $26,889 per student annually to $18,626.

Meanwhile, during the 1988–1997 period, the Girard Trust was found to have been investing in some questionable business projects. Among these: buying nine office buildings from Harrisburg to Chester for $25 million, purchasing a $1.4 million Center City Philadelphia building and leasing it to acclaimed chef Georges Perrier for his new Brasserie Perrier, buying a one-third interest in the former Bellevue Stratford Hotel (where the most infamous outbreak of Legionnaires' Disease had once occurred) for $4 million, and throwing some $19.9 million into an anthracite coal mining project.

The members of the Board of City Trusts (the Girard trustees) were appointed for life by a vote of the judges of the Philadelphia court of common pleas (themselves elected officials). The current crop consisted of city council members, judges—and Vince Fumo. In recent years, as the *Inquirer*'s Kauffman and Stets made clear, "the dominant influence" on the Board of City Trusts had been wielded by Senator Vincent J. Fumo.

Over the course of the next week, in page after page of the *Inquirer*, Kauffman and Stets pilloried the Girard Trust and the Board of City Trusts for alleged financial mismanagement, conflicts of interest, and racism. The chief investment officer of the $12 billion Glenmede Trust was quoted as lambasting the Girard for its subpar financial performance; and noted Philadelphia investor Paul Miller, the retired founding partner of the $53 billion Miller Anderson, agreed. The Girard was getting, at best, "below average returns," said Miller. Queried by the *Inquirer*, Senator Fumo said the Board of City Trusts had no intention of disclosing any of its investment plans for the future.

The *Inquirer*'s editorial pages—predictably liberal in the

post-Annennberg years and long hostile to Senator Fumo—concluded the series with a call for an independent investigation into the affairs of the Girard Trust and the Board of City Trusts. Particularly disturbing to the *Inquirer* were the charges of racism leveled against the Girard. What they got instead was a five-member Independent Girard Committee—appointed in December 1997 by the Board of City Trusts and its dominant figure, Senator Vincent J. Fumo. The co-chairman of this Independent Girard Committee: Richard Glanton. Not even then did she get it, recalls Niara Sudarkasa: "I guess I was just naïve. But I thought, 'What does that have to do with me?'"

Lincoln University, it's safe to say, wasn't a major concern for Fumo, but the Girard Trust certainly was. He was well aware that *Inquirer* reporters had been nosing into the Girard Trust's practices for over a year. The questions that they'd been asking centered on possible financial improprieties and alleged racial biases. From the beginning, it was a good bet that such were the underpinnings of the story as *Inquirer* editors envisioned it. And when the story appeared in print, it was sure to get prominent play on the front page and be run as a series. After that would come the outcry from reformers—led by the *Inquirer*'s editorial page—and a call for an independent investigation of the Girard Trust.

A smart politician—and no one ever accused Vince Fumo of being dumb—could have predicted all the above. And would surely have done everything in his power, if not to stop the series from running then at least to prepare a response to it. The best way around a truly independent investigation: appoint your own "independent committee." And who better to chair such a committee charged with "investigating" racial bias than Richard Glanton? He had every advantage Fumo could have hoped for: He was a Republican (where Fumo was a Democrat), he was black (where Fumo was white), he wasn't—yet—on the Girard Trust board (which Fumo dominated), and he was a smooth operator who gloried in down-and-dirty political machinations (the one thing Richard Glanton absolutely shared in common with Vince Fumo).

Sudarkasa might have been puzzled at the time, she says, but she isn't now. Glanton, she says, was sending her a pointed warning: *Don't you dare try to take the Barnes presidency away from me. You do, and I'll get you.*

Nonsense, Richard Glanton replies: "Senator Fumo was serving the public interest." (A spokesman for Fumo also denies the allegation: "Absolutely untrue. There was no connection between the two.")

Gene Cliett's take on the matter: Senator Fumo, he says, "was just doing a favor for Richard. And in return, Richard was going to do a favor for Vince."

CHAPTER THIRTEEN

SOMEONE HAS TO BE ACCOUNTABLE

Throughout the fall, Richard Glanton tried repeatedly—but unsuccessfully—to have Sherman White removed from the Barnes board. But when the Barnes board members met on October 9, says Sudarkasa, "We ignored [Glanton's] letter." Glanton, according to the Lincoln president, next tried to pressure White's bosses at the Mellon Bank into changing horses at the Barnes—also to no avail. The best he could do was a postponement of the December 1 Barnes board meeting, at which the annual election of officers would take place. It was moved to February 9. In the meantime, newspaper coverage was slowly but surely beginning to focus on the investigation going on at Lincoln University. It was no secret on campus that Senator Fumo's people—led by private investigator Frank Wallace—were nosing around the university, asking for confidential financial information and, in general, creating a level of tension not seen there since the early 1990s.

"I just didn't get it," Sudarkasa says. "I didn't put two and two together. I was dumb." At that point, the former Lincoln president recalls, she still "had no clue of the [Glanton-Fumo] connection." Meanwhile, she turned increasingly to Gene Cliett for help—"This was before I knew about the connection between Cliett and Richard," says Sudarkasa glumly. Cliett, she adds, was advising her to "send them [Fumo's staff investigators] the print-outs of all this raw [Lincoln financial] data." In a hurry to get off on another visit to Nigeria, Sudarkasa says, she acceded to Cliett's wishes.

When she got back from Nigeria, the Lincoln president discovered that Fumo's investigation was now in high gear. Sudarkasa put her fate in the hands of yet another questionable advisor, Lincoln trustee and state senator Hardy Williams. She endeavored, Sudarkasa says, to convince the well-connected Williams that the nearly $550,000 in renovation work on the presidential home had been devoted to "rescuing" it, making the house, among other things, handicapped-accessible. Her other— more important—goal, Sudarkasa says, was trying "to get him to stop Fumo."

Senator Williams, Sudarkasa says, advised her to forward copies of all the documents she and Cliett had previously sent to Fumo to her general counsel. About to go off to Florida on vacation in mid-December, Sudarkasa did just that. A Lincoln trustee who had supported Ken Sadler in the prior chairman's election— he was no fan of either Glanton or Sudarkasa and was contemptuous of Cliett (in conference calls, he'd put the vice-president in his place by calling him "Employee Gene Cliett")—says that this was typical of Sudarkasa and had much to do with her eventual downfall: "She let Richard know all her shit. So, yes, she's stupid; but Richard's stupid because of his arrogance—it's paper thin."

The trustee—he refuses to be quoted by name—claims that shortly after being appointed to the Lincoln board, he was approached by Glanton, who *"tells* me how to vote on an issue coming up." When the newly minted trustee demurred, Glanton bristled. According to this trustee, the general counsel's advice to him was delivered emphatically, "Don't vote like a nigger." Glanton's "game," this trustee says, can be summed up in one word: "Money! It's all about the Benjamins, baby."

For years, he adds, "There was a veil of secrecy around everything that had to do with Richard and Cliett and the president [Sudarkasa]." No longer. "It's like the Titanic—and they're all going down." Glanton, he adds, was starting to go around, "in his braggadocious [*sic*] kind of way saying, 'I'm gonna bring that bitch down.'"

In late December, Sudarkasa received a letter from Glanton, addressed to her and chairman Sadler, that, she says, shocked her. In it, the Lincoln general counsel recommended that, among other things, she reimburse the university for all the money it had spent renovating her home. Soon thereafter, Sudarkasa found herself on the phone as part of a three-way conference call with Glanton and Sadler. The Lincoln president was shaken "to the core," and asked Glanton: "Richard, what is this?" She continues: "I said, 'Richard, *what*? I'm not a lawyer, but after reading this, I'd guess that you expect me to resign, pay back $500,000, and go to jail.' I said, 'Richard, do you think I'm a fool? I wasn't born yesterday.'"

Glanton's reply, according to Sudarkasa: "I'm just trying to present the other side."

■

Fumo's investigators weren't the only ones looking into affairs at Lincoln. *Inquirer* reporter Rich Henson was, too.

It was early January 1998 when Sudarkasa gave Cliett a sensitive assignment—dealing with the pesky Henson. Sudarkasa's recollection is that Lincoln communications director Karen Warrington—former Mayor Goode's press secretary—came to her with the news that "someone has left on the *Inquirer*'s doorstep this big packet of information about Lincoln—the computer printouts [of the material given Senator Fumo]—and all this is traceable to Richard [Glanton]." Gene Cliett's recollections accord with Sudarkasa's. Warrington told her bosses, Cliett says, that Henson had called "saying [that] he had all these documents, alluding [to] how he'd gotten them from . . . another reporter who'd gotten [them] from Richard [Glanton]." Now, Sudarkasa wanted Cliett and Warrington to meet Henson at a neutral site, the cavernous Thirtieth Street Station.

When Cliett saw the documents Henson brought with him, he had no doubt as to what they were: "I look at the papers . . . and they're the same [financial] papers we'd given Fumo's investigators." Henson, Cliett recalls, "said he'd gotten them 'from a board member, yeah, your legal counsel.'" Cliett says he told the *Inquirer* reporter, "I can't believe it. These papers were never given to Richard. How could Richard have gotten them?" He was, Cliett says, "really taken aback." When Cliett got back to the Lincoln campus, says Sudarkasa, he had "turned very nervous."

Later, Henson would tell Sudarkasa, "All the lines go back to Richard Glanton." Sudarkasa passed the news on to chairman Sadler: "I told Ken, 'This isn't about Lincoln. It's about the Barnes.'" Henson, she now says, "was putting it all together: Fumo, Glanton, why they were putting the screws on the *Inquirer*."

Madame President was no longer happy with her general counsel—or with her vice-president. "After a while, it was like she and I were ready to square off every day, *every day*," recalls Cliett. Life at Lincoln, in the presidential and vice-presidential offices at least, had become heated, "more heated even than when John Clark was there." Sudarkasa, Cliett claims, called board members "and told them I wasn't supporting her, I was on Richard's side. One board member called me and told me. I said, 'Well, when it's all over and done, I don't have to take sides. I'll let the truth be my defense.'"

■

On February 4, news of the Fumo investigation into the "contro-versial renovation" of the Lincoln president's home broke in the *Inquirer*. Reporters Rich Henson and Christina Asquith quoted investigators from Fumo's office as saying that more than $350,000 had been spent on fixing up the house, described as "a large brick Victorian with peeling paint, drafty windows, a leaky basement, an old roof, and no furniture" when Sudarkasa first moved in in 1987. The *Inquirer* went on to quote former physi-cal plant director John Willis—already gone after disagreeing with his predecessor John Clark over priorities on the campus—as saying, "Mr. Clark told me it was the president's house, and when she said it should happen, it should happen." In other words: When the boss said fix it, you fixed it. The *Inquirer* reporters also quoted Cliett saying, "There wasn't a day when you walked through the campus that someone did not make a comment" about the work being done on the president's home.

That same day, Lincoln board chairman Sadler faxed a letter to university general counsel Glanton, ordering him not to com-municate directly with Lincoln trustees unless told to do so: "Please do not send anything to the board at this time. I'm in the process of discussing this matter with others to determine the next step."

Two days later, in a letter dated February 6, Glanton—con-trary to those orders—wrote all Lincoln board members "RE: Memorandum regarding senate investigation." The letter began: "I have been requested by Dr. Kenneth Sadler . . . to transmit this memorandum," and continued, "This memo attempts to sum-marize how the State would view the expenditures [on Residence 26, the president's home] in question and is also designed to fully disclose any adverse consequences that could result from this inquiry." But consequences to whom? That would be answered shortly.

"The question which arises is whether the money sent [*sic*] for Residence 26 was authorized when the Board approved the annual University budgets for the years in question. . . . If there is notice [of the expenditures on the president's home], and there was no inquiry, this raises issues of Board exposure concerning whether or not the Board carried out its financial responsibility." Even the footnotes in Glanton's memorandum spoke like cannons: "Apart from the potential issue of any liability, we must be equally concerned with being completely truthful. Any misrepresentations made can in and of themselves be actionable." The university general counsel thought it "prudent and obligatory to point out that criminal penalties do exist and can be imposed if there is a determination that the University spent funds appropriated by the state without Board approval, as required by law." He went on to suggest that the state auditor-general—Senator Fumo's ally, fellow Democrat Bob Casey, Jr.—might well want to involve himself in the investigation, and "any report could also be referred to the Attorney General of the Commonwealth of Pennsylvania," Glanton's ally, Republican Michael Fisher, "for further investigation." And, just in case anyone could have missed the point, there was footnote number seven: "The Board itself is not completely immune from potential liability in the event of adverse findings."

That letter was dated February 6; but, sent via UPS overnight delivery, it actually arrived in Niara Sudarkasa's office at Lincoln on February 9—the very morning of the very day that Glanton was ousted as president of the Barnes. The vote: 4-1, with Sadler, Sudarkasa, White, and Randy Kinder on one side; and Glanton on the other.

Even in the wilderness, Richard Glanton remained eminently quotable. His enemies, Glanton told *Inquirer* staff writers Leonard Boasberg and Julia Klein, were "like a vigilante Klan organization," "a bunch of weird racists masquerading as being concerned with the Barnes." He went on to criticize Sherman

White and "two former trustees"—obviously Cuyler Walker and the Mellon Bank's Charles Frank—for "working with [the Lower Merion] Township to prove the township's point that I was out of control." Glanton was unapologetic: He had raised a small fortune for the Barnes via the tour, while his opponents "sit there with their thumbs in their mouth [*sic*]." As for criticisms that Glanton had approved Barnes reimbursements for his meals at fancy local restaurants like The Palm and Le Bec Fin, Glanton scoffed, "What am I going to do? Go to my subordinates and say, 'Approve this for me?' Someone has to be accountable. I'm accountable."

■

It took the *Inquirer* a couple of days to catch up with the new leadership out at the Barnes. Unfortunately, the foundation's current president wasn't nearly as quotable as his predecessor had been. As the *Inquirer* reported at the time, Kenneth M. Sadler was a forty-eight-year-old dentist and administrator at the Winston-Salem Dental Care Plan in Winston-Salem, North Carolina. A colonel in the U.S. Army Reserve and four-term councilman in suburban Lewisville (population 7,500), Sadler was married to a physician and the father of two young sons. He was active in charities and had been the recipient of the Silver Beaver Award as a Boy Scout leader. A 1971 graduate of Lincoln with a degree in chemistry, he'd gone on to dental school at Howard and held a master's degree in public administration.

Sudarkasa's old nemesis Earle Bradford, the chairman of the Lincoln business affairs committee and, until now, a frequent critic, was hired as a consultant to help with the day-to-day management of the foundation. His fee: $1,000 a day. A resident of Villanova on the Main Line, Bradford, who had been the Arco Chemical Company's vice-president for public affairs, was fifty-one years old. He'd graduated magna cum laude from Dillard University in 1969 and held an M.B.A. from Cornell. A few days later, on February 13, Linda Marston quit her job at the Barnes, "citing Bradford's high salary and limited Barnes financial resources."

Back out at Lincoln, there was a new lawyer on campus: Blank Rome senior partner Christopher Lewis, secretary of state in the administration of former Democratic Governor Robert P. Casey, Sr. Lewis, as it happens, had also been Earle Bradford's lawyer in his contract negotiations with the Barnes. Now, he was being brought in as "special counsel" to the university with regard to the Fumo investigation.

Having reviewed the Lincoln board minutes from 1986 to the present, Lewis found, "The central issue presented by Senator Fumo's inquiry is whether the expenditures on Residence 26 were authorized. We conclude that the expenditures apparently were authorized." Attached to Lewis's report was a supporting letter from assistant U.S. secretary of labor for employment standards Bernard E. Anderson, the former Lincoln board chairman, to the same effect.

When the Lincoln trustees next met on February 20 to consider Lewis's appointment, the embattled Niara Sudarkasa found a vase with two dozen yellow roses awaiting her. With it came a handwritten note from the sender. It read: "Dear Niara, Let's move on. We have been good friends to each other. My preference is to work with you. Richard." Her reaction: "I was upset. Mr. Glanton had done so many thing to undermine me . . . I felt like it was an insult." She took the yellow roses—"yellow roses," Sudarkasa later testified, "are symbols of friendship"—and set them on a side table in the Lincoln board room.

Glanton, she says, didn't say anything to her at the meeting. But trustee Hardy Williams, a member of the state senate committee doing the investigating at Lincoln—"He never paid any attention to the university until politics came into play," insists Gene Cliett—did plenty of talking that day. Senator Williams, Sudarkasa recalls, was "very animated," speaking "with his hands as well as his voice. He spoke loudly" and passionately against the appointment of a special counsel—and against Sudarkasa.

There was considerable debate on the topic, with state representative Curtis Thomas, also a Lincoln trustee, arguing that the university had no choice but to hire a special counsel precisely because of the relationship that existed between Glanton and Fumo. The Lincoln general counsel, Sudarkasa recalls, "stated there *was* no relationship. Mr. Glanton stated [that] he understood his legal requirements—and would uphold them."

At the close of debate, the Lincoln board formally ratified Lewis's appointment as special counsel to the university "on all issues related to the Fumo inquiry." The board also adopted a resolution confirming that "the expenditures on Building 26, from Fiscal Year 1988, were authorized through the University's budget approval process."

Glanton held on at Lincoln until March 17, when he finally submitted his resignation as university general counsel to Sadler, "effective immediately." (It would subsequently be learned that Lincoln, with a permanent endowment of $13 million at the time, had paid Glanton's law firm, Reed Smith, $736,263 in legal fees for the years 1995–1997 alone.)

Less than two weeks later, the university's new co-general counsel, Christopher Lewis, commissioned KPMG Peat Marwick to do a forensic audit of past and present procurement practices at Lincoln.

Little more than a month after Glanton's resignation as general counsel, Senator Fumo's office released its own, long-awaited investigative report with a press release, "Democrats Oppose Lincoln University Appropriations." "At the urging of State Senator Vincent J. Fumo," the Democratic members of the appropriations committee had voted to withhold $11 million in payments to Lincoln. The so-called Fumo Report was full of allegations of overspending on the president's home, bid-rigging, and misuse of university employees. Somewhat surprisingly,

Sudarkasa's old saga with the Internal Revenue Service also found its way into the report, along with allegations that unauthorized Lincoln money had gone to pay for the president's tax advice. Senator Fumo's tax consultants on the Lincoln inquiry: Goldenberg Rosenthal, President Sudarkasa's personal tax accountants.

Fumo Report or no Fumo Report, Glanton was steaming. There would be numerous missives from the former Lincoln general counsel all that summer of 1998—with numerous recipients (the author among them) indicated on the letters and faxes that fairly flew from the laser printers at Reed Smith. Typical is this one, dated May 12, and addressed to Ken Sadler:

> *I am now following up with my response to your letter of March 12, 1998 regarding your initial decision to employ Mr. [Earle] Bradford at a salary of $260,000 a year, the retention of Mr. [Christopher] Lewis to represent Mr. Bradford [in his contract negotiations with the Barnes], and your purported waiver of the obvious conflict for Mr. Lewis's firm in connection with this representation of Mr. Bradford.*

Bradford, Glanton charged, was being "paid at a rate of $1,000 a day, $5,000 per week, $20,000 per month, or $260,000 per year" and had "every motivation to perpetuate his stay as Chief Administrative Officer at the Foundation." What's more, Glanton went on,

> *During the past 4–5 years, Mr. Bradford served as Chairman of the Business Affairs Committee of the Lincoln University Board of Trustees which has responsibility over the budget and financial affairs of the University. In that position, Mr. Bradford is one of Niara Sudarkasa's principal supervisors at Lincoln. At the same*

time, she is one of Mr. Bradford's supervisors in his sinecure at the Foundation, because of her role as a Barnes Trustee. . . . These relationships could be viewed by the Pennsylvania Attorney General as a potential cover-up and payoff.

CHAPTER FOURTEEN

A SUMMER
WITHOUT SHAME

In May of 1998, U.S. District Judge Anita Brody sent a letter to all counsel in the Barnes's federal suit. In her memorandum, Brody recounted how on November 21, 1997, she and her husband, Jerome (a physician), had filed a petition in the Montgomery County Court of Common Pleas requesting a reassessment on their property in Lower Merion Township. "On May 9, 1998," Brody continued, "it came to my attention that the Township of Lower Merion had intervened in the action." As a result, Brody was offering to recuse herself from the Barnes case. Of course, by now it was too late: Judge Brody had long ago ordered summary judgment with prejudice.

The outraged Bob Sugarman requested that Judge Brody not only recuse herself but also vacate her earlier judgment. The first part of his request was agreed to—and the case transferred to U.S. District Judge Ronald L. Buckwalter by order of Chief U.S. District Judge Edward Cahn—but the second part was denied.

Despite Judge Brody's rather tardy recusal, the Barnes was no better off in May 1998 than it had been back in September 1997. As for Glanton and Sudarkasa, they were both worse off—a great deal worse off.

They weren't alone in that leaking boat, either. Gene Cliett saw himself as in a no-win position: "stuck," he says, "between these two people, my boss and my friend." Just days before the KPMG report was to be released, Cliett resigned as vice-president of Lincoln.

On June 1, the Reed Smith lawyer received a letter from Kyle Anne Midkiff, the Philadelphia-based managing director of litigation and forensic services of KPMG Peat Marwick, asking for his help in the ongoing audit at Lincoln. Glanton faxed back an angry reply:

> *It is . . . my understanding that during the approximately last four months that [sic] your firm, together with Blank Rome [partner] Chris Lewis, at the direction of Niara Sudarkasa, have apparently run up charges in the hundreds of thousands of dollars which are being stockpiled to be billed at an appropriate time.*

Carbon copies of Glanton's letter went to Auditor General Casey, Commonwealth Attorney General Michael Fisher—and Senator Vincent Fumo.

The next day, the *Inquirer* ran a page-one story by Rich Henson detailing the findings from the KPMG audit. Suspect spending practices, it seems, abounded at Lincoln. The auditors reported finding numerous incidences of "questionable bid documentation," sloppy bookkeeping, and flawed oversight at the college. But the KPMG audit also revealed something else: a series of business relationships between two of the top officers of the college.

Lincoln officials, Henson reported, had subsequently informed

Republican Governor Tom Ridge of "questionable transactions," among them possible conflicts of interest involving the university's former lawyer, Richard H. Glanton, and its former top financial officer, Eugene L. Cliett, Jr. The KPMG auditors, it turned out, had discovered that Cliett, through his company ELCIS (Electronic Computing & Information Services, also known as Eugene L. Cliett Information Systems), had received some $174,000 in Barnes business between July 1996 and May 1997, payments that were, in fact, signed off on by Glanton. The work done by ELCIS consisted of $63,000 in computer consulting and equipment and $111,000 for the reproduction of Barnes-era books that had long since gone out of print. But because ELCIS wasn't in the printing business, Cliett had subcontracted the business to a real printer—Citation Graphics (which was also paid $250,000 by Lincoln for the fiscal year ending 1996). Cliett himself wound up pocketing $19,800, after paying the subcontractor.

Meanwhile, the KPMG auditors also found that Cliett was an investor in a company called Shooting Star Productions, which had been paid $13,750 by Lincoln in fiscal 1997 for productions of videotapes and consulting. The payments to Shooting Star had been approved by Cliett. What's more, Shooting Star owned a television antenna and transmitter and a Federal Communications Commission (FCC) license to broadcast on Channel 7. During the period January 1997 through July 1997, Cliett and Glanton collectively paid $185,000 to purchase a so-called Time Brokers Agreement (TBA) for the license to transmit television cable services, along with a transmitter and an antenna. KPMG also discovered the existence of a company named Digital Media TV, Inc., incorporated on July 11, 1997, with Cliett as CEO and Glanton as secretary. As the report stated: "Discussions with Mr. Cliett revealed that Digital Media TV runs infomercials on Channel 7 and a commission is paid to Digital Media based on sales."

Richard Glanton had been warned about the news a day earlier, but when the front-page *Inquirer* story came out, he went into a fury, writing chairman Sadler,

> *Yesterday about 4:00 p.m., I was informed by telephone for the first time that Lincoln University issued a report to the Pennsylvania General Assembly containing allegations of an alleged conflict of interest on the part of myself and Eugene Cliett, in his capacity as Chief Fiscal Officer of the University. I assume this report was the result of discussions of the Business Affairs Committee, which took place in the offices of [the Blank Rome managing partner] David Girard-diCarlo on Friday and Saturday of last week.*

Glanton wrote: "I do not now and have never had any interests in Mr. Cliett's computing company. Mr. Cliett and I were not business partners in any partnership during the period his company provided services to the Barnes."

The next day, June 3, 1998, the Pennsylvania state senate, goaded by Philadelphia's own Vincent Fumo, voted 44–4 to withhold two-thirds of Lincoln's annual subsidy. The stakes were being newly defined. At issue were the educational needs of a thousand-odd young men and women out at Lincoln, not to mention assorted professors, administrators, and staff.

Two days later, having already asked Glanton to deliver Reed Smith's Lincoln files to the university's new co-general counsel Christopher Lewis (of Blank Rome) and William Adams, Jr., Ken Sadler wrote: "In accordance with Rule 1.6 of the Rules of Professional Conduct [required of members of the Pennsylvania bar], I am instructing you, for the record, that Lincoln University insists that you uphold the confidentiality that attaches to the lawyer-client relationship and that you not reveal information relating to your representation of Lincoln." Sadler asked Glanton to return all Lincoln documents held by

Reed Smith, adding, "I request that you not retain any copies of these documents so that inadvertent disclosure of privileged information can be avoided."

On June 6, the *Inquirer*'s Henson quoted Glanton as saying that he'd hired Cliett's company to do work for the foundation because it "was the low-price vendor at a time when I had no involvement with him [Cliett] in any partnership, period. And he was the most experienced of the vendors. He gave me a better price than anyone else did."

Experienced? Experienced doing what? Subcontracting? For that's essentially all that Cliett did, adding his own $19,800 fee on to the actual printing company's charges.

That same day, Glanton wrote to Casey:

> *As a former General Counsel to Lincoln University, I am writing to request that you freeze any payment by Lincoln University to either KPMG for this alleged audit or to Blank Rome. . . . As I understand it, KPMG and Blank Rome have run up bills that may exceed $600,000 of tax-payers' money. It is my view that retention of KPMG was borne [sic] out of vengeance by Niara Sudarkasa, to smear the reputations of myself and others. . . . We [Cliett and Glanton] were informed by an individual also mentioned in the [KPMG] report (and who has agreed to provide us with a sworn affidavit), that one of the KPMG auditors stated to him that he would "like to get Richard Glanton."*

Much of the letter to Casey was, in fact, devoted to a detailing of the sins, real or imaginary, of Niara Sudarkasa's husband, former Lincoln University physical plant director John Clark: "It was recently discovered that during [Clark's] tenure, based upon statements by former and current University employees, he was responsible for allegedly dumping hazardous waste on Lincoln's property, as well as attempting to hide leaking underground diesel fuel storage tanks." An *Inquirer* story by Rich Henson three days later detailed virtually the exact same charges under the headline: "Glanton Pens Attack on Lincoln President."

Four days later, on June 16, Glanton elaborated on his mode of attack, writing a letter to Sudarkasa that began, again, with a reference to Clark and "the three contractors with whom Mr. Clark had developed a peculiar pattern of contract awards." These contractors, Glanton claimed, had "received more than three quarters of a million dollars in contracts during the relevant [KPMG] audit period. Virtually all of these contracts were of a no-bid nature, right under the $5,000 bid limit." No other department at Lincoln, Glanton argued, "had non-existent companies submitting bids except for the physical plant." Sudarkasa's tenure at Lincoln, said Glanton, amounted to a "decade of deceit."

That same day, June 16, Glanton wrote *Inquirer* editor Robert Rosenthal, expressing his disappointment in the paper's Lincoln coverage:

> *You have attempted to assassinate my character by carrying on the front page of* The Philadelphia Inquirer *allegations about a potential conflict of interest based on [the KPMG Lincoln forensic audit] at a cost of $600,000 of taxpayers' money by Niara Sudarkasa and a few Lincoln Trustees with [whom] she might have interlocking relationships.*

It was all so preposterous—Glanton himself having perfected the art of "interlocking relationships," especially where the Barnes and Lincoln came into play—but the letter had a chilling effect. When a litigious soul like Richard Glanton wrote threatening letters, an editor—any editor, anywhere—had to take him seriously; had, in fact, to wonder if his or her publication wouldn't be the next to be sued.

■

Less than a month after Glanton's letter to Rosenthal, the *Inquirer* ran a front-page story by Marc Kauffman (co-author of the "The Girard Legacy" series). The headline read, "Panel: No Evidence of Racism at Girard." Seven months after having been formed by the Girard trustees to investigate the Girard trustees, the independent committee delivered its considered opinion: "The good news has not been told."

At a City Hall press conference, the public face of the committee, CoreStates Bank CEO Rosemarie Greco, was forced to admit that the final report had been a "consensus, [in which] we did not agree, every one of us, every time." And, as it turned out, the committee had presented a draft report more than a month ago to the Board of City Trusts (the Girard trustees). Perhaps the most important recommendation in the draft would have limited trustees to fixed terms (rather than their current lifetime appointments). "There was," the *Inquirer*'s Kauffman noted, "no reference to term limits in yesterday's report." The *Daily News*, under the headline "Girard Board Cleared of Racism Charges"—and who better to do that than Richard Glanton?—reported that that news had been "warmly greeted by the Board of City Trusts."

On July 14, a letter went out addressed to Sudarkasa from A. Randolph Blough, director, Division of Nuclear Materials Safety, U.S. Nuclear Regulatory Commission (the same federal agency whose chairman was former Barnes and Lincoln board member Shirley Jackson). The Nuclear Regulatory Commission, Blough wrote, had "recently received statements that in 1991–1992, the director of the Physical Plant [John Clark] received kickbacks for burying low level nuclear waste from another facility behind the physical facilities plant on Lincoln University's campus." Blough went on to give president Sudarkasa thirty days in which to respond to the charges.

More ominous news was to come four days later, when the

Inquirer ran a story under the headline "Pa. Auditors Probe Allegations of Irregularities at Lincoln." The story went on to quote a high-ranking official in Casey's office, Peter Smith, as saying, "It is a major investigation. . . . We are really moving as fast as we can."

Marc Kauffman and Dan Stets's look into the behind-the-scenes activities of the Girard independent committee was the banner story next day: "Girard Study Made Softer, Less Critical. The Language in a Review Panel's Final Report Aims to Show Support for the School and its Management." Members of the independent committee, the *Inquirer* staff writers reported, "said the changes were made so the report would be more 'forward-looking' and constructive, rather than 'backward-looking' and judgmental."

The *Inquirer* obtained three versions of the report, indicating that the language had been progressively softened over the course of two months. CoreStates Bank CEO Greco told the paper that "the [Girard] board did not pressure the committee to make any changes, saying [Board of City Trusts] members were absolute Boy Scouts throughout this."

Vince Fumo? A Boy Scout?

More to the point, Kauffman and Stets reported, "Not all committee members were aware of the changes made in the final report." At least one member of the five-member independent committee told the *Inquirer* that she hadn't even seen the final report before it was released. And co-chairperson Greco "was surprised" to learn during her interview by the *Inquirer* reporters "that a particular observation in the May draft—that the Girard [College] instructional staff had few African-Americans—was not in the final report."

Most revealing of all, the *Inquirer* reported:

> *The committee members would not say exactly who wrote the final report, other than that it was done by committee*

members together and by consensus . . . At one point in the process, towards the middle of June, when several committee members were out of town, Glanton said in an interview that he was working on some minor changes he and the committee thought were needed.

And, "referring to the term-limits issue, Greco said that while some committee members did want to make recommendations, they ultimately 'reached consensus' around Glanton's point of view."

The same issue of the *Inquirer* also reported that the Lincoln board had met in emergency session the day before to consider the recent state senate action withholding funds for the university. Trustee Hardy Williams—state senator and appropriations committee member, Fumo fan, and Sugarman best man, not to mention Barnes lawyer extraordinaire (to the tune of $70,000)—told reporters that his former client Sudarkasa should consider resigning.

■

Inquirer art news reporter Leonard Boasberg had done a solid job covering the city of Rome suit; now, a younger colleague, Anne Barnard, was busy digging into the complicated Barnes-Lincoln, Glanton-Sudarkasa web. Barnard got far enough into it to ask many of the right questions. In a letter of August 10, Glanton replied to her request for answers: "I believe your inquiry is part of an active campaign by *The Philadelphia Inquirer* to disparage my reputation and to defame my character." Glanton went on to speak of "the malfeasance of the Lincoln board in supervising the President's management" and "the carnage at the University" and to warn Barnard that she and her editors at the newspaper "would have to account for any missteps you make." His purpose in writing to her, Glanton said, "is to put you on notice."

Under his management, Glanton claimed, the Barnes had been "run effectively, like a business, with checks and balances to ensure complete accountability." As for former Barnes trustee

Charles Frank, the Mellon banker: "I decided that while I was President, I would not reign while someone else ruled by controlling the finances of the Foundation."

I would not reign.

There were warnings galore in the letter to Barnard:

Your reference to any business relationship [existing between Glanton and former Barnes consultant Tom] Massaro is extremely misleading. I caution you that any defamatory article in this regard will be promptly addressed. . . . If you intend to do what you have done in the past, endeavoring to besmirch my reputation and cast doubts and innuendoes about my leadership, you shall be held to the same standard you are held to when you write about other cultural institutions in Philadelphia.

The letter concluded: "You are not objective enough to write about me or the Barnes Foundation."

A day later, Glanton complained to editor Rosenthal:

I am writing concerning two reporters on The Philadelphia Inquirer *staff and also to let you know that I thoroughly enjoyed lunch with you and Mr. [Philip] Dixon [at the time the newspaper's third-ranking editor]. . . . Because I think you are sincere, I am writing to express my genuine disappointment with the conduct of two reporters, Anne Barnard and Rich Henson.*

The two reporters, Glanton complained, had "pursued me like a mosquito [*sic*], seeking to draw blood by any means possible." Turning the tale on its head, Glanton added, "Someone needs to examine what is going on at the *Inquirer.* You are in a position to do so."

Glanton's correspondence with the *Inquirer* continued

unabated through August. (I was myself on occasion the recipient of copies marked "cc: John Anderson," among other names.) Surely the most revealing of the letters in the correspondence was a reply from deputy managing editor Dixon to Glanton dated August 28:

> *You claim that you can supply affidavits from others stating that "Mr. Henson falsely claimed that [you] gave the* Inquirer *information about financial mismanagement concerning Niara Sudarkasa and John Clark." My understanding is that you did supply Mr. Henson with such information. As I understand it, during a period from June through early July 1998, when you were in regular contact with Mr. Henson, you provided him with information concerning the alleged mismanagements of Ms. Sudarkasa and Mr. Clark. During this period, you also provided Mr. Henson with documents that you believed supported your charge. . . . Alternatively, you may be referring to documents that were delivered anonymously to Christine Asquith of the* Inquirer *earlier this year. . . . Mr. Henson has said that once you and he began to talk regularly, you called him, not infrequently, including at home on a Saturday morning, or on Sundays or even late at night.*

Whatever the reason—she's not sure—Anne Barnard, having devoted several months to a possible Barnes project, found herself summoned to a meeting with three *Inquirer* editors. She was told "in no uncertain terms," Barnard says, that she was off the Barnes project. Suburban editor Daniel Biddle, the man who once gave Richard Glanton the nickname "Killer," explained to her that "Downtown"—the paper's highest-ranking editors, including deputy managing editor Phil Dixon—wanted no part of such an investigative series.

■

As Sudarkasa's lawyer, Carl Singley, would later say of him: "Glanton is the definition of incorrigible." By now, the Barnes's appellate lawyer, Leon Higginbotham, had pretty much come to the same conclusion. In a letter to Glanton dated August 6 (with copies to the other trustees), Higginbotham expressed his frustration with the former Barnes president:

> *I believe the type of public statements that you are making will hurt the reputation of the Barnes and compromise the potential for settlement and ultimate resolution [emphasis in original]. It is difficult for me to see how these public accusations are in the best interests of the Foundation and consistent with your obligations as a Trustee. Is it asking too much of you to request that you stop talking to the press [in] regard [to] The Barnes for a period of 60 days so that we can try to get this matter resolved? Your comments have made the job considerably more difficult.*
>
> *You should not forget that it was because of your aggressive communications with the media that you became the victim of a defamation suit. . . . I am also concerned that I have called you on several occasions regarding your refusal to sign The Barnes' Conflict of Interest resolution. [To] my knowledge, I have never received a response. I am utterly perplexed as to why you have not signed the Conflict of Interest resolution that all the other Trustees have signed.*

No doubt Higginbotham had a very good idea why the former Barnes president hadn't signed the conflict of interest resolution, but he wasn't going to show his hand—yet. Instead, he concluded with some conciliatory words—"I would appreciate your efforts to bring sanity and rationality to the resolution of these difficult problems"—and signed the letter, "Very truly yours, Leon."

Little more than a year later, after a forensic audit of the Barnes had been initiated—its results still haven't been released to the public, though the report was delivered to the trustees in 1999—Glanton wrote Higginbotham a bitter letter of recrimination:

> *I know that Mr. Piccini [Louis Piccini, the former assistant U.S. attorney who headed the Deloitte & Touche forensic audit] as well as your firm [Paul Weiss] has [sic] been paid large sums of money, and Mr. Piccini obviously feels that having recently left a 25 year career as a mob prosecutor at the U.S. Attorney's Office, he must justify the $100,000 fee paid to his firm by the Barnes last month [November 1998], and I am concerned about the length that he and others might be willing to go to, to find something or anything to justify these large fees [that] Paul Weiss and D & T are being paid. As you know, I have initiated an action against KPMG and Blank Rome for the dishonest audit [at Lincoln], and I will not hesitate to take similar action against you, your firm, Mr. Piccini, and D & T if that is what it takes to deal with this attempted character assassination.*

I tried numerous times to interview Judge Higginbotham in 1997 and 1998, to no avail. He declined comment, acting in the most scrupulous lawyerly fashion. (I even showed up unannounced at his office at the Harvard Law School, hoping to catch him in a generous moment—he wasn't in that day.) Instead, Higginbotham had a young associate at Paul Weiss call me to say that the judge couldn't comment on the case. After all, "It might violate legal ethics."

Shortly after my last attempt to contact the judge, I learned of his death.

CHAPTER FIFTEEN

A MIGHTY
HEAVY BLOW

Richard Glanton had promised me a personal tour of the Barnes. The date we'd chosen for the occasion was Wednesday, August 19, 1998.

Two evenings before, like many another American, I'd watched President Clinton go on television and, at long last, admit to having had an affair with Monica Lewinsky. On Wednesday, as I waited for Glanton to show up for our 9:30 A.M. appointment, I listened as two female receptionists at Reed Smith debated about what *they'd* do to William Jefferson Clinton if they were Hillary Rodham Clinton. The elder of the two scowled as she commented on Clinton's televised appearance: "He knew he'd been caught with his hand in the cookie jar."

Just then, in came Glanton, smiling broadly: "Morning, ladies!" In return, they both answered: "Morning, Richard!" As we walked down the hallway to his office, Glanton turned to me, laughing: "Can you believe this shit? I feel sorry for that guy. I do." When we got to his office, Glanton's assistant handed him a stack of pink return-call slips. Had Channel 6 gotten hold of him yesterday? she asked. They had, and Glanton had brushed them off. Who did they think they were?

Well, they'd gone right ahead and aired that program, making mention of Glanton's own problems with Kathy Frederick. Glanton's face instantly clouded over.

Still visibly angry, Glanton led me into his big corner office, a handsome telescope in one corner, framed photographs of Republican presidents and governors on the walls, and a print of "The First Colored Senator and Representatives" prominently displayed. On a coffee table was a copy of *Great French Paintings from the Barnes Foundation*. As I flipped through the book and as Glanton looked through his messages, he told me that the Barnes presidency had been "the greatest job I ever had."

Ten minutes, later, we were in Glanton's Mercedes SLX navigating the Schuylkill Expressway. Though the outside temperature was already well into the eighties and the humidity 90 percent and rising, inside the car, the AC was on full blast while Mozart played on the CD. Glanton pointed out city landmarks as we sped along: Here the famous Waterworks, there Boat House Row. When we drove by the imposing Philadelphia Museum of Art, high atop a hill overlooking the river, Glanton grinned: "You don't think the Rishels [PMA curator Joseph Rishel and his wife, Anne d'Harnoncourt, the museum's director] wouldn't love to get their hands on the Barnes?"

Then, suddenly, without warning, Glanton's mood again shifted. He reached for his cell phone and began punching in numbers. When a secretary at Channel 6 either couldn't or wouldn't put him through to the general manager, Glanton fumed to me: "I was defamed!" He told the secretary that he expected a return call that day from the station manager. "You hear?"

In a sulk now, Glanton turned to another nemesis: "Anita

Brody is the stupidest fucking bitch on the federal bench. It sickens me that she wouldn't recuse herself. That bitch wouldn't know a conflict of interest if it smacked her in the face!"

It was only when we sped off the expressway and turned onto Latches Lane that Glanton began to cool down again: "Beautiful out here." When I said something about the neighboring "mansions," Glanton took obvious umbrage: "Ah, I wouldn't call them mansions. Most of these old homes out here, you couldn't get a half million for 'em."

One of the neighbors—a Jewish neighbor, as many were—was, Glanton told me, "nothing but a goddamn fascist. He and the rest of these good people out here, they don't care about [the] traffic. Just the Barnes. They care about that because African American people are running the Barnes."

Glanton went on to give me a tour of the now famous parking lot under construction—it *was* small, I had to admit—and then we pulled in front of the great stone chateau itself. "This is us," Glanton said, swinging open the massive wooden doors. There, looming over us from high across the way was Matisse's magnificent 1912–1913 painting *Le Rifain assis (Seated Riffian)*.

We spent much of the next three hours or so touring the Barnes, beginning with the basement, where Glanton insisted on showing me the much-improved infrastructure of pipes and boilers. On the ground floor, there were paintings everywhere, from floor to ceiling. Here Renoir's *Les baigneuses (Bathers)* sandwiched between two of the best Cézannes in the collection, *Red Earth (Terre Rouge)* and *Woman in Green Hat: Madame Cézanne*, there a pair of Modigliani women (*Portrait of Jeane Hébuterne Seated in Profile* on the right and *Woman in White* on the left) facing onto a cabinet holding no fewer than eighteen African sculptures: seven masks, six figures, and five smaller figures made of carved bone or ivory. I thought of what Matisse had said: "One of the most striking things in America is the Barnes collection, which is exhibited in a spirit very beneficial for the formation of American artists. There the old master paintings are put beside the modern ones, a Douanier Rousseau next to a Primitive, and this bringing together helps students understand a lot of things academics don't teach."

Obviously pleased with himself, pleased too by the sheer opulence of his domain, Glanton glowed with pride as we continued our tour. It was, I felt sure, the Glanton that his closest friends took such joy in: a man full of charm and spirit, still youthful even in his fifties, comfortable in his own shoes, delighted merely to be himself.

Pausing near a class given by Barnes teacher Nicholas King, Glanton commented to me on the "high quality of our people." Spying Glanton, King stopped dead in his tracks: "Let's give a big hand for Richard Glanton!" Glanton took it all in with a big grin. A couple of hours later, as we exited the gallery, he told me, "All I have is my good name. I have never profited a penny by my relationship to the Barnes."

So what, I asked him, was all the quarreling and politicking really about? His answer: "About who controls four-and-a-half billion dollars worth of art. Everything else is bullshit.'"

■

The rest of the summer was one long denouement—punctuated by hot letters and faxes between Glanton, Sudarkasa, and Sadler. Reeling, Sudarkasa eventually turned to Carl Singley for help. Singley's advice: Try to make peace with the township and the Latches Lane neighbors. On August 28, the Lincoln president wrote to Paul Rosen, the lawyer for the Latches Lane neighbors, asking him to "please accept my sincere apology for any discomfort or emotional distress any of your clients may have felt as a result of the published statements of Richard Glanton."

By then it was too late for Sudarkasa. The report of state auditor general Casey, dated September 9, finished her career at Lincoln. She was in the backseat of her car, Sudarkasa says, listening to the radio, when she heard a newscaster outlining the charges. Her first reaction, she says, was, "What university is this they're talking about?" But then she realized that it was Lincoln—"and I almost passed out—I was shaking the whole time." The report was, in Sudarkasa's own words, "scathing," focusing less on the costly renovations to the president's house than on charges of bid rigging. Casey laid particular blame at the feet of John Clark.

That afternoon, I talked to Glanton on the phone. He was clearly pleased by the results. The only reason the report wasn't harsher, he told me, was "because Casey does not want to offend a black woman. To me, that's politics. This woman should be accountable for the damage at Lincoln." The "appropriate person" for the report to be forwarded to, Glanton insisted, was the commonwealth attorney general, Republican Michael Fisher. "What you have here is just a watered-down version of what I've been saying," added Glanton. "I think the politicians watered it down so it would be palatable to black voters." When I asked Glanton how he would have shaped the report—had he been asked to—he told me he would have spelled it out: "Here are the crimes. Let's go. I would have couched [them] in terms where it would have been obvious how [attorney general Fisher] should prosecute the case."

Suffice it to say, Glanton said, Niara Sudarkasa "needs an attorney, whether it's Singley or a criminal lawyer, I leave to you to judge." He was sure, Glanton added, that Fisher would do the right thing: "Mike Fisher has impeccable integrity and will do what the law mandates. He has the highest integrity of any lawyer in the commonwealth of Pennsylvania."

Glanton clearly was on a high. His fourteen-year-old daughter, Morgan, had left for prep school at Exeter the day before—Glanton is a devoted parent—and he wanted me to hear something. It turned out to be Richard Glanton reading from a poem that he'd taped and sent to Morgan that very day and that read in part, "Never give up on your dreams."

Later that day, I talked to an official in the auditor general's office. The Lincoln report, he told me, had already been referred to the commonwealth attorney general's office. Sudarkasa, Glanton, and Cliett, he added, "were three strong people. Two of them were building power bases on a more or less parallel course until whatever it was that happened to destroy the alliance." Then he paused and said: "There's a lot that Mr. Cliett knows that someone with broader power than we have should be interested in."

It was a strange conversation—the auditor general's office report had, after all, focused almost exclusively on Sudarkasa (and John Clark)—made stranger still when the Harrisburg official added, "I think you may have the luxury—that's not the right word, I guess—to investigate this in a way that local reporters here can't. A lot of this is murky. Very murky stuff."

I didn't talk to Niara Sudarkasa until the next day, when she called me around a quarter of nine in the morning. Her first words: "I've been delivered a mighty heavy blow. What hurts me the worst is what they've done to my husband, John Clark. Without any smoking gun to hold up to me, they had to blast my husband." What particularly angered her, Sudarkasa said, was how "Richard came off with nothing. I was shocked."

Six weeks later, Sudarkasa responded to Casey's report with a 147-page reply, "When Politics Drives an Audit." In it, she strongly contested the charges leveled against her and her husband and claimed that at least some of the evidence in the auditor general's report had been fabricated. What's more, Sudarkasa charged Casey with failing to investigate the business relationships between Cliett and Glanton.

All to no avail. Less than a month later, Sudarkasa was gone.

■

After Senator Fumo threatened to cut off state aid, the university board demanded her resignation—and got it. On September 15,

Sudarkasa threw in the towel. For his part, Glanton announced that justice had been served when Niara Sudarkasa handed in her resignation. But it wasn't right, he added, that she was still on the Barnes board. She and Sadler, Glanton said, "should just go. Clean out their desks and leave quietly. They've done enough damage to Lincoln—and to the Barnes." Worse, said Glanton, Sudarkasa and Sadler were now determined "to spend a small fortune at a time when the Barnes needs every penny it's got" on the forensic audit launched by Judge Higginbotham.

On September 22, 1998—a week after Sudarkasa had turned in her resignation at Lincoln—I received a five-page fax at my office. The cover letter (on Reed Smith stationery) read, "From: Richard H. Glanton." Faxed with the cover letter—there were no remarks on the cover—was a copy of a letter from Glanton dated the same day and addressed to Lincoln chairman Kenneth Sadler. It began:

> *I am writing to you to impress upon you the urgency of two critical issues outstanding at Lincoln. . . . They are the immediate deaprture [sic] of Niara Sudarkasa, and the restoration of state funding to avert bankruptcy, in view of the $2 million deficit caused largely to pay [sic] for the $600,000 KPMG/Blank Rome audit excluding any references to alleged criminal activity in the physical plant, certified by the Auditor General.*

In the letter, Glanton recounted how only the day before he'd been in West Virginia and noticed a banner under which a college newspaper there was published. It read: "Little good is accomplished without controversy, and no civic evil is ever defeated without publicity." It reminded him, Glanton wrote Sadler, "of the unfolding tragedy at Lincoln University." The letter went on to spell out Glanton's displeasure with a host of Lincoln trustees and officials.

Sometime later that afternoon, I received a phone call: It was Richard Glanton. His enemies, Glanton told me, didn't know what they were in for: "These guys want to play hardball, and they're gonna get it." After all, "My heroes are Abraham Lincoln, Ayn Rand, and Theodore Roosevelt—and they didn't bend."

■

Glanton wasn't the only one taking a firm stand that summer. Sudarkasa also proclaimed her unwillingness to leave the Barnes board. With even his former business partner Randy Kinder now part of the new majority, that meant that Glanton would be out-voted 4-1, never more significantly than when in late September the board agreed to come to terms with Lower Merion Township and its commissioners. In its settlement dated September 24, 1998, the Barnes agreed to withdraw with prejudice all its claims in federal court and to pay the township $100,000. In return, the defendants agreed to drop their counterclaim in federal court. Glanton, who was outspoken in his opposition to the deal, promptly filed an objection to the settlement. In the meantime, the defamation suit in state court went forward.

That day, September 24, a news release went out from the Democratic side of the state senate appropriations committee: "Fumo Calls Upon Lincoln University Board to Act in Good Faith." Fumo's idea of "good faith": showing Niara Sudarkasa the door as quickly as possible. (Glanton had written to Ken Sadler on September 16—the day after Sudarkasa handed in her resignation—demanding that she be gone from the Lincoln cam-pus within two weeks.) That same day, Fumo also wrote to Sadler to say that he would continue to oppose the release of state monies to Lincoln until assured that Sudarkasa would receive no severance.

Five days after the Barnes settlement was announced, attor-ney Singley filed a $7 million suit in state court on behalf of Sudarkasa against Glanton, his law firm Reed Smith, and Gene

Cliett. Glanton, Singley charged, had "converted the Barnes into his own private slush fund and patronage haven, doling out millions of dollars in consulting, printing, and legal contracts at will." The former Barnes president, Singley argued, "was a virtual dictator with unfettered discretion [who] used the prestige and financial resources of the Barnes to curry favor with persons of power and influence and to punish his real and imagined enemies."

One of the most damaging charges in the filing concerned Glanton's role as general counsel of Lincoln: "From September 1997 continuing to the present time, Glanton . . . disclos[ed] privileged and confidential client information regarding Lincoln and Sudarkasa [to the press, to senator Fumo's investigators, and to the auditor general's office]. [Gene] Cliett provided Glanton with numerous financial documents and records for this purpose."

Less than a week later, the Lincoln trustees again met to consider a severance agreement with former president Sudarkasa. Also in attendance were Lincoln co-general counsel Christopher Lewis, Sudarkasa's lawyer Carl Singley—and Senator Vincent J. Fumo. The board voted 18-1 to allow Singley to address them. The only no vote was that of trustee and Reed Smith partner Michael Meehan, the chairman of the Philadelphia County Republican party—and son of the late William "Billy" Meehan, the longtime chairman of the Board of City Trusts (the Girard Trust). Senator Fumo was also allowed to speak: The Lincoln board, the appropriations committee chairman said, was to be commended for putting disgraced former president Sudarkasa on "administrative leave."

Sudarkasa, meanwhile, was still trying to get her case across to state officials—to no avail. Robert P. Casey, Jr., failed to respond to her counterstatement, "When Politics Drive an Audit." And, when, at Thanksgiving time, she wrote to the auditor general's father, former Governor Casey, Sudarkasa figured that their longtime friendship would count for something. She was hoping, Sudarkasa says, that the elder Casey would at least "get his son to read" her rebuttal. "He never replied."

■

As for the defamation suit in state court, well, there was one fewer defendant. Niara Sudarkasa. Having written a formal apology and having agreed to testify on behalf of the plaintiffs, she was dropped from the case. As a result of her decision, said Paul Rosen, "The cheese now stands alone."

As I wrote at the time in *The American Lawyer*: "He may indeed, but, meanwhile, says art critic Hilton Kramer, 'the Barnes has been turned into a veritable Bleak House.' Bleak House, that is, with a parking lot too—and a price tag for legal fees of more than $6 million."

CHAPTER SIXTEEN

I WAS
THE BARNES

Not quite three years after being forced to resign as president of Lincoln University, Niara Sudarkasa finally squared off in a courtroom in Philadelphia against her old antagonist Richard Glanton. The date was July 9, 2001. By then both Glanton and Sudarkasa were long gone from the Barnes board. Neither had been renominated when their terms expired. In that sense, at least, both of them were losers.

But the Barnes was a loser, too: In a front-page article by Doreen Carvajal, *The New York Times* had reported four months earlier, on March 6, that the foundation was so broke that its new leaders—president Bernard Watson (the former head of the Philadelphia-based William Penn Foundation) and executive director Kimberly Camp—were contemplating a proposal to move the Barnes brick by brick.

In words that would have made Albert Barnes turn in his grave, the *Times* recounted, "The vague outlines of the idea include some sort of relationship with the Philadelphia Museum of Art and a new location for the collection, perhaps even transporting the 75-year-old mansion and its graceful Doric columns piece by piece to a site in central Philadelphia."

Camp was the professional art curator the Barnes had never had, having been recruited from the directorship of an African American art museum in Detroit in the fall of 1998—at a time when Glanton and Sudarkasa were still on the board. Now, she was candidly talking to the *Times* about the Barnes's travails: "Have we thought about moving? Oh, yes, sure, absolutely. Who wouldn't in this kind of environment?"

The foundation had made an "emergency appeal" to raise $15 million in the summer of 2000. By the beginning of March, it had collected slightly more than $1.5 million, a sum which, as the *Times* noted, "amounts to mere life support."

Among the givers to the emergency fund were the Philadelphia-based Pew Charitable Trusts and the J. Paul Getty Trusts in Los Angeles. Each gave a half million dollars. In addition, the Wilmington Trust, a Delaware-based bank, pledged another half million over five years. Ironically, the largest single donation—$760,000—came from the Violette de Mazia Trust, where former Barnes education director Esther van Sant was one of three trustees. Needless to say, van Sant did not at all condone moving the Barnes. Others, connected to the PMA, however, did.

Philadelphia Museum trustee Stanley Tuttleman was quoted as saying, "I know that they move pyramids, and it can happen here." Like some other PMA trustees, Tuttleman favored moving the Paul Cret–designed mansion to a location on or near the Benjamin Franklin Parkway—virtually next door to the PMA. Put it there, said Tuttleman, and you "could get 150,000 visitors . . . a year."

Raymond G. Perelman, the multimillionaire father of billionaire Ron Perelman and himself the chairman of the PMA, seemed to suggest that, as far as he was concerned, the Barnes wouldn't even need to move its old home. And why should it? The elder Perelman had earlier helped lead a successful campaign to force out longtime PMA president Robert Montgomery Scott (whose position was left unfilled, therefore leaving the field to chairman Perelman, director Anne d'Harnoncourt, and her husband Joseph Rishel, the museum's curator of impressionist and post-impressionist paintings). More recently, Perelman had given $15 million to the museum to buy an existing Art Deco building on the Benjamin Franklin Parkway near the PMA. With all that additional space, the PMA could easily accommodate the Barnes art. As Perelman told the *Times*: "If that collection was moved to the vicinity of the Philadelphia Museum of Art, the [nearby Alexander] Calder museum, and the Perelman building, then the money is the least of the issues [facing the Barnes Foundation]. It would do so much for the city that all the foundations would respond."

And, of course, it would help fill up all the empty space in the Perelman Building of the PMA.

■

By the time *Sudarkasa v. Glanton and Reed Smith* opened in court, I'd already read through most of the pre-trial depositions. There were memorable episodes throughout. The former Lincoln general counsel, for example, at one point testified to his faithful service to president Sudarkasa: "In fact, I was like a Praetorian guard in the ancient courts of Egypt, protecting her when I was there."

Sometimes, though, the questions and answers proved revealing, as when Singley asked about the day the Barnes board stripped Glanton of his presidency. Glanton had left the boardroom with a press release already composed. Singley wanted to know whether Glanton had given the news release to the press or if the Barnes Foundation had.

"I don't know," Glanton replied. "I was the Barnes Foundation."

Singley also wanted to know what kind of training Glanton had that prepared him to run the Barnes. Had Glanton, for example, taken classes in art history, art appreciation, or art exhibition?

"Reading Picasso," Glanton replied, had prepared him to run the Barnes.

"Reading Picasso?"

Yes, Glanton replied. "It says we're born artists."

"Are you an artist?" Singley wanted to know.

Yes, Glanton replied. "In the words of Picasso I am."

■

The courtroom of common pleas court Judge Howland Abramson was small and dingy even by the standards of Philadelphia City Hall. Only the high ceiling with its gilt trim and the portrait paintings of early-twentieth-century jurists glaring down from the walls did anything to redeem the ugly carpet, the hideous fluorescent lighting, and roaring window air conditioners. The one podium in the courtroom came equipped with a big sign taped to it: "Property of Judge Abramson." If you looked carefully enough you could see where the chandeliers and gas lamps had once hung from the ceiling.

Sudarkasa v. Glanton and Reed Smith commenced on Monday, July 9, with opening arguments from both sides. So loud was the air conditioning that Judge Abramson ordered the units turned off. The heat proved stifling; Carl Singley nearly passed out while giving his opening statement. After that, the various court clerks spent much of their time shuffling to and from the window units, turning them off and on at the whim of the judge.

The real action began with the second day of trial, when Sudarkasa was scheduled to take the stand. By mid-morning as I crossed the street from my nearby hotel, the heat had begun to rise off the pavement in waves. The temperature read 90 degrees, and it wasn't even 10:30 yet.

Inside Courtroom 425, the crowd was as large as it would ever be in the course of the trial—perhaps three dozen spectators, most of them lawyers, with a smattering of reporters, among them Bob Warner of the *Daily News* and Stephan Salisbury from the *Inquirer*. One spectator, a young woman, busied herself by reading a long Nathalie Angier piece in "Science Times." The title: "For Some Creatures, Mating Dance Goes On."

The lawyers and their clients occupied the front row of the courtroom. At one end sat Richard Bazelon, lanky, athletic-looking, with an intelligent face and silver hair brushed back. He was representing Reed Smith. Nearby was Richard Glanton, dapper as ever in a navy blue suit, but also looking rather dour for a change. Next to him, often huddled in conversation with his client, was the irrepressible, curly-haired Bob Sugarman, perpetually rumpled, a sixties lefty turned sixtyish. After that came the plaintiff's side, beginning with the towering Christopher Booth, Singley's "second chair." Sitting next to him was Sudarkasa, a widow now, John Clark having died of kidney failure in June of 1999. The former Lincoln president was looking far healthier and many pounds thinner than when I had last seen her three years ago. This day she was wearing a black outfit, her hair cut stylishly short.

Finally, there was Singley himself: a tall, handsome man, dressed as carefully as Glanton himself, in a pin-striped double-breasted suit. Singley had come a long way since he first took on Sudarkasa's case: His friend, John Street, was the new mayor; and Singley, having been finance chairman of Street's successful campaign, was widely considered to be the most important behind-the-scenes player in the new administration. He was also now a senior partner at one of the city's biggest and most politically influential law firms, Blank Rome, where the managing partner was Governor Ridge's own closest confidant, David Girard-diCarlo, and where another partner was former Democratic secretary of state Christopher Lewis, the new Lincoln general counsel (and the man who initiated the KPMG forensic audit). Invariably polite outside the courtroom, Singley was, I well knew, a fierce advocate, shrewd and tough. Hovering behind him in the second row was an intense young Blank Rome associate named Matthew Lee, notebooks at the ready, and Singley's secretary, Mary Ann Nolan.

Sitting next to one another at the opposite end of the second row were two people who, I discovered, shared an intense interest in how the trial played itself out. One was Scheryl Glanton, the defendant's long-suffering wife; the other, John Unkovic, the in-house general counsel at Reed Smith in Pittsburgh. Scheryl Glanton struck me as youthfully middle-aged, elegant in her appearance, as precise in her dress as her husband was in his. Unkovic was pale and reed-thin, a small, intelligent-looking man with an enormous briefcase at his side that bespoke his calling—"corporate lawyer." He took copious notes throughout the trial. His specialties, I learned, were labor law and legal ethics.

Drawing a decent judge in common pleas court was a crap-shoot—and all too often luck wasn't involved. Singley, I had been told by others, had once feared that the fix might be in. He had good reason to worry. A decade ago, a sizable number of the sitting judges had been indicted and most of them convicted in the so-called Roofers' Scandal, the charges against them bribe-taking and worse.

As Fred Voigt, the executive director of the Committee of Seventy, a nonpartisan, good-government oversight group, explained to me: "In Philadelphia, common pleas judges are elected. To get nominated, you first of all have to contribute $10,000 to the party. That's the price of admission. After that, you have to have a sponsor. Probably a ward leader or a higher-up in the party. It used to be that you also had to pay your sponsor $10,000."

A few extremely powerful figures were said to control "three, four, even five or six judges," added a prominent local legal recruiter. "Those are your judge makers." The two most influential "judge makers" in town both sprang from South Philadelphia roots: Democratic ward leader Henry "Buddy" Cianfrani and the man who succeeded him in the state senate (after Cianfrani had been sent off to prison), Vincent J. Fumo.

Before the trial opened, Singley expressed himself pleased with the selection of Judge Abramson. He'd heard from other lawyers, Singley told me, that Abramson was "a fair-minded judge." After more than a decade on the common pleas bench—it was the rough equivalent of being a judge of district court in other states—Abramson had presided over few if any high-visibility cases. And, as far as anyone knew, Abramson wasn't associated with Fumo.

In the preliminary stages of the case, Singley, Sugarman, and Bazelon had argued over where the trial would be held. Sugarman and Bazelon favored Chester County, where Lincoln University was situated, while Singley was determined to keep the case in Philadelphia. Chester County was rural and predominantly white, Philadelphia was urban and increasingly black and brown. It didn't take a genius to understand why Singley took the tack he did. Though Glanton and Sudarkasa were both African Americans, Glanton was a wealthy partner in a predominantly white law firm, and Sudarkasa had been the president of America's oldest black college. Glanton, moreover, was a prominent Republican. In the end, Singley prevailed.

As the jurors and alternates filed into the courtroom, I studied them: five black men, one Latina, six black women, two white women—and not a single white male. Carl Singley, I remember thinking to myself, had the jury of his dreams. What was worrisome was the way the jurors looked. They didn't so much walk into the courtroom as drag themselves in. They radiated lethargy. By the end of the first week of trial—Judge Abramson had warned them that the case might require three weeks of their time, perhaps even four—the jurors looked dispirited. At least two were given to the odd siesta now and again, and one had once to be poked in the ribs when he began snoring gently in court.

There was a reason. That first week in the courtroom was almost entirely lacking in drama. Singley's lead witness was Sudarkasa; and the former Lincoln president was sure to be, as her lawyer no doubt knew all too well, a difficult sell. The questioning was fitful and uneven. If you knew the broad outlines (not to say the details) of the tale, it was irritating; if you didn't—and presumably not one of the jurors did—it must have been frustrating in the extreme. Much of what we heard was simply predictable: to show that Sudarkasa was an injured woman. With so strong-willed and opinionated a human being, that might not be easy.

Asked by Singley how she would rate her performance as president of Lincoln, Sudarkasa replied with a litany of accomplishments: Enrollment had risen from 1200 to 2000, SAT scores from a truly frightening 600 (combined) to a still pretty awful 900 in 1998. Meanwhile, Madame President received no less than thirteen honorary degrees, including ones from Oberlin, Franklin and Marshall, and Lehigh.

Her job, Sudarkasa thundered, had been "taken away from me UNFAIRLY! I had nothing but ACCOLADES until now!"

And so it went.

■

At 1:44 P.M. on the second Monday of the trial, attention shifted dramatically. Richard Glanton took the stand. Singley began by taking him through the usual paces: his age, place of birth, educational background, the date of his marriage (August 17, 1974), the number of their children—Singley asked archly, "Any *more* children?"—his history at Reed Smith, his annual salary (Objection, objection! Sustained), his standard hourly rate ($300), his corporate directorships (including Wackenhut Correctional Corporation), his business relationships.

Asked if he owned any businesses in Philadelphia, Glanton paused before answering:

"Philly TV News."

Asked who his business partner was, Glanton looked at the ceiling.

"It's not a partnership. So it is a corporation, it's not generally referred to as business partners."

Pressed by Singley, he eventually admitted that the president of Philly TV News was Eugene L. Cliett, Jr.

And as for Linda Marston, the former Barnes administrative director and wife of Glanton's fellow Reed Smith partner, it turned out that, yes, she too had worked for Philly TV News "within the last six months ago."

Singley went on from there to home in on Glanton's prior friendship with Niara Sudarkasa.

The Lincoln president, Glanton testified, had been "a business friend. . . . We would not socialize together. We would not go out to dinner together unless we had a specific agenda. We were not social friends."

Did you trust her?

"NO! I had seen too many victims."

Did she trust you?

"I was a good lawyer. . . . A good lawyer for the university. . . . Loyal service for the university was owed to the university, which is what it got."

After a lunch recess, Singley went to the heart of the matter, zeroing in on the KPMG forensic audit that had first revealed the Glanton-Cliett business relationships.

The KPMG audit, Glanton claimed, was aimed at making "me a scapegoat . . . a PATSY . . . for this outrageous conduct out there at Lincoln." Sudarkasa might not have been a criminal, Glanton said, but "she presided over it [criminal activity]."

When Singley began to bore in a bit too sharply, Judge Abramson admonished him to "be polite, because that's how I run this operation." Singley returned to the tale of the roses. What, he asked Glanton, did yellow roses symbolize? Friendship?

"Professional friendship."

"Weren't you more concerned about that $300,000 a year in legal fees you were getting from Lincoln?" sneered Singley.

By now, the jurors were at the very least awake. In a minute, though, they would be wide-eyed.

Did Mr. Glanton recall a January 1999 *Philadelphia* magazine profile by writer Mark Cohen?

Yes.

And did he remember saying of Sudarkasa: "I could swear the bitch said she was resign'n"?*

No.

"Did you call her a bitch?"

No.

He had, Glanton admitted, told Cohen that no one would "want to see her naked."

"But you didn't call her a bitch?"

No.

From my seat in the back row, I watched as Scheryl Glanton listened, her hands in a tight grip, so tight that you could see the muscles and the veins standing out in sharp relief. I also watched and listened as jurors stared at Glanton, reacting visibly to the word "bitch," a couple of the older black women loudly going, "Humpf!"

Philadelphia magazine's Cohen had quoted Glanton saying of Sudarkasa, "She's gotta be crazy. Who else would still be sitting there huffing and puffing like that, two steps from a damn jail?" Now Singley wanted to know: "Did you say that?"

Yes.

Had Glanton called Sudarkasa "a savage"?

---

*Quotes reflect the trial transcript and are slightly at variance with Mark Cohen's article.

"No, that would have been Mark Cohen's description."

Did Glanton know that "Niara" means "woman of high purpose"?

The Reed Smith partner glared back. Cohen, he said, "was venal."

Singley kept returning to Glanton's purported use of "bitch" to describe Sudarkasa: "You want that son of yours to talk that way?"

The jury, I noticed, was not only awake now. The women jurors, especially, appeared outraged.

■

Was it true, Singley continued, that Glanton had compared himself to Paul Robeson, the great African American actor, singer, and civil rights advocate?

"I said he was cursed and damned in life and praised in death," Glanton replied. And, no, he added, he was not ashamed of what he'd said in the *Philadelphia* magazine article.

Singley looked incredulous: "You want your son to read about you talking about somebody like that?"

Glanton glared at Singley. Scheryl Glanton sat bolt upright in her chair. John Unkovic scribbled notes furiously. Bob Sugarman shook his head angrily. Richard Bazelon looked up at the ceiling.

When Singley returned to the subject of Cohen's profile, Glanton testified that he had complained to then-*Philadelphia* magazine editor Eliot Kaplan: "I said the entire article was a pack of lies."

Asked by Singley if he had copies of those letters, Glanton said he did.

Where were they?

"I think they're at my office."

Over the next few days, Singley would continue to hammer away at Glanton's purported role as Sudarkasa's personal lawyer and his alleged part as mastermind of a conspiracy to bring her down as president of Lincoln. Asked about Sudarkasa's employment contracts and the negotiations leading up to them, Glanton continued to maintain that he was no more than "the court reporter, just writing down words spoken by others," nothing more than "a stenographer, exercising no independent judgment." As to Sudarkasa's tax probe, Glanton testified that he'd spent no more than "a moment or two" on it, most of it introducing Sudarkasa to the Reed Smith tax specialists who actually handled the case. "I would act as a greeter," was how Glanton put it. "I was the scribner." The terms of the contract, he said, had been dictated by Sudarkasa and former Lincoln board chairman Bernie Anderson.

Asked if the Lincoln board of trustees had voted to have their then-general counsel aid in the president's tax appeal, Glanton replied, no, but "there was a scribbled sentence by [business affairs committee chairman] Mr. Earle Bradford" authorizing the action.

Where?

"On a piece of paper. . . . Mr. Cliett sent it to me."

Did Glanton know who Vincent Fumo was?

"He's one of fifty senators."

How about Hardy Williams?

"He's a very revered man."

Had Senator Williams ever received legal fees from the Barnes Foundation?

"I don't think so."

Reminded that Williams had, in fact, been paid $70,000 by the Barnes for representing former trustee Shirley Jackson, Glanton retraced his steps: Yes, he'd authorized the payment, but the money itself came "from an insurance carrier, yes."

Did he know that Senators Williams and Fumo and attorney Sugarman were close friends?

No. It was news to him.

And did he ever tell Bernie Anderson, "If you support me for the Barnes board, I can make you chairman of the Lincoln board"?

No.

Did the former Lincoln general counsel ever try to influence the election of the university's board chairman?

Yes.

And was Philadelphia common pleas judge Gregory Smith—Senator Hardy Williams's son-in-law—the candidate Glanton supported in favor of Sadler?

"I didn't have a preference."

No?

Smith, Glanton testified, "was Niara's candidate."

"You were just doing her bidding?"

"That's correct."

Asked if trustee Cuyler Walker had objected to the Barnes's security contract going to Delaware County prison chairman Charles Sexton's firm, Foulke Associates, Glanton replied, "Not to my recollection. . . . If he objected it wasn't to me."

Asked about his contacts with *Inquirer* reporters, Glanton played coy. Yes, he'd met Christina Asquith in the snack car of an Amtrak Metroliner sometime in the fall of 1997. But their conversation that day had nothing to do with Senator Fumo or his investigation of the Lincoln president's home. "She said, 'What's going on there at Lincoln?'" Glanton recalled. He told her, Glanton said, that he couldn't talk about it. They then had a ten-to-fifteen minute conversation, he added, but about just what he couldn't remember. He did, however, recall what he ordered from the snack bar. (Glanton's performance that day recalled an earlier episode when Singley asked him about his initial meeting with Sudarkasa ten years earlier. What Glanton remembered most, he testified, was the food the Lincoln president served him: chicken, steak, and collard greens. "I thought it was weird," he added, as jurors snickered.)

Singley ranged far and wide. But the scope of his questioning was far more limited—and limiting—than might be imagined. Many, many a time, Judge Abramson would cut the former Temple law school dean off with the phrase: "We're not going down that road." *That* road included Glanton's expenses at the Barnes; much that had to do with the Foulke Associates, Charlie Sexton, Delaware County prison board, and Wackenhut Corrections Corporation connections; and, most importantly, Vincent Fumo and the Girard Trust. Judge Abramson, a bewildered look on his face, seemed unable even to fathom the connections that Singley was attempting to draw.

For anyone versed in the ins and outs of the Barnes saga, there was little new here, especially with Fumo, Williams, Wallace, and the former and present *Inquirer* editors and reporters absent from the witness stand. The one real revelation, though, was startling.

Way back in 1992, Glanton casually admitted, in the midst of Sudarkasa's first bout with the auditor general's office, he'd taken it upon himself to go to Harrisburg. President Sudarkasa was "asking for help," and he delivered it: "I went to see the auditor general [Republican Barbara Hafer, Casey's predecessor]. I told her [deputy] that I was up there to discuss the audit which had been the subject of a newspaper article, in connection with Mr. Clark's activities, in connection with the purchases that were not authorized or proper." Unauthorized, he told the court, to the tune of "roughly $225–240,000." Glanton made sure that the blame was heaped where it belonged: at the feet of physical plant director John Clark.

Eyes wide, mouth agape, Carl Singley blurted out: "Mr. Glanton, have you no shame?"

■

After Singley had quoted Glanton calling Sudarkasa a "bitch" and a "savage," I had little doubt where the jurors in this case were going to land. I watched them file into that courtroom day after day, watched them smile at Singley (if not always at

Sudarkasa) and avert their gaze from Richard Glanton.

On Monday, July 23, after three weeks of testimony, and without presenting their own case, defendants's attorneys entered a motion for dismissal. The next morning, to the dismay of Sudarkasa, Singley, and most jurors, Judge Abramson did just that, citing "a non-suit."

As to the charge of conspiracy, the judge found, "While the burden can be met by circumstantial evidence, such evidence must be more than speculation, conjecture, and supposition. Synchronicity constitutes supposition."

As to libel: "Here the defendant publicly held negative views which were shared and published by many, and ultimately by independent government officials. . . . It is the prism of the First Amendment through which this matter must be viewed in the greater good for the many."

The vast majority of jurors, as polled by the *Inquirer*'s Stephan Salisbury and the *Daily News*'s Bob Warner, were convinced that Glanton had lied to them. Most were prepared, they said, to vote in favor of the plaintiff. Several went over to shake hands with Sudarkasa and Singley afterward and commiserate. One juror made a point of saying to Sudarkasa, "We were gonna give you *a lot* of money!"

Juror Delores Smith expressed her "shock that this went this way. I didn't see the justice in not letting it go to the jury."

Juror Mary Palmer told Salisbury that she

> *was incensed that state legislators—including Sen. Vincent J. Fumo (D., Phila.) and Hardy Williams, a former West Philadelphia senator—whom Sudarkasa alleged conspired with Glanton to drive her from office were granted legislative immunity by Abramson and did not testify.*
>
> *"If you are involved in something this high-profile, you have a responsibility to explain it to people," Palmer said.*

*"Fumo and Hardy Williams are public officials. I under-
stand the right of legislative immunity . . . but if they have
a letter with [Fumo's] name on it, he can come in and
explain it, legislative immunity or not. I'm a voter."*

Palmer might have been a voter, but Howland Abramson was
a judge. And a judge with a past: His "sponsor," as it turns out,
was former Philadelphia city controller Joseph Vignola, "judge
maker" Buddy Cianfrani's cousin and a man who, like Cianfrani,
not infrequently found himself on the same side of internecine
Philadelphia politics with that other South Philly powerhouse . . .
Senator Vincent J. Fumo.

Stunned, Carl Singley left the courtroom vowing to appeal
the decision.

Judge Abramson made his farewell, thanking jurors for their
service.

For his part, Bob Sugarman was delighted: "I think the judge
captured it. First Amendment freedoms prevailed. People can
talk."

But it was left for Richard H. Glanton to put the final gloss to
his day of triumph: "I'm just happy Philadelphia is blessed with
a very, very professional judge. I can't say more than that."

EPILOGUE

A HAUNTED PLACE

When, in 1928, A. H. Shaw of *The New Yorker* took readers on a visit to the fresh and wondrous thing that was the Barnes Foundation, he memorably described it as "this paradise of art." Almost seventy-five years later, *The New Yorker* returned to the Barnes. The author this time was the legal correspondent Jeffrey Toobin.

According to Toobin, the foundation's consultants at Deloitte & Touche reckoned that the Barnes would need eighty-five million dollars "to guarantee its long-term stability," fifteen million of which would be needed over the next five years. An "adequate" annual budget would be four million dollars. So far, the money had not been forthcoming, at least not in any significant way.

The problem, as Toobin saw it, was that potential rescuers—like Barry Munitz, the head of the J. Paul Getty Trust in Los Angeles—"want to invest only in an institution that allows the world to see its collection. But [Lower Merion] township's restrictions, as well as those in Barnes's will [*sic*], make a substantial increase in attendance impossible. The spiral leads downward."

The person charged with solving these seemingly intractable problems is Barnes CEO Kimberly Camp. Prior to running the Barnes, Camp had served for five years as executive director of the Charles H. Wright Museum of African American History in Detroit. At forty-five, she is, in Toobin's words, " a large woman . . . with elaborately braided hair and the careful, soft voice of someone who has spent a professional lifetime in museum galleries."

She is also, as I found in the course of a series of visits to the Barnes, determined to try to preserve the foundation as a stand-alone cultural institution. When she arrived at the Barnes in November 1998—hired, she says, by "Ken Sadler. *Not* by Richard Glanton"—Camp "looked around" and realized that she'd "inherited an establishment in complete disarray." The Barnes, she adds ruefully, "was an eighty-year-old start-up operation." It was also, she discovered, "deeply dysfunctional." The litany of problems she encountered was a long one: "Hardly any development money was coming in, subsidiary rights were non-existent, the personnel policy was three and a half sheets of paper."

Worst of all, the Barnes was on its last legs financially. When she "came through the door" in November 1998, Camp recalls, there was $1.6 million left in the endowment. By April 1999, it was all gone. Today, she adds, "It's zip. We have no endowment." The last of the Barnes' endowment—$900,000—she explains, "went to pay for the parking lot. It was a very expensive parking lot."

There is, Camp points out, five million dollars in a separate "building endowment"—the remaining money left over from the great Barnes tour—but those funds are controlled by a judge in Montgomery County Orphans' Court. Without an operating endowment, says Camp, the Barnes has been forced to live hand-to-mouth: "We live on philanthropic handouts, virtually day to day."

One thing she could—and did—do, Camp says, "was to stop

the bleeding. Stop the continuous legal harangue that used to define this place." Then she adds, "I have never been in a situation so litigious as this."

Camp ticks off some of the other steps she's taken at the Barnes: "We've set up an advisory committee of distinguished outside curators. We've begun an oral history of the foundation and interviewed people who actually knew Dr. Barnes. We've done a full inventory of the collection, over eight thousand pieces, using the same system as the Getty [Museum]. We've added professional staff, from the Pew Trust and Bank Street." Her "reproduction rights guy," Andrew Stewart, previously worked at the Franklin Mint. In one year alone, the Barnes's profits from subsidiary rights from reproductions more than quadrupled. Meanwhile, Orphans' Court in the spring of 2001 granted the foundation blanket approval to lend any of its more than 4,000 works of art held in storage.

Still, Camp's biggest problem is the same as it has been since the day she walked through the door: Money. "I never, in a million years, dreamed that I would have had such a problem raising money," says Camp. "Not at a place like the Barnes!"

Sitting behind her desk on the second floor of the foundation's administration building—the room was Laura Barnes's study—Camp talks about the frustrations of her job. "The collection," she says, "is too good to be punished because of personalities. There are many of my colleagues in the museum business, many philanthropists, too, who are still punishing the Barnes Foundation because of Dr. Barnes."

Her reply to them, Camp says, is always the same: "He's dead. He's *been* dead for fifty-one years!" She manages a laugh.

Camp's eyes scan the room, from the stunning late-nineteenth-century Persian carpet—"not rare, but wonderful," as she puts it—on the floor to Dr. Barnes's two awards of the Légion d'honneur (knight in 1926 and officer in 1936) and his certificate of membership in the burgundian wine society, the Confrérie des

Chevaliers du Tastevin, on the wall. Turning in her chair, she can look up at an autographed portrait photograph of Barnes's great friend John Dewey ("To the Barnes Foundation, which puts in practice my beliefs and hopes for democracy and education"). But it's an exquisite Chippendale chair that she finally focuses on.

"I walked in here one morning, and overnight that Chippendale had exploded. It had *exploded*!

"You laugh, but it's true. This is definitely a haunted place."

The Barnes may well be haunted by the ghost of Dr. Barnes, but it's his successor who worries Kimberly Camp. Many of the same philanthropists and curators who haven't forgiven Dr. Barnes, she claims, "are also punishing the Barnes Foundation because of my predecessor." Her face curls into a frown: "These personality problems add up to major distractions." In the fall of 2001, Richard Glanton—despite the support of Democratic Senator Fumo—failed to gain appointment to the Board of City Trusts (the Girard Trust), but he was shortly afterwards put on the Lincoln board as the nominee of Republican State Senate President Robert Jubilerer.

Still, she says, "It's the [Barnes] collection [that] is the biggest distraction: Who *owns* the cultural patrimony?" When I ask her what she means by that, Camp replies, somewhat enigmatically, "The Barnes collection is, well, you know, very desirable."

Camp says she's gone repeatedly to the members of Philadelphia's cultural elite, "tin cup in hand," asking for money, to little avail so far. The Pew Charitable Trusts and the de Mazia Trust have given some money; but the individual big givers, the high-rollers at the Philadelphia Museum of Art, virtually none.

Had she been to see Ray Perelman, the chairman of the PMA, I asked?

"Many times."

And what did Perelman say?

"He stuck out his hand, and he said he'd be happy to give money, 'as soon as you give me this.' And I said: 'Give you what?'

And he said: 'The keys—the keys to the Barnes.' "

"What do they want?" Camp asks, mockingly. "*Want*? They want IT."

■

"Barnes Foundation Wants to Move," was the front page head-line in the September 25, 2002, edition of *The New York Times*. "The financially beleaguered Barnes Foundation," the newspaper reported, "is seeking court approval to move its art collection from its suburban Philadelphia home." As another front page account, this time in the *Inquirer*, put it, "The embattled Barnes Foundation has decided its best hope for survival is to build a new museum along the Benjamin Franklin Parkway and move out of its home in Lower Merion."

The Barnes, president Bernard C. Watson explained, had lost a total of $1.36 million in 2000 and 2001 and was projected to lose another $800,000 in 2002. The *Inquirer* reported that, "At the end of 2001, according to its nonprofit federal tax filing, the Barnes had $6.5 million in stocks, bonds, and money-market funds, and a growing pile—$703,437—of unpaid bills."

Relatively small though the numbers were, the Barnes was, nevertheless, broke.

"We have been walking along a financial precipice for some time," Watson told a *Washington Post* reporter. "Any rational person could see we weren't going to make it."

Within days of Watson's announcement, the *Inquirer* was reporting that "art supporters already have pledged at least $80 million of the $150 million needed to move the Barnes Foundation's stunning art collection from Lower Merion to Philadelphia's Benjamin Franklin Parkway."

While Kimberly Camp had had to make do with half-million-dollar donations handed out willy-nilly, suddenly, now, a host of generous white knights had come to the rescue. The new-found "rescuers" were led by Rebecca W. Rimel, president of the Pew

Charitable Trusts, and cable TV magnate H. F. "Gerry" Lenfest, head of the Lenfest Foundation—and Ray Perelman's successor as chairman of the Philadelphia Museum of Art. The other major player in the rescue: The Annenberg Foundation.

The three foundations, as the *Inquirer* noted, had together pledged $3.1 million in operating funds to the Barnes for at least the next two years—just enough, in other words, to keep the foundation solvent until it could move into the city. And they were believed to have pledged a total of $80 million toward the move itself. All of it, however, would be dependent on the Barnes seeking—and receiving—court approval.

Other philanthropic players said by the *Inquirer* to be part of the rescue effort include the aforementioned Perelman; Joseph Neubauer, chairman of Philadelphia-based Aramark Corp. (the big food supply company); Dorrance H. Hamilton, a Campbell's Soup heir and wealthy art patron; Paul F. Miller, Jr., the investment banker and former chairman of the University of Pennsylvania board of trustees; and Harold Honickman, chairman of Pepsi Cola National Brands, Inc. Miller, the *Inquirer* noted, "has promised to give $1 million himself and has asked others to contribute. He said he had been at the task for more than a year."

PMA chairman Lenfest waxed eloquent about the greatness of the Barnes collection, describing it as "fantastic." He had been, Lenfest added, "overwhelmed by it" when he visited the Barnes for the first time—in November 2001.

What neither the *Inquirer* nor the *Daily News* seemed to notice was that the rescuers were led by the very same Philadelphia cultural powerhouses that Albert Barnes had spent much of his life at war with: the PMA, the University of Pennsylvania, and the Annenbergs.

The *Inquirer*, however, did get at least one thing right. As the headline put it, "Big Money" was indeed "Lining Up to Support the Barnes." Among those jumping on the Barnes bandwagon was Philadelphia cable giant Comcast, whose executive vice president, David Cohen—former mayor Edward G. Rendell's chief of staff and law firm partner (both had been at Ballard Spahr where Cohen had until recently been chairman), he was the incoming Democratic governor's closest confidant—announced the donation of two million dollars to help with the move.

Needless to say, the editorial pages of the *Inquirer* and its tabloid sister publication the *Daily News* ("The People Paper") were thrilled at the news—especially at the economic potential of it. Just think of all the out-of-town visitors pouring into the Parkway! All the extra tourist dollars! Or as the subtitle of an *Inquirer* account so succinctly put it, "Officials see more visits to Parkway site."

Legal papers filed in Montgomery County Orphans' Court on September 24, however, revealed that the Barnes Foundation trustees had more in mind than just moving the collection. Quoting from the Barnes's own proposed decree ("In RE: The Barnes Foundation, A Corporation"): "The proposed new Bylaws no longer include Dr. Barnes' Indenture of December 6, 1922 as part of the Bylaws." In other words, the trustees would be free not only to move the collection, but to take it on tour when and if they liked, to charge whatever admission fee they liked, to lend works of art—even to sell paintings from the collection.

And as for the trustees, there would be a whole new set of them as well. To quote again from the petition: "Among the changes to the Bylaws will be expansion of The Foundation's Board of Trustees from five to fifteen members. Lincoln University would continue to have the right to nominate four trustees. Mellon Bank no longer would nominate a trustee or serve as a Trustee. Upon adoption of the new Bylaws, the present five trustees would immediately elect three additional trustees, expanding the Board to eight members. Those eight trustees (by means of a nominating committee) then would recommend seven additional members for election to the Board, but, for the election of those seven persons only, Pew and the Lenfest Foundation would jointly have the power to approve the nominations. . . ."

In other words, with the stroke of a judge's pen, control of the Barnes would pass from Lincoln University to the Pew Trusts and the Lenfest Foundation. Future Barnes board members, the petition states, would be chosen for both their "integrity" and their "potential value to The Foundation."

And just who were the current board members of the Barnes who signed off on these changes to the foundation's bylaws? Bernard C. Watson, the president, was, it turned out, not only the former president of the William Penn Foundation (whose Web site motto is "Advancing Greater Philadelphia"), but also "Presidential Scholar" at Temple University, as well as the most recent winner of the Spirit of Philadelphia Award for service to the community. Watson also happened to be both a director of Comcast and the current chairman of the Pennsylvania Convention Center Authority, which only one month earlier had asked for $464 million in state and city aid to double the size of the Philadelphia Convention Center.

His predecessor as chairman of the Convention Center Authority (1990–1995): fellow trustee and Barnes Foundation vice president Stephen J. Harmelin, the managing partner of Dilworth Paxson, Judge Bruce Kauffman's old firm—the one that collected $1,593,414.14 from the Barnes over the course of four years, 1992–1996. Among the Dilworth firm's most important clients: the Annenbergs.

The other trustees included retired Howard University dean Jeff Donaldson, Philadelphia Common Pleas Court judge Jacqueline Adams, and Goldman Sachs Foundation president Stephanie K. Bell-Rose.

In the weeks that followed, Richard Glanton professed himself highly displeased by the Barnes board's action. He could see some merit in moving the collection to Philadelphia's Parkway, the newly appointed Lincoln trustee told reporters, but he was adamantly opposed to the university losing control over the Barnes. Glanton's proposed solution to the financial crisis: sell some art. The painting he had in mind to sell was Matisse's *Joy of Life*.

Glanton wasn't the only Lincoln trustee voicing opposition to the proposal. According to the *Inquirer*, Barnes president Watson informed university officials of the Barnes board's plans only hours before the press conference at which they were announced. Lincoln board chair Adrienne Gray Rhone told the press that the university would contest the petition in Orphans' Court.

When University of Pennsylvania Law School trust specialist Bruce Mann suggested that breaking the Barnes indenture might not be a cakewalk—"a tough nut to crack," was his exact phrase—the powers that be in Philadelphia professed themselves surprised and appalled. The Barnes's new lead attorney, Schnader Harrison partner Arlin Adams, was quoted as saying, "It [the move] seems to make so much good sense that it's hard to visualize somebody objecting." Of course, the former longtime judge of the U.S. Third Circuit Court of Appeals was quick to add that, "I'm not going to rule it [opposition] out."

For its part, the *Daily News* proposed that the Lincoln and Barnes boards should reach out to an "impartial arbitrator," someone like Mayor John Street or Governor Edward G. Rendell—whose best friend Cohen's company had just given two million dollars to fund the Barnes move. Surely, the *Daily News* editorialized, there must be some kind of "win-win" solution to the impasse at the Barnes.

On October 24, 2002, Judge Stanley Ott of Montgomery County Orphans' Court announced he would be holding hearings to adjudicate the matter in the spring of 2003. Meanwhile, of course, the clocks again ticked at law firms all over Philadelphia.

The battle of the Barnes had only just begun.

INDEX